Love Letters

ONE FATHER'S WISDOM (*OR NOT*)

CHRIS GORDON

Love Letters

© 2021, Chris Gordon.

Print ISBN: 978-1-66780-6-822
eBook ISBN: 978-1-66780-6-839

Contents

Preface

THIS IS A LOVE STORY. IT IS A TALE OF LOVE AS reflected through the actions of individuals, of groups, of communities, and of strangers. Ultimately, it is a story of life lived with a sense of urgency, with meaning, with purpose, with value, and with hope. It is a reflection of several truths made self-evident to those who were participants in the story. It was reality—a reality that included truths that changed forever many who bore witness to these events, as truth often does. None of the participants within the story will ever be the same again. It can be no other way.

It is hoped by the author, if he has done his job well enough, that through the telling and reading of this story, those who experience it secondhand, will, too, never be the same again. Life is like that. Truth is like that. In the end, hope is all there is.

Chapter 1

BAD THINGS HAPPEN IN THE WORLD. THINGS YOU don't expect, things you don't deserve, things for which you can't prepare. Unexpected events blindside you as you progress through the experience called life. These experiences "rock your world," they leave your imagined sense of normalcy in tatters. You are forced into a mode of physical and emotional survival, a psychological state where you act out of instinct, an instinct informed by an internal sense of belief, grounded essentially in hope—the hope of survival, the hope of control, the hope of a future sense of safety. An intense focus comes from existing in the moment as you try to move and act from minute to minute, knowing that each act, each decision matters. This focus is similar to that of a person who finds himself suddenly adrift in the ocean with no life support system: he must swim or drown. There is no other option. The castaway must decide which direction provides the best chance of reaching the safety of shore—and then he swims in hope, stroke by stroke, knowing that to succumb to physical exhaustion or emotional despair means inevitably sinking into the depths, never to return, defeated, overtaken, lost. Thus, it was for us on Monday, March 2, 2009.

* * *

I was in my office working in between classes at my job as an instructor of music at Bevill State Community College in Fayette, Alabama, when my telephone rang around noon. Although I receive many calls during the course of any ordinary workday, a call from my wife, Pam, is rarely one of them. When she does call, something at home is askew. I picked up the receiver on the first ring and heard her voice, fast, high-pitched, and breathless, saying, "You have to come home! Dr. Bobo just called and wants me to come to his office with Anna. He thinks it's leukemia!"

All I could mutter as a response was, "I'm on my way!"

I ran down the hall toward the campus dean's office, bypassed the secretary, then stuck my head into the dean's office, interrupting a meeting already in progress. "I have to go home," I said. "The doctor called Pam. He thinks Anna has leukemia!"

It was the first time I had spoken the words out loud; doing so nearly caused me to fall down. My voice broke as I spoke. In my mind I was screaming, *How could this happen! She only has a cold, for Christ's sake! Surely he's wrong.* My heart raced, my chest tightened, my breathing turned shallow. I raced to the car, telling myself to calm down, to take it easy. I still had an hour's drive ahead of me: I did not want to drive like a maniac, succeeding only in making things worse. I knew I was panicky because Dr. Phillip Bobo of Tuscaloosa's Emergi-Care Clinic was rarely wrong, and Pam and I both knew it.

I drove south on Highway 171 toward Tuscaloosa, my mind racing. I did not associate leukemia with anything in particular; I barely knew what the word meant…only that it meant cancer! While I drove, the only reference to leukemia that came to mind was the Debra Winger movie *Terms of Endearment.* And in that movie Debra Winger's character dies!

"Oh God…Oh God," I kept saying to myself, my stomach turning in knots. "This can't be happening! Why, for God's sake?"

Deep in thought, barely conscious as I drove, and twenty miles into the sixty-mile one way commute, my cell phone rang. Pam said: "Dr. Bobo told us to leave his office and go straight to see Dr. John Dubay, an oncologist, at Druid City Hospital. We're leaving for his office now. Just meet us there."

"What did Bobo say?" I asked.

"He said he thinks Anna has leukemia, but to be absolutely certain, he wants us to go see this guy so he can double-check. He said not to talk to anyone, and not to read anything on the internet; it will just scare us to death. So, we're on the way there now. They will have to take some more blood and do the labs, so we'll not know anything for a little while. Just be careful!"

"Is that all he said?" I asked

"Yeah, but he was upset. I've never seen him like that."

"How do I get there?"

"Just go in the front door of the hospital, pass the elevators, and go down the hall to the right until you get to the doors marked *Oncology*. We'll be in the waiting area, I'm sure."

Pam hung up. My mind raced again, saying, *Oh God … Oh God!*

I do not remember much after that until my car found a parking place and I rushed into the hospital, following the directions Pam had given me. I stumbled into the set of offices marked *Oncology* and saw Pam and Anna sitting among several other people in the waiting area. I grabbed my twenty-one-year-old daughter and hugged her, trying not to hurt her with the force of my embrace or to convey the hysteria I felt. I hugged my wife, too, knowing instantly we felt the same terror. We did not talk much, for talking opened the door to panic, and instinctively we wanted to remain strong, in control, showing Anna we could handle the situation. Fortunately, the receptionist called Anna's name not long after my arrival. We stood in unison. Anna calmly followed the nurse into the area, where a nurse took vials of blood samples. These were sent off to be analyzed, scrutinized, and processed: we were told to go home and return to Dr. Dubay's office on Wednesday morning to receive the results.

Wednesday! I thought. *That's forty-eight hours from now. We have to wait forty-eight hours before we learn anything?*

The three of us went home, slowly, in separate cars, and in silence. Each of us looked as if we had just been slapped, and slapped hard, not knowing who—or *what*—had done the slapping. Tori, our youngest daughter, seventeen and a senior at Bryant High School, would be returning home soon. We would have to tell her the news, of course, engulfing the whole family in emotional uncertainty.

Anna was in her senior year of undergraduate study at the University of Alabama. She was pursuing a double major in psychology and Spanish while maintaining a minor in The Blount Undergraduate Initiative Studies Program, a concentrated curriculum centered in Western Civilization, including its history, literature, philosophy, and arts. She was two months away from graduating an institution she loved—and one that loved her! She was a star student, seriously minded, intelligent, ambitious. She was on track to graduate summa cum laude, and she had already been inducted into Phi Beta Kappa and numerous other undergraduate academic honorary institutions.

Surely the doctors are mistaken, we thought.

Anna had been battling a cold she had contracted in December of the previous semester. The symptoms had persisted ever since: a runny nose, sinus infection-type ailments. As she always did, she went to see Dr. Bobo at the Emergi-care Clinic seeking relief. Pam and I had taken the girls to the clinic for years, seeking treatment for ordinary minor health issues. Everyone knew Phillip Bobo was the best diagnostician in town—and probably in the state—when it came to family medicine. For Anna's symptoms, he had prescribed the usual antibiotics to treat a sinus infection, and then he had prescribed strep medications, as both girls had a long history of strep infection. But those regimens did not seem to help. Anna's symptoms persisted for over two months.

Irritated to find herself heading into March with the same old malady, Anna again went to Dr. Bobo for a checkup, seeking relief. This time, Dr. Bobo delved more deeply into the situation, taking blood, examining the slides himself, intending to figure out Anna's condition once and for all. That was when he called Pam.

When we arrived home that Monday afternoon, the three of us sat in the den, the family gathering place, and stared at each other. No one wanted to say a word that might reinforce the existence of what Dr. Bobo had already warned us about. No one wanted to give it legitimacy; no one wanted to shift into a phase of acceptance. We had reflexively gone into fighting mode.

Not this girl! Not in our family, we thought collectively. *Nothing is going to threaten us and get away with it!* We would beat this—if it even existed.

* * *

We are fighters and competitors. It is part of our nature. Pam and I are professional musicians; she is a pianist and I am a trumpet player. Both disciplines require a lifetime of dedication, continual practice to improve our technical ability. We had mastered the ability to focus, to work, and to execute the most challenging of musical literature within our fields: we knew how to perform in the moment, in real time, combining technique with artistry and taste to provide a memorable performance each time we performed. Our girls, too, had been raised artistically and athletically with those same attributes. They were both academically disciplined, driven to achieve; moreover, beginning in her first year of Eastwood Middle School, when students had their first opportunity to try out for one of the sports teams, Anna wanted to try out for the softball team. Neither Pam nor I had experience with organized school sports, and the school had a brand-new teacher/coach. She knew little more than we did about how to build a program or teach the requisite skills. After the closing of "tryout day," Ms. Ray, the coach, asked each girl which position she would like to play. No one volunteered for pitcher, the one necessary figure in fast-pitch softball. The game cannot be played without a pitcher! Someone had to step up and be the face of the team.

When nobody responded to Ms. Ray's question, Anna spoke up. "I'll give it a try, Coach," she said.

With that brave gesture, stepping into the unknown, with no idea of what lay ahead, Anna and our entire family began a love affair with fast-pitch softball. From that day forward Anna and I began the process of learning how to pitch. I became, by default, her first pitching coach. Neither of us had a clue as to how to proceed. We attended softball camps, found a pitching instructor, attended lessons, and got out into the street next to our house, the only level ground available on which Anna could practice, every day that spring semester. I was her catcher, her motivator, her live-in coach, reminding Anna during practice sessions of the instructions her private pitching coach had given her during the previous lesson. Anna put in the effort, honed her skills, and put in the time necessary to at least begin her first season in the circle when the team began play. She was brave. She was determined. But, due to her inexperience as well as the team's and the coach's inexperience, the Eastwood Middle School softball team did not win a single game—for two years!

Often embarrassed, sometimes humiliated, occasionally discouraged, Anna trudged onward. She would not quit! Something got under her skin that buoyed her competitive spirit. She was determined to succeed, to achieve, and to receive respect from her coach, her team, and the opposing teams she continued to face in county competition. Slowly she improved, gaining control of form and technique, mastering ball placement and the ability to control speed. As she progressed, she added different pitches to her arsenal: fast ball, changeup, curve ball, screw ball, rise ball, and drop ball. Pushing through sweat and blisters, hours and hours of practice, with single-minded determination, she willed herself into a competitive softball pitcher, winning a starting position on the Central High School softball team as she matriculated into the ninth grade. Here, for the first time, she had a knowledgeable softball coach in Billy White. Her teammates, often older and more experienced, were more highly skilled—and they were competitive. Collectively, they expected to win, and they began the processes necessary to make it happen. Anna thrived in this competitive environment. She gained confidence in herself as she received more and more support from her team. If she could take care of her shortcomings as an athlete, minimizing mistakes and maximizing consistency, her teammates had the skills and determination to establish a solid defense behind her, providing the components necessary for overall team success. Anna improved not only her pitching but her hitting as well. In the two years she was on the Central High School softball team, 2002 and 2003, she garnered awards for Best Batting Average and Most Valuable Player.

Some degree of success caused Anna—and all of us—to catch the softball "bug." We expanded our family's participation in the sport. Living in Tuscaloosa, home of the University of Alabama, both girls were fortunate to be able to participate in the softball camps held each summer by Patrick Murphy and the University of Alabama softball coaching staff and players. Age-appropriate camps that used national high-profile college players as coaching assistants and counselors combined with college-level coaching instruction from pitching coach Vann Stuedeman fueled a fire in Anna.

Tori, too, began to play softball, first in church leagues, the city recreation league teams, and then University of Alabama softball camps. Four years younger than Anna, Tori had the distinct advantage of watching everything Anna did as she grew up, including competing athletically, allowing her to excel far more quickly and at a younger age than Anna. Given the family's exposure to competitive instruction, the four of us chose to take the next major step: joining the world of travel softball.

The world of travel softball competition is for the serious-minded developing athlete. Teams are formed of those individuals and families who wish to compete at a higher level than school-ball teams provide. In this world, teams hold highly competitive try outs, allowing only new members who are devoted to achieving a high level of competition, discipline, and participation. This is true not only for the player, but for the entire family.

Anna and Tori joined travel ball teams by 2002, starting at the local Tuscaloosa level. Both of the girls were accepted onto the same fourteen-and-under team, the Bama Express, coached by D.J. McMahon. The team was our introduction to tournament softball, played at city parks all weekend. A world where winning was paramount—or at least the desire to win. Girls and coaches put in hours of practice preparing for the next weekend's tournament, where getting to and staying in the "winner's bracket" was the quickest road to a championship trophy. Each team, at least locally, chose to play in a range of between five to nine tournaments each summer.

If a team was highly competitive, the team chose to participate in fall ball travel tournaments as well. This elite group of teams was the most competitive, playing six months of almost weekly tournaments. Fall tournament season bled over to high school softball in the spring semester, which led back to summer ball again: a continuous calendar of yearlong softball. As Anna and Tori progressed, both came to desire an ever-higher level of team ability and competitive drive. We went through several travel-team changes, progressing from the Bama Express to the Tuscaloosa Tide, which then branched out to more regional tournaments, and finally to the NSR Express sixteen-and-under and fourteen-and-under teams.

NSR, the National Scouting Report's newly franchised business, formed in Birmingham in 2003. Their teams comprised elite athletes from all over the state of Alabama who were interested in being recruited by colleges across the country as softball players. The NSR sixteen-and-under team, which Anna joined, and the NSR fourteen-and-under team, which Tori joined, served as the showcase teams for elite tournament play by young recruits seeking the attention of college coaches: the teams competed across the southeastern United States in the biggest and most prestigious tournaments being offered. The NSR sixteen-and-under team became the best travel ball team in the state, for a time eclipsing the previously established traditional powerhouse clubs like the Birmingham Vipers and the Sharks from north Alabama.

Anna became one of three pitchers for the Express who were among the best in the state and the southeast region. The team's hitting, fielding, and pitching abilities were envied by many, and their track record regarding tournament wins during the 2003 and 2004 travel ball seasons was virtually unmatched. Anna was an expert reliable hitter. Although she could not be counted on to hit the long ball, she could be counted on to achieve hits that moved runners on the bases ahead of her. In the pitching rotation, she was not the fastest pitcher, throwing only in the high fifties, as clocked on the radar gun, but she had a combination of skills. She possessed six different pitches that she could place on any of the nine quadrants of the strike zone on a daily basis, and she had a devastating change up that created between a twelve and fifteen mile-an-hour difference in ball speed as compared to her fast ball. She was smart and competitive; she often caused opposing batters to ground out into the gloves of her team's magnificent defense. She was going to be hit by batters; they were just not going to hit her well! These skills, combined with her desire to get the best of any hitter who stepped into the batter's box and the mental toughness to do it, meshed extremely well with the higher pitch velocity achieved by the other two girls in the team's pitching rotation.

During the summer of 2004, the NSR Express, now called the CSXpress, earned the right to compete at the highest level in the country: the American Softball Association's sixteen-and-under national tournament. Dozens of teams from across the United States participated in the tournament, including those who were historically most advanced: teams from the western part of the country, where established competitive youth softball began twenty or more years before the phenomenon took hold in the southeast. The south and Alabama was playing catch up with the west, and we were making large strides in that competitive direction.

The CSXpress family traveled to Bloomington, Indiana, during the summer of 2004 to see how we stacked up to the nation. Over six days of continuous competition in August, on eight or ten softball fields hosting up to ten games each, teams from California, Oklahoma, Kansas, Michigan, Illinois, and many more states including Alabama, competed in the long and arduous elimination tournament. College and university coaches from across the country prowled the fields during every game, scouting the athletes to determine those they might desire to offer player scholarships. Our proud CSXpress got hot and began a winning streak of five straight games, rising in the rankings, before losing their first game in the double elimination tournament. With a final record of six wins and two losses, the CSXpress earned the highest ranking of any team ever from Alabama to participate in this tournament.

Anna pitched three games in the tournament, two starts and one game in relief, including winning the game against a highly touted and historically competitive team from California, the San Jose Sting. When the CSXpress won the game, as the team and families were packing their gear, onlookers (usually teams and their fans waiting for the next scheduled game) began saying to our fans, "Do you know what you just did? They're incredible! They usually finish in the top four, year after year, and you just beat them. Amazing!" We were finally put out of the tournament in the evening of the next to last day. When the final tally of rankings was posted, the CSXpress 16U team finished seventh in the country! No Alabama team had ever placed as high: Anna's team had eclipsed the previous Alabama team by eighteen spots. Anna faced forty-two batters in eight and a third innings, pitched with one win and one loss, giving up five walks and tallying six strike outs. Her batting average in ten at bats was .500, including scoring the only run in the 1-0 victory against the San Jose Sting.

After that travel ball season, Anna played in her senior year of high school but retired from travel softball. She did want to play college softball, but by this time, she realized her real interests lay in academic pursuits. She possessed a Division 1 mind, but she was not as attractive an athlete on the D1 level. She was not tall, did not throw extremely hard (throwing in the high sixties and low seventies was required to catch the attention of big-name coaches if you wanted to be deemed a true D1 pitching prospect); but she did get college attention from smaller schools, including a scholarship offer from Spalding University in Louisville, Kentucky. This small private Catholic university made Anna an offer of a four-year scholarship to pitch for their school. It was the first scholarship offer ever made to a student from outside the state of Kentucky. Tuition and room and board were included, totaling $20,000 a year at the time, bringing the total scholarship value to $80,000!

Anna and our whole family went on an official visit to the campus, where we met the coaching staff and those players still on campus. Everyone was gracious, pleasant, sincere, and genuinely warm. When Anna returned home, however, she had a decision to make—whether to play college sports at the NAIA (National Association of Intercollegiate Athletics) level of competition, or to enroll at the University of Alabama, where she was interested in academic pursuits. She chose the life of the mind rather than the life of the body.

Athletics had taught her hard work and confidence. It had challenged her mind, body, and character. She learned to face fear, perform with courage, even in the face of adversity. She learned she was tough, she could perform—and she was a winner. She would need this competitive state of mind during the forty-eight hours we waited to receive the test results from Dr. Dubay's office.

*　*　*

On Wednesday morning, Anna, Pam, and I drove to Dr. Dubay's office at Druid City Hospital in Tuscaloosa to learn the results of the blood tests. We were escorted into the doctor's office by a nurse/receptionist. Dr. Dubay was sitting behind his desk looking at a folder containing Anna's lab results. He motioned for us to sit. As I recall, there were three chairs. Anna sat in the middle, flanked by Pam and me. He left his desk to sit in another chair closer to us, still looking at the folder.

I remember looking at him, this young man who appeared to be in his early forties, quiet, unassuming. But as he sat near us, in a chair like ours, he looked more intently at the results he was holding in his hand. His body language told us everything we needed to know. This poor man was in emotional distress as he prepared to speak. He turned his body toward the wall, facing it at an angle. He crossed his legs and leaned forward, bowing from the waist, crouching just over his knees. He had contorted his body almost into a pretzel as he lifted his eyes from the paper; he turned it toward us and quietly spoke directly to Anna.

"Anna, I am sorry to say that you have acute myeloid leukemia. This is a very serious disease, and we need to begin treatment as soon as possible."

Chapter 2

We were stunned. It took a minute for Dr. Dubya's diagnosis to sink in. Dr. Dubay waited patiently but quietly, in obvious emotional pain himself. But only he knew what it meant. It would all be new to us. Slowly, questions formed; all of us asked them in turn.

"What does that mean?" asked Anna.

Dr. Dubay explained that leukemia is a cancer of the blood cells, which are manufactured inside a person's bone marrow. In Anna's case, something had gone wrong in that process: abnormal cancerous blood cells were being produced. Dr. Dubay further explained that there are four major types of leukemia, two of them chronic, or long-term, slow-developing types, and two are acute, or fast-growing, more dangerous types. Anna's form was the most dangerous and the fastest growing; therefore, treatment had to begin immediately.

We asked what the treatment options were. Dr. Dubay said that chemotherapy would be used to kill all the bad cells in Anna's blood: three rounds of the therapy, each taking twenty-eight days to do its work. So, Anna would have to be in the hospital for most of three months to achieve remission, or the state in which no more cancer would be present in her system. We asked where Anna should go to receive the treatment, and Dr. Dubay, who had been trained at the University of Alabama in Birmingham, recommended that we go to that institution to have the procedures done. He was confident in their physicians' abilities to treat Anna's disease.

He informed us that he could make the necessary referral and that we could meet with Dr. Baird, who would be Anna's treating physician at the Kirklin Clinic in Birmingham, the next day to begin the treatment. He told us that the process would be long and difficult, but that there had been many advances in the ways acute myeloid leukemia was treated, and that the therapies used were much more effective now. He did caution, however, that there were no guarantees and that Anna's condition was serious and life-threatening. These were the words that almost stopped us from breathing. There were some audible gasps, mouths left hanging open, and frozen stares with fixed pupils as we processed the words Dr, Dubay had just uttered.

This can kill my child, I thought as I waited for my body to take its next breath. Tears of fear silently slipped out of the corners of some eyes. When the numbness caused by what we had heard began to dissipate, it was replaced with a zombie-like behavior: our bodies seemed to move of their own accord, as if guided by an automated pilot, while our brains were disengaged from the captain's seat, concentrating instead on processing and analyzing what they had been told. It was in this state of mind that all three of us began our social routine of exiting the scene. We went through the motions of engaging in the social pleasantries necessary to exit and walk toward the office door, and from there out into the lobby, where we slowly, methodically found our parked car.

When we reached the car, we discussed where we should go, home or some other location, to talk. Anna suggested that she was hungry and requested that we go to the Waysider Restaurant, a Tuscaloosa culinary tradition, specializing in breakfast fare, usually reserved for lazy Saturdays, Sundays, or special occasions. Today it would serve as comfort food: a place where we could talk, plan, and strategize regarding how we were to function now that our lives had been turned upside down. Plans were smashed. Life goals had been altered and interrupted. We were now on a road no one had expected to travel nor even thought possible; yet, here we all were, without a roadmap, a GPS, or even a friend or acquaintance who had ever driven the road we now were required to travel along.

We realized we needed the whole family present for the conversation. Pam called Tori at school and did the things necessary for her to meet us for breakfast. With our small family of four seated around one of the Waysider's signature round tables, surrounded by coffee, diet Coke, the restaurant's legendary biscuits and honey, we let ourselves respond to what we had heard. While in a very public eating establishment usually reserved for life's celebrations, we quietly fell into our first experience encompassing a corporate-like family fear: a mixture of self-doubt, shock, and controlled panic. Everything about what lay ahead for Anna—for *us*—was unknown. What would the chemotherapy procedures be like? Would Anna survive? Was our health insurance adequate? Everything surrounding our new circumstance was confusing; in our numbed state of being, all we could do was to try and stay together, physically, mentally, and spiritually, to do what must be done in the immediate future.

It immediately became clear that the situation was something we could not handle on our own. We needed to share the news with family, with employers, with friends. We needed their support, their encouragement, their help and their strength to navigate everything that needed to happen.

After we finished our brunch at the Waysider, we decided to go to my parents' apartment at Capstone Village, a retirement community on the University of Alabama campus, to tell them the disturbing news. Logistically, they were the easiest family available to tell because they lived in the same city as we do. Our midday visit was highly unusual, especially because all four members of our family entered their apartment at the same time. My parents were immediately concerned: obviously something significant was happening.

We told my parents that we had just received the news that Anna had been diagnosed with the most aggressive form of leukemia, a cancer of the blood cells, and that she would be moving to the hospital at the University of Alabama in Birmingham for treatment right away.

Grandparents are allowed to fall apart, but not parents. There were gasps, tears, and silence as the weight of our words settled into my parents' minds. The family's oldest grandchild, the first grandchild for either side of the family, was in jeopardy, the outcome of Anna's life unknown. My mother responded with a typical grandmotherly embrace of her grandchild: she wrapped her arms around Anna as tears fell. But then she did something I did not expect but by which I was not surprised: she assembled the family into a circle and began to pray.

She prayed to God for Anna's healing and for the sustaining of her life. She prayed in earnest for Anna to be able to continue with her purpose in the world, beseeching the Almighty to not be finished with her yet. It was a type of prayer spoken in a broken but confident voice that was sternly speaking to her God, as one would expect a grandmother to pray in a moment of serious need. But I would have imagined that this energetic and declaratory voice would be reserved for the silent thoughts and prayers designed for God alone to hear, an intimate conversation between two entities familiar with each other. To hear such a prayer in a loud voice spoken with confident words masking an internal fear, the voice of a mother praying for the sustaining of the life of the child of her child caused me to break emotionally deep inside: I began to weep loudly and uncontrollably at the poignancy, power, and personal intimacy of the moment. Pam, holding my hand, squeezed down on it, hard, yanking me back from the abyss of emotion and self-indulgence and back into the reality of a battle for parental self-control. She did not want Anna to become further disturbed or frightened by her father's loss of control and emotional discipline. A mother's protective instincts had roared into overdrive to an extent I had never witnessed before, brought out by the sudden threat to the safety and the well-being of her oldest child. Although my initial reaction to her yanking me back into the moment was one of outrage—how could she be so insensitive to my pain and fear!—I quickly realized she was in fact protecting the emotional state of her child, desiring that nothing occur to increase Anna's despair or fear. Pam knew instinctively that everything from this moment forward was about Anna. Anna and no one else. She did not care who it offended. She was shifting her role, roaring into becoming Anna's protector, her defender, her nurturer. She would make every person and every circumstance bend to what she as a mother thought was best for Anna, regardless of relationship, status, or title. For Pam, everything from this moment forward was about Anna, her health, her state of mind, her restoration.

Shaken but determined, we collected ourselves and exited, returning home to again talk, plan, prepare, and pack for the trip to UAB. The phone call came, informing us that Anna was to report to the Kirklin Clinic to meet with Dr. Baird, who would oversee her care and implantation of her chemo regimen the next morning. In that meeting they would explain procedures, perform tests, and take labs that would be used to diagnose the exact form of the disease raging in Anna's body. Then they would order the specific chemotherapy indicated by the diagnosis, and wait for the mix of therapeutic agents to be created and delivered. Then they would begin the regimen.

Following the phone call, Pam left the house to go to the University of Alabama's School of Music, where she taught class piano to undergraduate music majors and coordinated the school's piano accompaniment needs for its students, to meet with its director, Charles "Skip" Snead. She needed to inform him of the situation and to inquire about making arrangements that would allow her a leave of absence from her position for the foreseeable future. Skip was immediately sympathetic and encouraging, telling Pam the faculty would jointly assume her duties for as long as was necessary. She did not need to worry about losing her job, Skip said; she should focus her attention and energies only on what lay ahead. These were the best words for Pam to hear, full of empathy and strength: she walked away from her job—and from her students, who loved and adored her, as she did them—not knowing when or if she would return.

Anna wrote an email to all her professors at the University of Alabama, informing them of her diagnosis and letting them know she would be forced to leave school immediately, in the middle of the last semester of her senior year as an undergraduate, to receive treatment that hopefully would save her life. As she composed the email, the realization that that she might be forced to delay her graduation or possibly never be able to finish the final eight weeks of her undergraduate degree dawned on her. She might never graduate. The thought of not graduating was devastating. Anna's entire personality and self-image was centered on her skills as an excellent student. As she sent the email, she collapsed on the bed in her room, sobbing uncontrollably. Fear and doubt merged with a raging anger stemming from the realization that the disease was stealing her life and all its pleasures. I think this latter realization was the more emotionally devastating one for her to process. The fear of disease, of pain, of death seemed easier to handle than the anger caused from the interruption of her classes, her plans, her goals, her achievements, her dreams. It was completely unacceptable.

* * *

Anna Gordon was born to learn. She possessed an enormous curiosity and thrived in the classroom from the moment she stepped into first grade. Maybe her scholastic bent derived from the fact that both Pam and I were university faculty, or perhaps its origins can be traced to my parents, who were both career elementary school educators—my mother a first and second grade teacher and my father an elementary school principal before becoming director of instruction for Alabama's Jefferson County Public School System, which was a system administerial position.

Not only did Anna love a great teacher-student relationship, but she also enjoyed the tedious work of reading and writing, doing math and science, historical research, and the like. She excelled at them all. Her successes came not only from natural aptitude; she enjoyed the processes of work and the benefits it produced. Achieving good grades came as a result of not fighting the process that was necessary to earn them. Over her lifetime as a diligent student, she developed a laser-like focus that made the effort required to study produce the best possible results. With it came the best recall and memory ability I have ever observed.

Anna's ability to recall information constantly astounded the entire family. It never seemed unusual to hear Anna quote whole passages from novels, academic texts, and journals, or to recall dialogue from movies she had seen only once. The winter when she was barely two years old, Pam and I took her to see the Ringling Brothers Barnum & Bailey Circus perform in Birmingham. Anna was fascinated by the clowns, staring, pointing, laughing, amazed by their antics throughout the show. To capitalize on her excitement, I bought a very large full-color program to take home as a remembrance. Along the bottom of each page ran a continuous listing of every clown's full name along with his or her portrait. All the clowns in the troupe came from Slavic countries, or so it seemed, and each had a multisyllabic Slavic name, filled with consonants and unusual sound combinations. Every night, Anna looked at the clowns' pictures, page after page, and asked me to pronounce their names while she pointed to the clown to be identified. In only a week's time, I could point to any clown's face, randomly selecting one from the various pages of the program, and she would joyfully yell out their name, correctly pronounced, building in excitement with each one, until all twenty-six clowns had been identified. Then, as if it were a game, she would squeal out, "Again! Again!"

* * *

The morning after Anna sent the email to her professors, we packed two cars full of everything we had been told we would need for the extended stay the first round of chemotherapy would require, and we drove to Birmingham to check into the UAB Hospital. I knew an extended hospital stay meant I would have to keep many people up to date, including family members, employers, colleagues, and friends. I could not imagine doing this task adequately if I used phone calls as my primary means of communication. I hate talking on the phone. I always have. Furthermore, I do not communicate well over the phone due to my annoyance with the medium. Instead, I chose to email a specific list of people who would receive daily news of Anna's and Pam's activities. After I had set up the email list properly, it would allow me to communicate only once, from any location, without having to worry whether I missed telling an important piece of news to someone or not. At first, I listed only family and essential employers, along with a select group of friends. As time wore on, requests to be added to the list grew on a weekly basis.

*   *   *

3-5-09

Folks,

Many of you have asked for the mailing address here in the UAB hospital.

UAB Medical Center
Wallace Spain Building/West Pavilion
619 19th St. South
Room W940
Birmingham, AL 35249
Attn: Anna Gordon

As far as visitors, she is allowed visitors especially early on, when we get to day 10-14, she will be prone to outside infections, but the doctors will know more when we get closer to that time.

Today, Anna had a bone marrow biopsy to determine her exact strain of the disease, and to determine her exact chemotherapy treatments. These she will start in the morning and tomorrow is "DAY 1." She also had a heart EKG, some X-rays, and lots of blood work. To make her therapy treatments easier, she will begin the

day surgically implanting a "port" IV, allowing the free flow of infusions without having to go through the skin and the pain associated with that process.

Anna, as well as Pam, Tori, and I feel your prayers and positive thoughts and energy that are being sent her/our way. We are humbled by your concern and support. We love you for it.

Please feel free to forward this info sheet along to whomever has inquired. I am trying to get out as much information as possible to many people at once, but I may leave folks out by mistake, so I ask your help in spreading the word as we go along.

We love you,
Anna, Pam, Chris & Tori

*   *   *

Pam decorated Anna's hospital room with personal items brought from home to make the environment less clinical and more inviting. These objects included additional lamp lighting to soften the light in the room and avoid having only depressing overhead florescent lighting. Framed photographs and Anna's personal bedding, complete with comforter and matching sheets, were also unpacked. As cards arrived in the mail, they were taped to walls and windows so that Anna—and anyone who entered her room—immediately understood how much she was remembered and supported. As time wore on, almost every available space in the room was used to display cards and other mementos offering well wishes.

Earlier, Pam had planned to sleep in Anna's hospital room, in order for her to be the best caregiver possible for Anna by remaining on the frontlines of battle. But we immediately discovered that no bed was available for her to sleep in. Instead, she was expected to sleep every night in a chair that could be dressed in sheets and blankets. While both the chair's pull-out footrest and the headrest could be lowered into a horizontal position, the chair was still a chair. Furthermore, the chair's width was confined by its two arm rests, which would now serve as baby-bed confinement rails whenever Pam was ready to sleep. There was no way for her to turn. She would have to adjust to sleeping on her back, in only that one position, prostrate on a bed made of cheap hotel-stock plastic-covered recliner cushioning—every night, for as long as the hospital stay required! The price Pam would pay emotionally and physically to be the best caregiver possible to Anna as she and our family endured the frontlines in the battle for Anna's health was immediately clear to me. It was one of the primary unpleasantries of the daily journey that was about to unfold for us.

* * *

3-7-09

Folks,

I think I have finally made an email list that will make my communications updates more stable.

Day 1 (FRIDAY 3-6) recap—Anna had surgery for the "port" installation—(this is where all IV things including chemo will go). She did not eat well or on schedule due to anesthesia effects and interruptions and unappetizing hospital food. Later in the day she got nauseated and was given something that made her feel very "drugged," also not a good thing. She felt the reality of what she was about to go through and mourned the news regarding the loss of her hair (which will take place in about 7-9 days). Then chemo began at 9:00 pm that evening. All in all—not a good day!

Day #2 (3-7)
She slept well for most of the night, ate a good breakfast and feels much more perky this morning. Her attitude is much more positive in the new day and she and David (bf for those who do not know) began walking the halls and playing UNO! :)

*For those who have asked about flowers/gifts/etc... Flowers are ok early on but will be removed from her room by day 7 due to bacteria, mold, and other natural disease-causing agents. Balloons, etc., are fine.

Again, we are overwhelmed with your concern for Anna and the rest of our family, and we cherish your prayers and signs of concern.

Much Love in return.
Chris

*   *   *

3-9-09

Folks,

Sorry the update is later than usual, but I went back to work today driving to Fayette, then went to Birmingham to see Anna and Pam and just returned home 8:00 pm. All medicines are working well, as was planned, with the white cell count now over 90% eliminated already! She had an up and down night last night due to the weakening of her system in response to the chemotherapy, as expected. While she had a good day today, walking and eating well, she is tiring more easily and readily, and we expect this to be the case for the next week or more before she begins to rebuild healthy blood and the energy that goes with it. She had several visitors, and we hope for a restful night tonight.

We are eternally grateful for your constant prayers and positive thoughts and wishes for her and our lives. Please know that they are felt, they are cherished, and we could not endure without your support and love. Thanks be to God!

Chris

* * *

3-10-09

Folks,

Anna had a rough night last night and a hard time this morning.
Seems like the chemo is working as expected and killing all the
white (bad) blood cells. It also kills all fast-growing cells in the
body, good and bad. Therefore, it is expected that she will decline
in energy, in attitude, and experience physical difficulties. Some
of those began last night with her blood pressure dropping and
causing her to feel weak and a faint/fall risk. Dr. Baird ordered
the nurses to put Anna on a neutropenic diet, where any food that
[came in contact with] the ground during the growing process
[has been eliminated] due to dangers of bacteria exchange. They
removed the flowers for the same reasons.

In response to her dropping blood pressure episodes, they put her
back on IV fluids that they had removed the day before. This has
stabilized her pressures and she has felt better this evening and
afternoon. The prayer shawl arrived via Rev. Bryan Sisson today
and she adores its beauty and softness and mostly all the prayers
and well wishes that anointed it with its special quality!

Many thanks to all of you who participated in the special event on
Sunday in Fayette at my church, Fayette First United Methodist.

The white blood cells are almost gone! Prayer works! Thank you
for yours.

Chris

* * *

I first took the position of director of music at Fayette First United Methodist Church in 2005, the year Anna entered the University of Alabama as a freshman. At my teaching job as instructor of music at Bevill State Community College in Fayette, I taught every course in music the college offered and I conducted every ensemble the college offered: concert band, jazz ensemble, and choir. My piano accompanist at the college was also the pianist for the church and had been for many years. One day she approached me at work, telling me that the church had an opening for its choir director, and she inquired if I would accept it. She thought I would be ideal for that position. At first, I declined to even entertain the notion. I had never had a church job, and I never really wanted one. But then I thought about Pam. She taught piano privately to multiple students. She taught at the University of Alabama as well. She played in various churches, where she served as organist. And she had done this for our entire married life. Moreover, I had previously surmised that our expenses would be rising because at that time our first child was entering college. Because my accompanist and I worked so well together, and because I liked and admired her as a person, I ultimately concluded that the position at the church was the perfect opportunity at the perfect time. I interviewed for the position with the head of the Pastor Parrish Relations Committee, who was also a church choir member. I was offered the position, and I accepted.

I began in the fall. I learned quickly what was expected of me, and I learned how to maintain a routine that would balance my home life with the additional hours to my work week and my commute required. Now, not only would I be commuting from Tuscaloosa to Fayette five days a week to teach, I would also be adding Sundays to my commute *and* adding additional hours to my day by having to stay in town on Wednesday evenings for choir rehearsals. The additional workload was daunting, but I believed it was worth the effort because of the additional income the new job provided. What I did not expect was that I would also come to love and enjoy the people of the church. They welcomed me instantly into the congregation and embraced me as their own. Just how much the church loved and supported me became obvious four years later, when Anna was suddenly diagnosed with the worst known form of leukemia.

The women of the church had a committee of ladies who gathered to knit "prayer shawls" as gifts to be given to any member of the church who was experiencing a difficult illness or required a hospital stay. The tradition of service to the church community by these women dated back many years. I was not aware of the practice until one Sunday in early March, just after Anna began her chemotherapy treatments at UAB. I was absent from the service that morning as I had immediately taken some time off from the church to support my family during the first weekends after our cancer journey began. However, I was told by my Sunday School teacher, who was also the assistant pastor of the church, that on Sunday, March 8, the finished prayer shawl the ladies knit for Anna Gordon had been brought to the service to be dedicated by the church as a gift of comfort, and also as a reminder of their support for Anna and our family during this time of need. When the final hymn of the service was completed, the pastors invited any member of the congregation who wished to do so to approach the altar during the organ postlude and touch the shawl, which had been placed quietly on the altar, and to offer their prayers of healing for Anna. They then exited the sanctuary, as was their custom, to take their places outside the doors of the church to greet members of the congregation once the service had concluded. The sounds of the organ died away as the organist finished the postlude, and the pastors readied for the throng to begin making its way to their cars. However, in that silence no one exited the doorway. The pastors waited and waited before climbing the stairs to peer back into the sanctuary to see where all the churchgoers were. When the pastors looked inside, they saw the entire congregation gathered around the prayer shawl, touching it, or touching one another close to it, to be connected to it, while they each in their own way offered their prayers of healing for my daughter.

* * *

The nurses of the ninth floor of the Kirklin Clinic, where cancer patients are housed for chemotherapy treatments, were kind and helpful. Many developed sincere relationships with Anna and Pam as they held more and more conversations with each other and the familiarity grew between them. Nurses are truly the catalysts for caring, compassionate, efficient, and knowledgeable treatment. They are often the explainers of unfamiliar procedures as well as the ones left to implement those procedures. They provide invaluable insight for the patient and family regarding what they can expect in relation to physical symptoms or the internal effects of the chemotherapy, allowing the patient to know whether their feelings and reactions are common or unusual. Physicians who come in and out of the patient's hospital room are typically there only a few minutes, informing the patient of the procedures and tests they are performing and why they are performing them; but they rarely remain with the patient long enough to discuss anything more than the patient's immediate queries. As the patient and family process what they have been told, questions invariably arise after the doctor has left. Many feelings can emerge as a result, ranging from high anxiety to elation to the promise of high hopes depending on what the physician says and how they say it in the short time they are with the patient. But the nurses are there to explain, to calm, to rejoice, to problem solve when conditions change from hour to hour. They are the first to diagnose any change in symptoms or any events that fall outside the normal range of expectancy. It is the nurses who first notify the physicians whenever it is necessary for them to address a patient's pain, nausea, or fever, or to prescribe an antibiotic or medications specific to the patient's therapy. In terms of the consumer's perception of both the therapeutic experience and the hospital experience, competent, caring, friendly, communicative nurses mean *everything*.

In the battle zone of the hospital room in which a cancer patient is residing, the air is continually filled with emotion, with smells, with clutter, with sounds. A barrage of noise is constantly emerging from the hallway, where ceaseless banter presses through speakers broadcasting instructions to doctors, nurses, and other hospital personnel. A multitude of mechanical pumps and other medical equipment emit a myriad of warning beeps: disturbing sonic blasts that come from inside the patient's own room as well as from the hallway where other patients' alarms are ringing, each demanding a response from the nurse's station. Between all of the beeping and the conversation and the fast walking through the halls and the squeaking of sneakers on the tile floors from the feet of rushing nurses who are answering patient calls and beeping alarms, the rolling of wheels on food carts or mop buckets or computer carts, the cacophony becomes mind numbing and anxiety producing for patients and caregivers alike: they remain confined to a small eight-foot by twelve-foot space for months on end, where the patient endures poison being pushed into their body, suffering its physical effects in their room's semi-light and the constant sound-bombardment every hour of the day. The hospital environment never alters during its twenty-four-hour cycle. The nurses eventually get to leave the hospital, recovering in some space representing normalcy and relaxation, then return refreshed, ready to be cheerful and professional all over again. But the patients and their caregivers never get to leave.

Chapter 3

AT THE TIME ANNA WAS DIAGNOSED WITH AML, both Pam and I were working multiple jobs, trying to do what was necessary to raise a family and have enough money to pay for all of its expenses. In addition to our teaching positions, we each had a church job we worked on weekends, Pam as organist for the First Presbyterian Church in Aliceville and I as director of music at the Fayette First United Methodist Church. Both of our church jobs were out of town, requiring us to travel an hour to reach our respective churches. I also drove two hours to teach each day; in fact, to maintain my teaching career, two of my weekdays entailed a three hour and twenty-minute commute. We were on the road a lot; I was driving almost fifteen hours each week. All just to earn a living for ourselves and our family.

When the situation regarding Anna's illness first became known to all of our coworkers, there was a tremendous outpouring of help and well wishes. Both of our teaching institutions bent over backwards to be supportive in any way they could. The University of Alabama's School of Music immediately raised over a thousand dollars in faculty contributions; the money was for us to fund any necessary increased expense, such as the increased expense for gas and food. While Pam and Anna were entrenched on the ninth floor of UAB Hospital, dealing with chemotherapy treatments and their aftermath, I continued driving to work each day. I also continued my church job on the weekends, also driving a two-hour commute to visit the girls most nights at the hospital. When I returned home, I spent as much time with Tori each day as I could, checking on the school day's activities and making sure she was fed and ready for the next day. Doing the laundry, feeding the pets (an elderly dog and two cats), as well as writing the email updates regarding Anna's condition, were all parts of my daily routine. While I was tired and every minute of my day was filled with responsibility, I felt that it was nothing in comparison to what my daughter had to endure physically and emotionally, as well as what my wife had to witness and endure twenty-four hours a day.

Because I mingled with people throughout each day, I often heard words of encouragement from colleagues, students, or church members. Pam relied on the telephone and Facebook for emotional release and the support of friends. Her only genuine conversations with people each day were with the medical professionals who entered Anna's room. I was busy, very busy, working and traveling to the next place I had to be to keep our world balanced and spinning. For Pam, as well as for Anna, time often seemed to stand still as the monotony of space, furniture, view, sounds, and even air never changed.

*　*　*

Not long after Anna began chemotherapy treatments on the ninth floor of the Wallace Spain Building of UAB Hospital, Pam's telephone rang. As Anna slept, Pam answered her phone, accustomed to hearing the voice of a family member or close friend on the other end of the line. She was therefore surprised to hear an unusual and unexpected voice: Dr. Robert E. Witt, president of the University of Alabama, was calling to pass along important information affecting Anna. Dr. Witt told Pam that Anna's professors had gotten together and conferred with each other regarding her academic situation, namely, that she had left school to receive treatment during the middle of her last semester of study. The faculty agreed among themselves—and had confirmed their consensus with the dean of the College of Arts and Sciences—that Anna's stellar academic performance during the semester and all previous semesters was sufficient for them to conclude that Anna need not worry about returning to school at the University of Alabama to complete the remaining weeks. She was officially graduated from the University, and she would keep her status of having earned the highest academic honors and graduate summa cum laude!

Pam began to weep as she listened to Dr. Witt speak to her. She wept at the realization that the president of the University of Alabama had wished to personally deliver his message of hope to us, and that with his words he was removing an overwhelming anxiety for Anna, the possibility of her losing all that she had worked so hard to accomplish during her undergraduate years. The fear was now gone. These were tears of joy. Anna now needed to concentrate only on doing her part to get well and move on to the next phase of the academic regime she loved so well.

*   *   *

Anna Gordon and Dr. Witt established a friendship in the summer of 2005 in Tuscaloosa through a circumstance no one could have predicted. These two very different people crossed paths and recognized something inside the other that would end up inspiring them both. Watching the relationship grow and mature over the five years after they first met was fascinating. The relationship was made even more amazing by its unlikely beginnings.

Fresh from her decision to pursue academics rather than college athletics, Anna exerted a great deal of energy investigating and pursuing scholarship opportunities at the University of Alabama the summer after high school graduation. To her bitter disappointment, she discovered that due to her mid-range ACT score of twenty-three the university offered nothing that would be of help financially. The discovery that ACT or SAT scores were the determining factor when institutions of higher education decided whether to award scholarship money to a prospective student infuriated Anna. It seemed to her—it seemed to all us—that this evaluation method was the easiest method to use in order to quantify a student's overall suitability for a scholarship, and to sift through a large numbers of applicants; but it was neither the best nor the most accurate method available.

To her mind and to ours, this method seemed successful in identifying students with academic potential but appeared sorely lacking in its ability to identify candidates who could be counted on to produce actual scholastic results. As a result of both Pam's career and my career as faculty in higher education, we had taught a variety of students, those possessing high academic potential and those with lesser degrees of cognitive ability. We had observed that student success is related to self-mastery in combination with discipline and desire. Cognitive potential is a gift that can aid greatly in this success, but it is not a guarantee. Only those who can harness that potential through actual work can achieve success and inner growth by doing good work on a consistent basis. This fact seemed sorely lacking in the selection process for awarding financial assistance to students.

Many evenings in our house were spent discussing the learning process and the habits of successful students and successful people. Our conclusions always resulted in the opinion that success and greatness are obtained through a record of consistent results. To truly award deserving student applicants for scholarships at an institution would require a more labor-intensive process of investigation into each applicant's record of success over an extended and challenged period. Obviously, this method of evaluation would require more man-hours and extend the time spent on decision-making by any institution. We understood the reasoning behind emphasizing test scores as the determining factor, but Anna thought that the investment results for the institution, in terms of the return on their money as reflected by the quality of their student body and the student body's achievement levels, could be viewed as less than optimal.

This awareness was the center of Anna's frustration. The reality was that her record of success over many years as a student and as an athlete was being overlooked as a justification for monetary reward. Hard work and dedication, focus and sacrifice, had born fruit in regard to her record up to that point, and she knew students who were being awarded money by the same institution she wished to attend who possessed a lesser record of actual achievement than did she. It was during this period of frustration with the real world of academia that she received an invitation in the mail to attend a recruitment reception hosted by the University of Alabama in honor of high achieving, academically gifted, students in the Tuscaloosa area. The reception was an attempt by the university to influence "local" students to not leave home to attend the Vanderbilts, the Emorys, the Harvards, and the Princetons, but rather to stay and bring their academic skills to the University of Alabama.

Anna and I attended the reception, which was held at the beautiful home of Weldon and Deloris Cole on picturesque Lake Tuscaloosa. Anna was already firm in her decision to attend the university with or without financial assistance via scholarship. But we attended the reception out of curiosity, and with Anna believing the reception would be the only means of benefiting and gaining recognition of her "local" accomplishments. She was not going to *not* accept the gift.

Over one hundred prospective students and their parents attended the event. It was held on a beautiful Sunday afternoon in August of 2005. Soon after the group's gathering, the prospective students were escorted to a downstairs area where they interacted with ambassadors and recruiters from the university staff and the student body. The parents remained upstairs to listen to a speech given by President Witt encouraging us as parents to keep our children home and to become part of a growing trend toward academic excellence that had been established since Dr. Witt became president of the university two years earlier. I listened, uninterested, knowing Anna would begin in the fall semester, and that her future was well established. I felt that Dr. Witt's message really did not apply to us.

When his short speech concluded, Dr. Witt began to mingle with the adults in the room, talking and encouraging each family in turn to invest in the university's future growth in academic excellence with their own children's gifts. I investigated the tables of food and waited for Anna to reemerge so we could make our way home. In the time it took for me to make it through the throng of people crowded into a confining space, I turned a corner in the house just as Dr. Witt was finishing a conversation there. He turned directly into me. He immediately shook my hand and began again to deliver the conversational pitch to the parent of a prospective student. It was obvious he had replicated the pitch countless times that afternoon.

I let him talk and I listened politely until he came to his conclusion. I replied that he did not have to worry about Anna. She had already decided to give up athletics by turning down an eighty-thousand-dollar athletic scholarship to a private school in another state to attend the university here and pursue an intensive academic tract. I did take the opportunity to inform him, however, that his university would not be giving her a dime of scholarship money because, according to its policies, she was not qualified for any financial aid. Yet, she was qualified to be invited to this reception, and she was attractive enough to the university for it to attempt to keep her here.

Dr. Witt looked amazed. He was genuinely taken aback by what I said. He asked me for my daughter's name, and then he handed me a business card. Then he told me something that took me aback once more. He said, "Ask Anna to write me on Monday. I will look into her situation myself." Then he departed to continue his recruitment. I thought to myself, *Yeah, right. I'm sure he tells everyone something like that.* But the longer I thought about what he had just told me, the more intrigued I became.

Shortly, the students ascended the stairs from down below, and we began our exit back outside. As Anna and I were making our way to the front door, I told her what had happened, and a thought occurred to me. I wanted Dr. Witt to have a face he could match with the name of the prospective student who would be writing to him tomorrow. So, I steered us over to where he was standing; he was again shaking hands as people exited. We waited briefly as we made our way up to him, but when we were face to face, I said, "Dr. Witt, I want you to meet my daughter. She is the one I was telling you about." Immediately, he took my daughter's hand and called her by name, remembering the details of our specific conversation, one out of many dozens he had had in the last hour. "Anna," he said, "I'm Robert Witt, and I want to welcome you to the University of Alabama."

He continued: "I want to tell you a story. I went to college at a small school in Pennsylvania. I am sure you have never heard of it. As I approached graduation, some of my best friends and I began thinking about graduate school, and we wanted to attend Dartmouth College. We all applied, but I was the only one of my group who got accepted. I was confused because my friends all had better test scores and better grades than me. They were upset when we all got our letters in the meail, and I was mystified. I promised myself that when I arrived on campus that I would find the graduate school dean and ask him why they had chosen me and not my friends.

"Well, as it happened, I did run into him, and so I asked, 'Why me?' He replied by asking me a question. He asked, 'How did you begin your day every day?' I was confused, and then he filled in the answer himself. 'You began by washing dishes in the cafeteria, didn't you?' By now I saw what he was saying— and yes, I had done that so that I could receive my meal plan for free. 'And tell me how you ended each day.' I replied that I spent it emptying trash cans in the dorm because in doing so, I received a discount on my dormitory housing bill. 'Exactly,' he said. 'So, we knew that you were capable of hard work. Your friends did have slightly better test scores than you did, but they had an easier time of it. You had to work two jobs—and you were still able to maintain good grades. Frankly, Dartmouth had never recruited a student from your college before, and we had only allocated one scholarship. I wanted someone who I knew could work hard and someone who had proven it. That is why we accepted—you.'" Then Dr. Witt looked Anna straight in her eyes and said, "Anna, you just need a little help in getting over the fence. Write me an email tomorrow and I will look into this myself." He pulled another business card out of his coat pocket, and he handed it to her. "I look forward to hearing from you," he said. And we were off.

The next day, Anna wrote the email and sent it off with curiosity. She went about her regular schedule, almost forgetting the situation. But then one day, in the mail, came a letter addressed to Anna from the Office of the President, the

University of Alabama. Dr. Witt had written a personal letter on his stationery, explaining that he was awarding Anna a five-hundred dollar "Future Leaders Scholarship." Moreover, he encouraged her to write him at the end of her first term and let him know how things had gone, and he asked her to stay in touch. In August of 2005, Anna enrolled and began double-majoring in psychology and Spanish with a minor in "The Blount Initiative," an intense exposure to the great literatures and philosophies of the Western Civilization and the world in general. She worked very hard, day after day, tirelessly but enthusiastically pursuing mastery of each subject the best she could. By the end of her first semester, she had received all A's and had a perfect 4.0 grade point average, of which she was very proud. She had proven to herself that she was up to the task of advanced college work, and her initial success removed any remaining fear she had that she might be overwhelmed with college-level demands.

In gratitude for the president's investment, and with pride in her accomplishments, Anna wrote Dr. Witt an email in December, thanking him for his investment in her academic potential. She told him she had been successful in her first semester's work, as she had promised, and she thanked him once again for his kindness and consideration as she closed the email. We thought she had brought full circle the perfect closing to the chance encounter between president and prospective student, and then we relegated it to the archive of family lore that would be pulled out and retold over and over.

In January of 2006 Anna began the second semester of her freshman year with optimism and high energy. She was well into her first month of study when she received a second letter in the mail from the Office of the President. To everyone's surprise, Dr. Witt was doubling her scholarship amount, adding another five hundred dollars to her student account! He told her that she had demonstrated the resolve to achieve the results she had predicted for herself and that he wished to support her efforts with this reinvestment. We were stunned. The president had not let go of his relationship with Anna when he had the opportunity to unencumber himself with an overly bold freshman by washing his hands of her and merely filing away her thank you note, feeling smug about his skill in successfully navigating an embarrassing the public relations blunder into which he had earlier stumbled. Rather, he was curious about this young lady and the possibilities her future might hold. He was demonstrating that he would be watching her; he told her so in the letter. He closed the note by encouraging Anna to stay in touch with him and to contact him if she needed him in any way in the future. This realization was a wonder for Anna and our family. Dr. Witt wanted an extended connection, and he was inviting it with the second award.

With an even higher degree of enthusiasm and determination, Anna dove into her semester's challenges. The gauntlet was laid down; she would pick it up and run with it—and run with it, she did. She completed that semester with another perfect grade point average. It was not easy...at times it seemed impossible. But she persevered, working diligently every day, often keeping long hours deep into the night. When May of 2006 arrived and she finished her final exams, she knew she had done what was necessary to remain at the top of her academic game. When her grades were official, Anna wrote the second thank you email to the president, and he responded with pride in her accomplishment and informed her that her scholarship would continue at its present level for next academic year!

In the summer before her sophomore year, Anna decided to apply to become a resident advisor for the university's Office of Student Housing. She enjoyed her freshman experience in the dormitory and believed she would enjoy the job of RA. She felt that she could be good at it. She was accepted as an RA; it was very rare for an entering sophomore to be entrusted with this responsibility, and Anna began intensive training in the weeks prior to student arrival. The training was fast paced and often hard as she logged long hours, often being assigned "on call" assignments where she was the first responder to any dorm resident's problem over a twenty-four hour or forty-eight hour period, especially on weekends. To her mind, the primary perk of being an RA was the furnished apartment she received, which provided her privacy: she did not have a roommate. Also, there was a small monetary stipend each month representing additional payment. The RA position reduced the amount Anna was paying to attend the university, and it made her "Future Leaders" scholarship go even further because her previous housing bill, which accounted for almost half of her college expense, was now eliminated.

The degree of energy and focus Anna's sophomore year required for her to remain successful at the level she desired (as both a student and an RA) was truly daunting, yet she stubbornly maintained her success, refusing to be overcome or to allow her resolve to be broken. By the end of the academic year, she again had received the highest marks possible over both semesters of that academic year, and she was awarded the "Most Valuable Player" award by the Office of Student Housing in recognition of her efforts as an RA. Again, as requested, she wrote Dr. Witt what now was becoming an annual report of her student experience, and she updated him on the highlights. She also thanked him, saying that his investment in her was paying dividends.

One afternoon in July of 2007, just prior to the beginning of Anna's junior year, the telephone rang at our home. Pam answered. She heard for the first time the very excited voice of the president of the University of Alabama: he was calling our house from his office. He asked to speak to Anna, but Pam had to tell him she was away from the house. He went on to say that he was calling to tell all of us that he had just finished typing a letter to Anna, and that she would be receiving it soon, but that in the meantime he wanted to personally tell us he was awarding Anna a new scholarship in recognition of her single-minded achievements. Dr. Witt was now giving Anna "The Crimson Achievement Scholarship," which carried a two-thousand-dollar award! This new scholarship would replace the one she previously had been awarded, and it would continue from year to year. Pam began to weep as she listened to the excitement in the president's voice, and she was barely able to finish the conversation. What a wonder! We realized that not only did the president maintain a personal and ongoing interest in Anna, supporting and encouraging her efforts, but that the new monetary award, in combination with Anna's RA housing credit, brought our daughter's college expenses down to a nominal level. Eureka! The tale of the personal connection between Anna and Dr. Witt that ran through our family's lore was ever expanding!

* * *

3-11-09

Folks,

A good night's sleep but a rough tough morning as Anna had several issues with revolving blood pressure due to her vagal response which overwhelms her central nervous system when traumatic things happen to her, and traumatic things are happening to her insides with the 6th day of aggressive chemo down and 1 more left to go. She is beginning the physical reactions that were predicted that cause her to be weak, anemic, tired, and open to infections. She has continued the day on a neutropenic diet and flowers are leaving the room, and all must wash and sterilize hands before entering the room as a guard against infections.

The best news today is that there was a terrific report regarding the bone marrow biopsy's "cure percentage." Anna is very lucky to be in the top 5% of all people who have the best cure rate percentages for this type of leukemia. This means for her that if/when she leaves the UAB hospital with all leukemia gone, she will have a 60-70% chance of it never coming back again!!! We are thrilled with that news, and we again hold all of you up as an example of the power of prayer to create desired outcomes. God is blessing all of us together—us in that he is restoring our daughter to health, and you for helping to make it happen—caring people becoming Christ for one another!

Words cannot express....
Chris

* * *

3-12-09

Folks,

Day 7—tonight marks the end of the infusions of chemo!!! First
step over with, after the next bottle that gets popped and placed
upside down on the rack that carries all chemo, all IV fluids, all
nausea meds, all antibiotics, etc. All of these have been going at
any one time today as she is still having some blood pressure sta-
bilization difficulties, moving down as she changes positions with
her head from up to down, etc. To help her feel better—they have
given her two units of blood which should improve her energy
level. She has some recurring nausea this evening as well.

Her blood has arrived at the bottom levels of where it was expected
to go, so now is the beginning of the "bad days!" Even though the
chemo has been infused inside her body, it will do its work for
another week or so. The doctors feel that the bone marrow tests
will confirm no more bad cells and instead of repeating the bone
marrow biopsy on day 14, the doctor wants to move it up to possibly day 10—we will see.

She is mostly sleepy now with some windows of regular energy
levels, but we hope that these periods of normalcy will lengthen
and increase with the blood transfusions.

Thanks for your food, your good thoughts and wishes, your
prayers, cards, and phone calls...all are being consumed in this
battle. We will win!

Chris

* * *

3-13-09

Folks,

Day 8, Friday the 13th, is not as bad as it sounds but not great either. She did not sleep well last night and thus had to catch naps all day. She received a platelet transfusion today because her clotting ability has been reduced below what they want to see. These blood products, today and yesterday, require them to give her Benadryl to ease the body's reaction to them. The Benadryl makes her sleepy, so not much is going well for her to feel good but there are no major problems. She did begin to run a fever today, as expected. She is very tired and will be for a week or more. The blood levels have bottomed out on all the numbers, and they have arrived in the cellar and will stay there for a week or more before they climb up in her third week at the hospital.

David flew in from California and he will remain for a week or more to be with Anna during the roughest period of her treatments. His presence makes Anna more animated, and we are grateful for his desire to be here. Also, Alabama Power has provided us an apartment located literally across the street from the parking deck into which David and I will stay, sleep, do laundry, and recoup. We are grateful for the Carver family and all of those who arranged for it to be available for us this next week!

We feel your prayers and good wishes. The doctors and nurses feel it too and have already established a strong bond and caring for Anna. We thank you all for your support.

Blessings to all of you in return...

Chris

*   *   *

In the fall semester of 2009, Anna, now a graduate student at the University of Georgia, was asked by her professor to write an autobiographical paper explaining how she had experienced in her own, real life any of the "learning theories" her class was studying. While the extensive paper contains academic explanations and specific references to an abundance of learning theories and texts, it also includes several long passages of biographic narrative that let us, the readers, experience her story in her own words. In the following excerpt, she tells how she and her boyfriend David came to meet and their history together. Also included in this excerpt is Anna's telling of her diagnosis experience from her first-person point of view. (The following is an excerpt from "Theory Practice: A Developmental Autobiography," an unpublished paper by Anna Gordon, written for the University of Georgia.)

It was during my third go-around of RA training that I met David. He had just been hired as the new hall director of the athletics residence hall and was a graduate student in accounting for the Culverhouse College of Business. I found it hard to believe that a guy as good-looking and confident as he would struggle with walking up to a girl and asking her name, but still, he tells me he did. It worked, I guess, because at our first meeting I was blown away by him completely. I had never met anyone like him before. He was handsome, charming, quick-witted, and fiercely dedicated to his goals. He was well liked by his students, connected professionally all over the country, and was crazy about me. On the outside, our relationship was a match made in the movies, but it took me a long time to recognize the flaws that would eventually break it.

For two years we maintained a long-distance relationship. As I continued working toward graduation, David traveled across the country as a business consultant. We frequently talked about the future and our plans for pursuing our graduate educations together, and eventually, moving toward engagement. However, as my final year in college steadily waned and I began to complete applications to various higher education and student affairs programs across the country, David became more and more unwilling to compromise on a school that would meet both of our needs. He eventually determined that he would only apply to one program: The Keenan Flagler MBA program at The University of North Carolina at Chapel Hill. He cogently argued for me to apply to nearby universities such as the North Carolina State University (since Chapel Hill does not offer a higher education program of any kind), while I protested that I should not have to compromise the quality of my education to accommodate his. Despite the tugging on my conscience, I applied to North Carolina State, as well as the University of South Carolina, in addition to the other universities that I was actually interested in attending and promised David that I would consider them as an option.

In February, I fell ill with strep throat and found myself unable to recover completely. Nevertheless, I continued to attend classes and make progress toward my graduate school decision as I traveled to the University of Georgia as well as Indiana University to complete my program interviews. On March 1st I received a call from Lesley Atchley in the Department of Student Affairs Assessment at the University of Georgia, offering me the graduate assistantship for the office. I was delighted by the offer but hesitated to accept it immediately know-ing that I had so many more campus previews left to go. During my interviews, my health only continued to deteriorate, and after several follow-up visits, my physician suggested that he test my blood for signs of mononucleosis. Thinking little of the test, I went home when it was over to make myself a sandwich (since I had no food in my dorm at all). As I took my first bite of grilled cheese, I noticed my mother's car pull into the driveway. This was unusual since I knew she worked incessantly all day during the school week. Another car pulled into the drive behind her, and two women stepped out. My mom exchanged a few words with the women before they hugged her, got back into their vehicle, and drove away.

I knew in that moment something was wrong. My mom looked obviously upset, as if she had already been crying, and seemed to be as completely surprised to see me at home as I was to see her. I immediately begin to inquire what was wrong, but she evaded my question by asking me about my day. The more I began to inquire, the more upset she became, until she finally sat next to me on the couch and said almost inaudibly, "We have to go back to the doctor." "Why?" I asked, relieved not to have heard something more frightening than that. "I already went this morning. I have a new prescription and everything." "No," she said, before hesitating, "Dr. Bobo just called. Your blood work came back. He thinks it could be leukemia."

I was stunned. I do not even recall really what I thought in that moment because I was so surprised. It seems strange, but in some ways, I was almost relieved that the news had to do with me and not someone else in my family. Because it was me, I was almost certain I could handle it. We immediately drove back to my physician's office, where he explained the news to me and phoned the hospital to set me up an emergency appointment for an oncologist to examine me. Afterwards, my parents and I went straight to the oncology clinic, where a nurse took my blood a second time. "Do you have a port, honey?" she asked. Do I have a what? I screamed aloud to myself, but I'm pretty sure I managed a quick "No." Whatever a port was, I didn't have one.

As I waited to see the doctor, I glanced around the waiting room at the elderly and sickly-looking adults that were also waiting to be seen. I could not help but reason over and over to myself how I didn't belong there, and that this was all going to turn out to be just a terrifying premature diagnosis that my family and I would discuss over the dinner table on holidays and special occasions from now on. I was healthy, in good shape, and took care of myself. There was no way that this could be happening to me.

As it turned out though, it was. Dr. Dubay, now my designated oncologist, confirmed the diagnosis when he walked into my examination room the next morning and announced grimly, "The news is not good." Being the converger that I now know myself to be, I immediately interrogated him about a plan of action; I wanted to know what it was, and I wanted to start it fast. The plan was that I would begin intensive chemotherapy immediately at UAB hospital in Birmingham, where I could expect to be hospitalized for no less than a month. Because the hospital did not have a room available that day, I waited for twenty-four hours for one to come available. In the meantime, I began to look for any and all ways to take action against my illness. The morning following my diagnosis, my mother and I went straight to the mall, where we must have bought every nightgown, pajama set, and pair of slippers we could find. We bought books, movies, games, snacks, journals, and thank you cards for the care packages that we knew would come. I began to treat the illness like I would a class assignment: I would meet it head on, knock it out, and move on to the next thing.

We arrived at UAB at eight o'clock in the morning the following day. A nurse checked me in and escorted me to the ninth floor, where she left me in a cramped room filled with scary-looking medical equipment that hung on the walls. When the nurse left the room and closed the door behind her, I let the bag I had been carrying drop to the floor, sat on the stiff hospital bed, and thought to myself about how much time I would be spending in it over the next month or more. I looked over to my mom, who had been mostly quiet and calm until this point and saw that she was beginning to sob. Seeing her so upset, I began to cry too. We held on tight to each other, much like we did that day in the car nearly four years ago [when I moved in to the dorm to begin undergraduate school], again not ready to begin the newest and most difficult transition that either of us had yet to face.

That first day in the hospital faded into a week, a week into another, and another, and another. I began a seemingly endless cycle of treatment, illness, fevers, allergic reactions, biopsies, and blood transfusions. Guests came and went; flowers and food were brought, displayed, and eventually thrown away. My life had become a whirlwind of fear, pain, disappointment, bitterness, and frustration combined with a sense of determination, hope, and appreciation for the ones I loved who surrounded me. By April most of my acceptance letters had begun to arrive. Each time a new one was delivered, I opened it, read it, and hung it from a corkboard in my room. I looked at those letters alongside a poster which I brought with me for every hospitalization that read, "I Ain't Never Been Nothin' But A Winner," a famous quote by Bear Bryant, Alabama's most beloved football coach. Both the letters and the poster helped to remind me every day that I had things I was going to do, and that I was not going to let a little thing like cancer get in the way of doing them. I may have been stuck in a hospital in Alabama, but I had my family, a diploma, and Georgia on my mind....

I experienced a different experience when I learned of my diagnosis of leukemia. Unlike my experience of matriculation to the University of Alabama, leukemia was an unanticipated event that carried with it a significantly higher impact. Not only was my day-to-day life altered, but it was also turned upside down completely—and to be perfectly honest, my doctor could never say definitively whether or not I could expect to keep my life at all. Additionally, when I was first required to make this transition, I had far fewer assets than liabilities in terms of the situation, myself, my support, as well as my strategies for facing the situation. In terms of the situation itself, I knew the duration of my transition would be indefinite, the timing of it was entirely uncharacteristic, I had no control over the situation whatsoever, my role had changed permanently from that of an undergraduate student to that of a cancer patient, and I was additionally experiencing concurrent stress with my relationship with David as well as my decision about how to proceed toward my goal to attend graduate school. In terms of my support, I had my immediate family and one or two steadfast friends that stood with me throughout my entire journey; most, however, dropped off along the way. It happened slowly at first, but they disappeared steadily as the weeks turned into months.

David was one of those. I am not sure if it was the stress, the fear, or the final strain on an already tenuous relationship, but whatever it was, it broke us. Some of my oldest friends did it too. Some came at first, cried with me and told me how much they cared. But when they left, they went back to their normal, healthy lives, their spring break beach vacations, their petty complaints about work and school, and eventually, they forgot their friend on 2nd floor West DCH. Others never came at all.

…My lingering in Gilligan's second level of moral development often manifested itself in my relationship with David as well. Because I tended to put his needs above my own, I began to make decisions that were not in my best interest, but in his. Because I cared so much for him and for the sustenance of our relationship, I began taking steps toward sacrificing the quality of my graduate educational experience, such as applying and considering schools such as North Carolina State, so that I might allow him to have the kind of experience that he wanted. I eventually made the transition From Goodness to Truth, and remained dedicated to my stance that my need to attend an excellent graduate program was essential not only to my career, but to my happiness as well. In that situation with David, I was forced to make one of the most difficult transitions I will likely ever have to face: I chose to give up my relationship in exchange for independence at the weakest point of my most vulnerable and isolating experience.

* * *

3-14-09

Folks,

Saturday is both a good day and a bad day! On the good side, she has been taken off all IV fluids and she is free to move about untethered to a pole for the first time in 9 days! That means that her blood pressure dropping issues of the last few days have ceased and fevers have subsided. Her blood numbers are at the bottom of where they will be, and she will stay here at this level for the remainder of the week before they begin to move up again in week three.

On the bad side—last night she had a hallucination (brought on by Benadryl that was mainlined into her IV, whose purpose was to ease any blood product issues before they arise since she had platelets given to her yesterday). Pam was having a conversation with her in the middle of the night and Anna was referring to events and conversations in the day that did not happen. Pam had to call the nurses and two came in and worked with Anna for a couple of minutes before she came back into this reality. They are going to dilute any subsequent Benadryl meds.

Also, right around noon, after they had taken out her IV lines, Anna began a nosebleed that lasted for 3.5 hours!—There was considerable packing and other procedures undertaken to stop the bleeding caused because of her low platelet count from the chemo. They had to rehook up the IV and give her another platelet transfusion to get it to stop bleeding so she could eat the lunch that Kathy Wilson brought her at noon (Anna had requested one of Kathy's famous recipe chicken pot pies which Kathy made and drove to the hospital from Tuscaloosa to give to her). So ...finally the day got back on track after she was able to eat something she likes since the food here is beyond bad! Things were stressful for the four hours as they worked to get it to stop, but the day has turned back around to being tolerable, made that way because of special visits from her university professor, Dr. Jennifer Jones, and Kathy Wilson, Frances Huffman, and Scott Tucker—all family for the Gordons. One good thing about crisis times is the reunions that occur on the side!

David and I are enjoying the apartment provided by Alabama Power, which is serving as a center of clothes washing, sleep, showers, and the refrigerator stores food for future use. Thanks for the many notes and cards, balloon bouquets, emails, etc., expressing thoughts of sentiment and good cheer. They are working!!!

Chris

* * *

3-15-09

Folks,

Today marks the beginning for the bad days they say. Days 10-14 should be the low points, we were told, and it sure does seem like that is what is occurring. Anna had a very rough night last night and a difficult morning today, but she has rallied, and the afternoon is the best part of the day so far. Last night, she began what has turned out to be a 14- to 16-hour stretch of fever ranging from low grade to 102 or more and moving all around. This was predicted, and she has had fever on and off for the last several days but nothing lasting this long. In the attempt to combat the fevers, she was given a powerful antibiotic and the dreaded Benadryl again last night. Anna had a strong reaction to the antibiotic which caused her to feel "as if my skin had poison ivy and was sunburned at the same time from the inside out! I want to scratch everywhere." This started with a localized reaction on her chest then spread throughout her body, enflaming as it went. Her head and face began to swell, and her lips swelled, and her eyes swelled almost shut!!! The night nurse, who will remain nameless, seemed unconcerned and was difficult to contact in the middle of the night for any relief or attention. When he did enter, he grunted something about Anna had brought it on herself by asking to take the Benadryl pill rather than the mainlined shot, which she had hallucinated on just the night before!! He implied that she was to blame for her own body's reaction and that he should not have been bothered. Pam threw him out of the room and asked that he be taken off Anna's room assignment immediately—and he was!! Two different antibiotics, two nursing shifts, Benadryl, and Tylenol and 15 hours later, she began to rest and sleep. Pam and Anna had little to no sleep last night and I hope they make it up this afternoon.

This afternoon, however, Anna has walked, slept, eaten, and played cards with David. I returned to Tuscaloosa to meet Tori who gets in from a weekend church trip and I will be a parent to the other sibling. We ask for your focused prayers and positive thoughts as we enter this week of low period where the dark things are that Anna must do battle with and we can only watch, like parents on the 50-yard line at the state championship game. Thank you to our church families in Aliceville and Fayette who have been gracious to let us remain with our daughter during this time. We also thank all of you for your support!

Chris

* * *

Anna's relationship with David was the first serious romantic relationship for her, serious enough that its value to them both caused each of them to consider what life after graduating from the University of Alabama would look like. Making plans, including selecting graduate programs for them both while considering the location of the universities and the content and reputation of their programs, filled Anna's last semester, even before Anna's diagnosis in early March. Anna's leukemia was an enormous disruptor to the plans. She was now consumed with efforts to reclaim her health so she might still be able to obtain the future she wanted. Meanwhile, David was unsure how to act: Anna's plans had been interrupted, and his had not. He wanted to be supportive of Anna's path to remission. He cared for her and wanted them to be together when they began a new school in the fall. But the clouds of uncertainty regarding where they should relocate, the tension created because David's choice of institution was not aligned with Anna's goals, and with the looming uncertainty of her health situation, the resulting storm proved too much for the relationship. It could not endure. David knew he had to move on to where he deemed his future awaited him. Anna's immediate future had been suspended; the uncertainty as to whether she would have a future was palpable. Because the situation could not be overcome, when David left the hospital at the conclusion of his visit, it marked the ending of his relationship with Anna. Cancer had not only cost Anna a healthy body, it had cost the ending of her first real love.

Chapter 4

NURSES ARE THE HEART OF ANY HOSPITAL. THE
empathy they possess and the efficiency with which they execute their duties
determine the quality of care a patient receives during their hospital stay.
Nurses can boost morale, ease suffering, enhance recovery, and diminish
patient and caregiver's anxiety by helping them to see the need for various
procedures and tests. They often also explain the meaning of a physician's
words when the patient or caregiver has time to develop questions following
a brief doctor's visit. Nurses often see the patient's physical changes first, and
they determine whether it is necessary to call a physician to come evaluate a
new health-related situation or to consider a new medication or procedure.
Nurses who are not successful in displaying an optimal degree of concern for
the patient can increase the patient's anxiety and hinder a patient's progress
to recovery. Anna and Pam built relationships of trust and affection for many
of Anna's nurses, and those nurses responded in kind. As a result, genuine
friendships developed.

Doctors, on the other hand, are often less personal when interacting
with patients in a hospital setting—at least that was Anna and Pam's experience. I do not know whether doctors are taught during their training to
be so removed from their patients or whether most doctors are too busy to
engage more personally with them. Perhaps they risk expending too much
emotional energy when engaging with patients? Regardless, the doctors
Anna encountered almost universally maintained their emotional distance

from her, never inquiring as to her life, or her interests, or her goals. When they spoke, it was to address her condition or its treatment. As soon as the conversation regarding her immediate health concluded, they tended to exit the room hastily.

The hospital associated with the University of Alabama in Birmingham is a teaching hospital. It is associated with UAB's medical school, which is one of the premiere medical schools in the country. Thus, in addition to the primary physicians on staff who oversee patients' care, a parade of medical students entered Anna's room.

Medical students endure four years of education and training before they receive their degree. The first two years of study consist mostly of classroom instruction. During the third and fourth year, would-be doctors "shadow" primary teaching physicians who work in various disciplines of medicine, providing hands-on experience with the processes and information associated with the major specializations of modern medicine. They "rotate" in small groups, spending a few weeks experiencing the focus on— and content of care for—each discipline before progressing to the next concentration. These rotations expose each student to the various branches of medicine practiced within a hospital setting; the exposure also serves to inform the student as to which medical branch they are most interested in. After graduating medical school, they will each have to select one of these disciplines to specialize in. The student then receives their degree and begins a "residency" at another hospital, where they will perform supervised work exclusively in the field they have chosen. After completing the residency program, either the new doctor will be hired as a working physician within their chosen field, or they may choose a "fellowship" program where they receive even more specialized instruction and experience prior to beginning their working career.

Typically, during their rotations medical students visit patients early in the morning, asking questions and collecting vital signs and other medical data regarding any overnight event the patient might have experienced.

They also prepare a written update on each patient that will be delivered to the attending physician regarding the patient's condition just prior to the physician's daily rounds, when the physician visits each patient with a herd of students in tow. The students frequently remain at the hospital until late in the evening, executing any orders given by the physician during the rounds earlier in the day, writing reports and documents, and updating records. Because it is common to develop connections with those people you see the most, Anna and Pam came to love the nurses (mostly), and also to enjoy the medical students. They interacted with Anna's actual doctor the least.

Anna and Pam were fascinated by one medical student in particular. Robert McDonald was older than the other medical students they encountered—older by at least a decade. He was also easy to talk to not only about medical issues and conditions, but about more personal matters. Rob had some unusual life experiences, and Anna and Pam found him to be unconventional. They discovered that Rob held an MBA degree and that he had been a hospital administrator. He was the director of an AIDS clinic in Africa, and he told them of those people he had encountered, their medical problems, and their culture. He shared that while in Africa, he felt a strong empathy for the patients he met. Over time, he became dissatisfied with his role as a mere administrator; instead he wished he could take a more "hands on" role, so that he could be more helpful when his clinic cared for its patients. He came to recognize a growing desire to return to school and become an infectious diseases specialist; in so doing, he could become more useful to those enduring the ravages of AIDS. Here he was, in Anna's hospital room, having abandoned a career he had already established, replacing it with the long and arduous process of become a doctor. While Rob's oncology rotation was seemingly short—he would soon move on to the next specialty in his rotation—his impact as a person on Anna and Pam, and the sharing of his humanity with both Anna and Pam, made him unique, welcome, and memorable.

* * *

3-16-09

Folks,

I am happy to report a good day!! Day 11 seems to be a rest from the turmoil of the last several days in that Anna and Pam had a good night of sleep and a good morning before receiving a transfusion of platelets and a unit of blood in the afternoon due to a low white count and a low red count. Fevers have been down, and she has tolerated the antibiotics well today that have caused her difficulty early on. In fact, Anna touched her right ear and felt wetness coming out of it and asked the nurse about it. He then looked at it and called the doctor who looked at it and declared that she had a "blister" that had emerged and burst. In other words, the reaction and burning she felt from the heavy antibiotics the other night literally did burn her from the inside out!!! I had never heard of such a thing. This makes the insensitivity of the offending night nurse regarding Anna's "whining" even more ridiculous!

We had many visitors and well wishes, and the mail bag brought in today was amazing—filled with cards and letters and gifts and well wishes from many of you in Fayette, Gordo, Tuscaloosa, even Oklahoma, Texas, Arkansas, Louisiana, and other places beyond our imagination. Pam, half joking, half not, wanted me to get a map of the world and pin the locations of all the mail, cards, phone calls, letters, emails, and gifts because not only have they come in from the places I just listed, but from New York to Los Angeles, Alaska to Daytona, Russia, Japan, Taiwan, Africa, and Scandinavia. Surely the Lord moves in mysterious and amazing ways! I can honestly say there is nothing as impressive and humbling as the concentrated, focused, and intense caring, praying, and nurturing of Christian people acting as Christ for ones who need it. Every day God comes to us disguised, wearing your faces, leaving his mark through your signatures, speaking through your voices, and ministering through your actions—and to think he planned it that way...

So, I will thank Him by thanking you, each day! Thank you!!!!

Chris

*   *   *

3-17-09

Folks,

Day 12 was a very good day, probably the best day since she has been in the hospital! Blood counts are low, and she is still receiving preventative meds, but she was full of energy and was untethered to IVs for much of the day. Anna sat up, got out of the bed, and sat in a chair for half the day or more, saw many visitors—even Claire Goodson from Anna's softball playing days came by to visit with her mother! Anna was even feeling well enough to complain about how I was portraying her in these updates—that is a good thing!!!

The bone marrow biopsy is scheduled for Thursday to see if she is "clean," and we should have the results back by Friday!

Tori and I got to go up together for a long visit today and Pam's sister Kay got to come by for a bit also, leaving her mother for the first time in two weeks after her mother's back surgery. A good day is much better than a bad day any ole day!

Chris

*   *   *

3-18-09

Folks,

Today was a good day for Anna. She had visitors from UA and enjoyed old family friends. She had a small nosebleed today that was a minor concern but got it stopped quickly. She had 2 units of platelets and 2 units of blood today, in preparation for the bone marrow biopsy scheduled for the late morning (Thursday.) We will see when these results return, possibly on Friday, whether she is "clean" in her blood stream and marrow—this has been the goal of the chemo! Please remember her tomorrow as she endures this difficult procedure, done this time with low platelet and white counts to battle with.

Chris

*   *   *

3-19-09

Folks,

Today was the second bone marrow biopsy—exactly 14 days after the first. Anna tolerated it well, again, and now we wait for the analysis to come in, hopefully, tomorrow. The goal is to have 0 cancer cells, and if they see that amount reached in the marrow, then they will begin to pump her up over the next week or two in preparation to go home. If they see even one cell, they say they will start her on a 5 and 2, meaning they will do the same two-chemo drug treatment they did over 7 days last week [but this time they will do it] over 5 days, with the second pushed in over 2 of those 5 days.

It is agonizing to sit and wait, hope, and pray for the results we all seek. Many of you have been praying along with us today and over many days and we must trust the Lord to work out His goodness in His own time. Whatever the outcome, we thank you for your support and concern and we know that it is with your help that we endure—thank you!

Chris

*   *   *

3-20-09

Folks,

The doctors just left the room and Anna Gordon is CLEAN!!

No more Leukemia!!!!!!!!!!!!!!!

Thank God and Thank you,

Chris

*   *   *

3-21-09

Folks,

I hope everyone has heard by now that many prayers were answered. Anna's second bone marrow biopsy results came back indicating no Leukemia anywhere in her system! It is not predicted to come back either, thank God! We are now looking forward to Anna's return to a healthy building up of blood levels that will enable her to return home sometime soon! She is resting well, and she is looking forward to happier days. Her hair is now beginning to let go, as expected, and she is remaining positive about it.

We are mindful of all your help to make this a successful outcome for Anna. Without your concern, which you turned into regular, powerful prayer for Anna's health and our strength, our being at this pleasant point might be in serious doubt. What a wonderful, comforting experience it is to know we have this level of support.

Thanks to you all and thank the Lord for His goodness to us!

Chris

* * *

3-22-09

Folks,

Anna spent the morning sleeping, recouping from the last two days' emotional rollercoaster. She is perky today and animated, indicating good healthy feelings of relief, acceptance, and optimism. Her hair continues to let go, but this is expected. She got another unit of blood platelets this morning, replacing the killed ones, keeping her platelet count up. It needs to stay at or more than 20 and the chemo is keeping hers around 8 or 9, creating a bleeding risk due to the inability to clot. So, she will regularly get platelet and blood units all through this recovery process.

Many of you have asked what is the treatment path now? She will be in the hospital for another week or two—to get her blood counts up to a healthy level so that she can enter the outside world without fear of infection. When we leave the hospital, she will stay home for 3 weeks then return to the hospital for a week of additional chemo (but not as intense or extensive) to keep the system clean of Leukemia cells. This cycle will continue for 4 months—3 weeks at home and 1 week in the hospital. During the 3-week periods of time while she is home, she will also have to come twice a week to the Kirklin Clinic in Birmingham to get blood checks, monitoring her blood counts and given additional platelets or blood units when necessary.

Chris returned to work at his church in Fayette this morning and was greeted with warm and wonderful, caring people. I had an emotional day being around people who helped pray for Anna's health, and I felt at home. Pam will remain on hospital duty, and I will go back to work teaching Monday morning. I am sure it will take many weeks and months to come to adequately process all the events of the last few weeks. We are just glad to be intact and still going and we will let time do its work in all its wonders.

Chris

* * *

3-24-09

Folks,

Somehow yesterday (Monday) I missed sending a report. I guess I was so busy getting to where I needed to be next, since I went back to work that day and made a trip to Birmingham for a short visit (4 hours in the car), that I collapsed in bed before I could write it. Please let this email be for both days.

Anna is feeling much better, and she is beginning to improve in her blood counts, spiking up a good bit today!! The doctors said this morning that she might be able to go home as early as Friday, depending on her upward progress, of course. So, the recovery is going very well. Pam counted [your well wishes] today and Anna has received well over 200 cards and letters in just 19 days. No wonder the doctor was quoted as saying when he first looked around her room, "Who are you?" She is someone well loved, well cared for and cared about by so many people and well prayed for.

We thank God and we thank you for all your interest and concern shown throughout these many days. We are truly Blessed!!

Chris

* * *

3-25-09

Folks,

Today Anna experienced almost the remaining hair letting go in large traumatic chunks, exposing the scalp in various places. She is scheduled to have a hair stylist shave the remaining scalp tomorrow, completing the loss of hair process. It has been letting go gradually for many days and the pace has accelerated to this place. I know you can tell yourself it will grow back soon, and it will, but it is still traumatizing for a young woman to deal with yet another blow to the self-esteem.

She is scheduled to have several visitors from the UA campus today, later this afternoon. Her blood counts have not skyrocketed today like they did yesterday, but they have not dropped lower either. We are still waiting for the word on when they will be up enough to go home. She was to get lessons today on the care of her "port" so she will have several days to practice under nurse supervision before going home. She was also taken off all antibiotics today, a good thing.

Now the mental adjustments will begin, and we appreciate your support in that process.

Chris

* * *

3-26-09

Folks,

Anna had a long day of sleeping then visitation. The previous couple of days caused her to need to recover sleep which she did until about 3 o'clock, then she talked with Dr. Jennifer Jones for a long time into the evening about graduate school possibilities as well as many wonderful topics. Dr. Jones is such an engaging conversationalist that the evening breezed by. Anna's blood counts dipped back down to 0 in her important count that determines when she can go home so she will not be returning home tomorrow as first thought. It could be this time next week. We will just have to let the bone marrow do its job and get her back up to speed. She is adjusting to her new hair style, and she is experimenting with various scarf-tying techniques.

She also enjoyed going through the mail today which had several packages of caps, wigs, and other items to try on. We thank you for all your kindnesses in helping to make her feel more comfortable in her new reality.

Chris

*   *   *

3-27-09

Folks,

Today was a hard day because the doctors came in and announced that they think they see blast cells in the daily blood slides (blast cells are cancer cells). They also announced that they felt we should know. But they said the same thing on day 13 and when they did the second bone marrow test, on day 14, the pathologist read it and said she was cancer free. The thing with this time is that the next scheduled bone marrow biopsy is for 10 days or so from now. We must wait each day to see if they think they see a pattern of blast cells from now until who knows when. Also, the doctors did not even look at the slides, I think I was told a lab tech did. I wish they would have a little more concrete evidence in hand before they come in and announce that their "cancer free" diagnosis might be incorrect at this point!

Therefore, as you can tell we are stressed somewhat with this possibility and the not knowing of any facts! Please continue to hold
Anna up—we need a positive outcome to all of this and as Anna's
T-shirt from Jeanie Hindman says "... this too shall pass—now
would be nice!"

Chris

*   *   *

3-28-09

Folks,

As I had hoped, the doctors came in this morning and reported
that they saw nothing unusual in Anna's daily blood slides. This
is as we had suspected and had been led to believe ever since the
last bone marrow biopsy was read by the pathologist and declared
"cancer free." It seems as if what they thought they saw yesterday
was an anomaly. We are grateful for the removal of the stress that
they placed on us yesterday. Do you hear that roller coaster coming into the loading dock again?

Another good news this morning was that Anna's blood count
numbers were going up as finally expected, at least the white
counts and average count. The reds were down a little and she has
received a unit of blood this afternoon. But they are talking about
her going home by Monday. That would be wonderful, but as we
have come to find out, things can change quickly, so we hope they
continue to go up. I apologize for any shared stress that yesterday's
note may have caused—just remember you wanted to know... so
you get it as we get it! Thanks for being there! :)

Chris

*   *   *

3-29-09

Folks,

Anna's blood counts are going up! The average count is now about half what it needs to be but they still say that tomorrow, Monday, she will go home. We are preparing by packing and organizing all the many food items, gifts, cards, and clothes that people have sent or brought since we arrived four weeks ago. The doctors say that they still see some blast cells, but they are not worried about them at this point. I do not know what that means because I associate their "blast cells" with cancer cells, but that is not exactly the case, and the difference has yet to be explained well enough for me to understand it. We are waiting for the positive news that we trust will follow the next bone marrow biopsy which is now scheduled for April 8.

I am preparing at home for their arrival by cleaning and stocking up groceries and making plans to add some alterations that will make Anna's being at home safer and more manageable. While her counts are encouraging, Anna was very tired today having not slept well and because her body is working hard to make new healthy cells, it zaps all her energy.

Tomorrow, if they return home, we will begin the second wave of treatment—that two- or three-week at home stay interrupted by a week in the hospital for chemo consolidation. This will repeat for four months. We are excited and apprehensive, wanting to do it right and cross the path to normalcy efficiently and quickly. We thank you for your continued support and remembrance in your prayers.

Chris

* * *

3-30-09

Folks,

Home Sweet Home!! Tori and I got to UAB hospital at 1:00 pm and after 4 loads of double layer luggage carts filling two vehicles (the van and the Jetta) like we were going to the beach, we finally got checked out and arrived home at 6:00 pm. A wonderful roast-beef dinner with all the trimmings was ushered into the door at 7:00 pm by Tom and Debbie Albright (Tom had already cut my grass) and we are soon to sit down and enjoy the first meal as a family all together in 26 days or so.

Everyone is grateful and overwhelmed to be home at least for a short while, resting in their very own beds, pillows, and comforters. We will rest and sleep well tonight!

"God Bless Us Everyone..."

Chris

Chapter 5

Dr. Robert Witt, president of the University of Alabama in Tuscaloosa, informed Anna in March of 2009 that the provost and Anna's professors had conferred with each other and determined that Anna had already fulfilled the requirements of her coursework; she was a candidate for graduation in the forthcoming commencement ceremony in May. In consideration of Anna's special circumstance, Dr. Witt called and invited Anna and our entire family to sit in the president's box. It was a magnanimous gesture. Anna thanked Dr. Witt for his kindness and thoughtfulness, but she decided that because her immune system was still rebuilding itself and was not yet one-hundred percent back to normal, it would be best if she declined the offer and did not attend graduation, which would entail the customary thousands of parents and graduate candidates occupying the same space and breathing the same air. Instead, on the day of graduation, the whole family made its way to the president's mansion for the scheduled pre-graduation reception. So as to not make her lack of hair an advertisement for her medical condition, which she viewed as an inconvenience, Anna dressed comfortably but beautifully and donned a summer hat that prevented her still-balding head from the view of onlookers. She walked up the outer stairs of the mansion just as the entry queue shortened to two students. Dr. Witt himself stood at the front door, greeting each student who entered his home. Quickly the two students in front of Anna passed through, and Anna found herself embracing her mentor and friend. He recognized the symbolism of Anna's effort to be present at the reception, and he embraced her with warmth and caring. Although Anna did not enter the house, which would have risked exposing her immune system, she had wanted to thank Dr. Witt, yet again, for his help, his concern, his mentorship, and his encouragement during her undergraduate sojourn. Their friendship had given her the opportunity to discover her purpose in regard to a career: he had inspired her to be a university president so that she could affect future students in the same way he had affected her.

* * *

Before Anna's diagnosis on March 2, 2009, she had already begun the graduate school application process. Her discussions with Dr. Jen Jones ignited a fire that blazed with enthusiasm, encouraging her to evaluate potential schools that offered graduate programs in higher education and concentrations she desired. She researched each school online, conferred with Jen, then narrowed her list to five schools. She knew that she would have to update her resume, list references, and submit letters of recommendation to each school. There were obvious choices as to whom she would ask to write letters on her behalf: leading professors in her concentration of study at the University of Alabama, supervisors of undergraduate research, even supervisors of her work as a resident advisor in student housing. However, she also asked Dr. Witt to write a general letter of recommendation on her behalf. Dr. Witt readily agreed to do it, writing his remarks on official letterhead, bearing the title of his office. Anna included the letter in all five of her applications to graduate school. Now *that* is something a graduate school applications committee does not see every day!

Part of the selection process by the graduate schools Anna applied to was an in-person interview with the applications committee. Naturally, this required Anna to schedule trips to each of the five schools on her list. The visits gave the prospective school the opportunity to see if they wanted Anna Gordon, and it gave Anna the opportunity to evaluate if she wanted them. Anna visited the schools late in January and February of 2009. She hoped to be offered a graduate assistantship from each institution. The assistantship would include tuition expenses plus a monthly stipend in exchange for performing whatever duties were stipulated by the terms of the assistantship. In the end, the national ranking of the University of Georgia,—along with the school's reputation and the terms of the assistantship it offered Anna—persuaded Anna to go to Athens in the fall. Her enthusiasm was palpable as she moved toward graduation. Then leukemia happened.

* * *

4-1-09

Folks,

Anna has been home for two days, adjusted to her own bed after a month away, and she has had two full nights of uninterrupted sleep! Amazingly, that is the hardest and most valuable thing to

acquire in the hospital. She has had a constant set of visitors at home on each of her two days here, from friends to relatives to university faculty. She ventured into wearing makeup today, the first time since the beginning of her chemo, and she looks powerful and wonderful—like a flapper from the roaring twenties in her white hat!

Another basket of gifts and goodies came from yet another Sunday School class from the Fayette First Methodist Church. It was filled with so many wonderful presents of scarves, books, snacks, stationery, and fun stuff! All our friends, many who have never even met Anna, have been overwhelmingly generous with their support and encouragement!! We cannot express adequate thanks for your outpouring.

As I got in late tonight from work, 9:00 pm, I found her ordering Alabama football tickets online!!! You have got to be feeling optimistic if you are planning the football season activities for the fall—Roll Tide!!!!!!!!

That's My Girl,
Chris

* * *

4-3-09

Folks,

Today Anna rested. She slept until 1:00 pm, recovering from a long couple of days with lots of company. How she/we enjoy the visits, but they do take their toll on her limited energy supply. She had no visitors today, but the family did get to resume some normal activities that we enjoy. We, all four of us, went out for a drive late in the afternoon, finding the van heading through the drive-thru at the local TCBY yogurt shoppe. Then off to get gas and the van washed—most people just do not know what fun is...lol. Anyway, it was Anna's first trip out into the world—into spring, facemask, and all.

While there were no visitors today, there were still deliveries and mail. Flowers, presents, cards, and letters found their way from many unexpected sources to our door, bringing support and well wishes. While disease and difficulty are not something you wish upon yourself, sometimes, if you look, you get to see the very best in people and of people, parts that they do not always display in the day to day. Compassion works that way; it never ceases to soothe and amaze those who need and receive it.

Chris

*   *   *

4-7-09

Folks,

There has not been a lot to tell in the last several days, so I have not written. Anna has still maintained a healthy schedule of visitors almost every day and she has even ventured out into the world going to one of her favorite restaurants for the evening meal on Wednesday last week, dawning jeans for the first time in a month and sitting in a public place eating Japanese food at Bento. She has rested as much as possible and she and Nathan Smock and some others have begun work on a 1000-piece jigsaw puzzle she received. She has worn most all her hats and scarves by now, finding matching clothes in her closet to go with the things she has received. She is keeping her mother busy, who is trying to make all her favorite foods before she must return to the hospital to begin consolidation chemo treatments soon.

Tomorrow, Wednesday, Anna, and Pam go to the Kirklin Clinic in Birmingham to see her physician, Dr. Baird, and she will undergo the third bone marrow biopsy. We all hope it goes well and the news is positive. Please remember them tomorrow.

Thank you for your continued support and friendships,
Chris

*   *   *

4-10-09

Folks,

FINALLY!!!—After a long two-day anxious wait, with the entire world waiting to hear the news, the nurse called to report that the blood marrow is clean!! Anna is still in remission. They were still waiting on the chromosomal analysis, which takes longer, before they thought to call. Pam called the clinic and got them to trace it down before the entire staff left for the holiday weekend. But the most important information we did get [the news that her blood is clean of cancer cells]. The other [news of the chromosomal analysis results which we did not receive today] tells of her prognosis over time. Now we can all enjoy the Easter celebration!

We went to Anna's Honors Day activities at UA in the Psychology Department, where she received awards for Academic Excellence in a Psychology Major with a 4.0 GPA over 150 hours and Excellence in Honors Psychology Senior Research Projects. It was bittersweet for her, getting to see many of her professors and friends, while at the same time not being able to have the day unfold as she had foreseen it a year ago with the altering of her future due to cancer.

We celebrate with her and with all of you, getting good news on Good Friday!! Enjoy blessings now and each day!

Chris

* * *

4-15-09

Folks,

I have not written much since Anna has been home, other than to report the results of the 3rd bone marrow biopsy as being very good with no cancer indicated. I can now report that the chromosomal report came back to us on Monday, indicating perfectly normal DNA, causing her doctor to declare Anna in "complete remission"! That is the final piece of great news and it lays the foundation for her to complete the "consolidation chemo" and continue with her life.

Pam and Anna returned to the UAB hospital today, Wednesday, (room # 938 West Pavilion) for 6 days of "consolidation," which she began tonight at about 9:00 pm. From what I have heard from Pam tonight, it is the equivalent of 1 day, or 24 hours, of [the] drip that she received in the first round of chemo, accept that this is fast dripped into her "port' in a matter of three hours. She could potentially become more ill with this than she was with the original dosages. We will see as the night progresses, and I will report how she tolerated it in the email scheduled for tomorrow.

We are grateful for your support and prayers, and we thank you for your interest and comments!!

Chris

* * *

4-17-09

Folks,

Anna is off today from the "consolidation" chemo. The routine is to take the amount of chemo that was done over a 24-hour period during the original chemo sessions and increase the speed of it so that it is pumped into her in 3 hours. They wait for about 8 hours and do it again, then give her 24 hours off. She has responded fine to this (so far 1 day down of the 3 that she will have the chemo drip) but she has slept a good bit, but this is her only symptom yet regarding its internal effects to her system. She is walking and Pam and Anna walked a good bit while I went out to Surin West to get their lunch as the hospital food is still not appetizing.

I came up this morning for the first time since they arrived on Wednesday since I have been hosting Dr. Donald Shetler this week, whose biography I am writing. The University of Alabama brought him down from his retirement home in Charleston, SC to lecture to 5 classes of their music education majors. I believe they enjoyed getting to meet him and listen to him discuss many aspects of his career that have made him one of the preeminent figures in music education in the country in the twentieth century. I am grateful to the University for their interest and kind support. I was especially glad that he got to attend the Druid Arts Award ceremony last night at the Bama Theater and see the Tuscaloosa Horns receive the award for "Musician of the Year." He also got to spend some time at the Westervelt-Warner Museum of American Art, where he and I and Dr. Ken McGuire of the University faculty received a private tour by the owner of the collection himself, Jack Warner. They hit it off right away and we spent 2 hours talking and exchanging stories. Don even pulled out his cello and played a mini concert for Mr. Warner, Ken, and me in the George Washington room. Dr.

Shetler's visit was prearranged many weeks ago and Anna's current chemo treatment just happened to fall at the same time, making it difficult to do all that was necessary to get through the week, but we made it.

We hope that the remainder of the week goes as smoothly with no complications as [Anna] begins the descent down to the lowest levels of blood chemistry. We thank you for all your many comments of support and cards and letters. They have already begun to arrive. Just before Anna left for UAB, she accepted the University of Georgia's offer of a graduate assistantship assigned to the Vice President's Office of Assessment for the University. Anna will enjoy attending and working in a new and exciting area of interest to her as she will begin her master's degree in Higher Education Administration in August in Athens, GA. Anna will be a Georgia Bulldog and she is thrilled to be going to such a fine school and they seem excited to have her there as well.

God is good!!

Chris

* * *

4-18-09

Folks,

Anna has spent almost the entire day sleeping. She was interrupted 4-5 times in the evening by nurses doing their chores after having just finished chemo at midnight, then they started again with the chemo at 8:00 this morning and finished at 11:00 or so. She has had little time to sleep because of the hospital schedule, plus, the chemo itself is very concentrated, some 30 times the strength of her March chemo recipe. I guess the doctor is trying to overwhelm the system with high intensity, short-term infusions designed to penetrate everything, even the brain with this concoction. The doctors come in every morning and have Anna do coordination skills, testing to make sure the brain has not been affected. I wish they would leave her brain alone; it was just fine before they started messing with it. She has the day and night off today and the Sunday day off before she begins again with the chemo on Sunday night.

We hope this is all working and doing what [it] is supposed to do—seems like a lot of high power for a system in complete remission. And to think, we still have three more sessions before we are through... ugh!

Chris

*　*　*

4-19-09

Folks,

Anna and Pam had a difficult night last night being awakened 14 times before 7:00 am. They are indeed ready to come home ASAP. The doctors have nothing to say other than the perfunctory platitudes and "... all looks fine," but then again there is really nothing for them to say since it is just "consolidation." All that is required is to get the meds inside her and get them out again. In a way, it is anticlimactic in comparison to the March madness where some drama regarding the outcome of the procedure existed. There is no battle to fight here, just leaving troops in occupied territories to "mop up," as they say. This leads to boredom and frustrations, knowing that there will be 3 more months of this.

It is almost disappointing, beginning the descent of her blood counts toward "0," after she felt good again in the interim time since she returned home and made plans toward the future. To return to the depths of energy and health due to controlled toxins invading her blood stream is a bad joke, and the reality turns to nightmare when one contemplates doing it three more times when she would rather be making new plans and new beginnings! Yet wait she must, and we must with her. But there is hope as even our Lord asked "...if this cup pass from me?" We all would like to change things and make them different from what they are in the present. Patience is a virtue for a reason, and we pray for more of it.

Chris

* * *

4-20-09

Folks,

The girls came home today, a day early!! I think they were thrown out for bad behavior, or at least that is what they say. But I do not care, and they do not either—at least they have "broken out of the big house" for three weeks! They are appreciating being at home among their stuff and their people and their freedom.

They made the decision to go [to] DCH Cancer Treatment Center in Tuscaloosa for all her blood counts, lab work, and any transfusions or platelets if necessary. This will cut down the number of hours involved in having to go to the Kirklin Clinic in Birmingham. They can do the same thing here with less time and fewer people involved. So, things are looking up! Although they say that 70% of patients must return to the hospital due to infections as they attempt to recover at home, we hope that Anna will be in the 30% of those who pass the test. We will see.

Anyway, at least for tonight, the car is unpacked, the sheets are clean and fresh with [the beds] made, the Olive Garden was very good, and the Samsung is HD and on. Simple things are very comforting!

Chris

*　*　*

4-27-09

Folks,

Anna has been at home living as normally as she can in recent days. It has gone well, and this is slightly different, the "consolidation" process, than the original chemo healing process. We have been expecting similar timetables and similar events in the way she feels and her activity levels, but this has been its own thing, forcing us to pay closer attention so that we might be able to predict her reactions in the next three months. She has reacted better overall with the "consolidation." She has had more energy, felt better, and been able to sustain a daily schedule of activity that is normal.

Today, Anna and Pam had an appointment to go to the Cancer Treatment Center, here in Tuscaloosa, for blood counts. She is now neutropenic again, as expected, which means her blood counts are very low and she must return to a specialized diet to keep clear of foods that may cause infections or reactions. This also means that her platelet levels are low, causing her to be a bleeding risk if she were to fall or have an accident. When the platelets fall to these levels, they give her platelet transfusions and that is what they did today at the Cancer Treatment Center here.

I was pleased to hear that their first experience with the brand-new center was fabulous and everything that you could want in a specialized facility. As compared to the famous Kirklin Clinic, the experience was night and day, leaving Tuscaloosa shining in the sun! We are grateful for caring nurses and volunteers that made their day not only efficient but memorably pleasant! Congratulations DCH!

More when there is something to say,
Chris

* * *

5-1-09

Folks,

Tough day and night! Yesterday, Thursday 4-30-09, Pam and Anna were scheduled to go to the Cancer Center in Tuscaloosa for routine bi-weekly blood work. Her blood counts are in the basement, as expected by this time of the week, and she received a transfusion of platelets, preceded by Benadryl to ward off any blood reactions during the process. That went as expected and they returned home by midday. Anna felt tired and lethargic all afternoon and into the evening spending the time mostly lying on the sofa. By bedtime she drifted off to sleep with no fever or blood pressure issues all day. I proceeded to bed and packed my bag and horn to leave this morning at 8:00 on my way to perform in Houston and New Orleans over the weekend.

At 2:00 am, Anna came into our bedroom and announced that she had a fever of 102.9!!! She is to go to the hospital immediately when her temperature rises to 100.5 due to her low white blood cell level counts and the inability to fight any outside element in that condition. We ran out of bed, called the UAB cancer nurse who told us to go to the Emergency Room in Tuscaloosa and get antibiotics, which we did. Five minutes later we were in the ER of DCH being handled by people who seldom see a cancer patient for this type of regimen of treatment. They go into high diagnostic mode and order CT scan and chest X-rays attempting to locate the source of the fever, while listening to her symptoms of only fever and painful headache. The zealous ER physician, in his attempt to do everything in his power to rectify the problem, begins talking of Spinal Taps and Spinal Meningitis, scaring us to death. Thankfully, the CT scan came back quickly indicating an acute sinus infection. Well, yeah!!! We know that. She has had one since January AND IT IS STILL HERE!!!!!

I sent Mart a text canceling my trip at 3:00 am. Then when we discovered that it was the sinus which she has had for a long time and not something new and scary, I texted him again at 6:00 saying I would go on and play since it would be difficult and awkward for him to find someone new in such a short time. I left DCH at 7:30 am to go meet the "fellas" at Lowe's and we packed the van and headed out on our trip when the phone rang!! Pam was saying amid a bad cell signal and break ups that they had hooked Anna up to a heart monitor and that its alarm was going off constantly!! They had never done that at UAB, and we did not know if she had something new that needed attention or what. We were on the on-ramp to the freeway when the call came. Mart stopped the van, turned around and went back to Lowe's parking lot, kicked me out of the van with all the guys verbalizing love and affection for Anna and the family and headed off to Houston without me. I should have never accepted the gig in the first place.

I returned to DCH to find the girls out of the ER, in a holding area, awaiting admission as [hospital staff tried to] find a room for her.

At 10:30 am we finally got her into a room on the oncology floor, room #222—for all you old 70's TV fans. Now she is on the antibiotics appropriate to the infection, and I hope it gets rid of it once and for all!!! We should be here at DCH for today maybe tomorrow as well, then return home to the regular schedule. The heart monitor just seems to be DCH's standard procedure. UAB never did that sort of thing, so we were not accustomed to it and thought the worst right away. Live and learn. Panic and relax, such go the ebb and flow of a family living with cancer. I hope we get some sleep today!!! :)

Drama still lives...
Chris

*   *   *

5-03-09

Folks,

Anna had pains shooting through her back and legs at 4:30 am, because of the Neupogen shots she was given on Friday and Saturday. These shots are designed to "stimulate" the growth of white blood cells, something you need when you are near the bottom of the blood counts so you can fight infections like the sinus infection that sent her to the hospital Friday morning. However, the side effects of the shot are that there is pain associated with the bone marrow as it quickly puts out the new cells. Anna described it as like the bone marrow biopsy pain, a little less but constant and moving around to different places. The price of getting out of the basement in her blood counts came with a physical payment that requires her to have some narcotic pain medication to endure it. But her counts skyrocketed quickly, and she and Pam came home at 2:00 pm. Talk about the roller coaster effect!

DCH has been a joy. The nursing staff has been very efficient and sensitive to our needs. They are consistently staffed with the patient having the same nurses each day on the same shifts so that you are not constantly learning new people and they are learning you and your condition. It is a breeze being 5 minutes from home and the food is good! Throw in the state-of-the-art new Cancer Treatment Center and we in Tuscaloosa have much to be proud of and enjoy!

We hope for a quiet week filled with rest and no drama!—I will write again when there is something to report. We thank you for your interest, prayers, and concerns.

Chris

*   *   *

5-27-09

Folks,

I have not been able to write as quickly as I had wanted because I was out of town playing and did not return until Tuesday evening. Then I had to return to work this morning for the month of June, but I did want you to know that Anna and Pam returned to the hospital, DCH room 225 in Tuscaloosa, on Monday and they will be there most of this week due to fevers Anna has been having. In the process of treating the fever, she has also received 2 units of blood and 1 unit of platelets along with IV antibiotics and fluids. This is [in response to] the infectious part of the blood counts being down due to the chemo regime she had a week ago. The blood counts seemed to have gone down more quickly than expected this time around however and we seem to be in a revolving door at DCH—having only left there last week at this time from her regularly scheduled consolidation #2 treatment.

So, they are battling feeling bad and [the] mental fatigue of existing within four walls! Thanks for your support.

Chris

*   *   *

5-27-09

Folks,

Anna has had a Neupogen shot this evening and still had 101 temperatures as I left the hospital at 8:00 tonight. The Neupogen shot is to stimulate the bone marrow to manufacture white cells more quickly so that the counts go up and her immune system returns to its regular capability. However, in the stimulation of the marrow, it feels like a bone marrow biopsy [that] lasts for two days rather than 20 minutes! So, to feel better faster, you must feel worse now—go figure! Maybe it will help the fever also, who knows.

She has had antibiotics today and has had times of no fever and rising fever—up and down—up/down all day for three days. Cancer and cancer prevention suck!

Chris

*   *   *

5-28-09

Folks,

Another tough day at the hospital—temperature of 101.5, another Neupogen shot, cold/hot, hot/cold, 3 blood cultures, IV antibiotics (two different IVs alternating every 8-12 hours), sweats and shivers—and NO INTERNET!!!!! Fever broke just before I left the hospital at 8:00 pm. Anna ate little all day until Indian take-out tonight and a piece of Holli Moss's chocolate pie!!

The doctor says that she is at the bottom of her counts today. She has no white cells at this point. Therefore, no immune system at all. Therefore, she has been having fever all week; her body produces a fever to fight the invading bacteria by raising the temperature past which it can survive because they [the bacteria] are temperature sensitive. The shots should boost the whites' regrowth soon, and maybe in two days from now she might feel better as things begin to return more to normal levels. Let us hope her body can keep the invaders at bay until the white-celled calvary can come to the rescue for this month!

Chris

＊　＊　＊

5-29-09

Folks,

Anna had a better day today, sleeping through most of it, rising at 3:00 pm! She still has some fever, from the 99.5 -101.5 range, but the white cells are beginning to rise slowly from 0 to 0.5 today. The neutrophils, a combination of white cells and other stuff—I should have paid more attention in biology—is the key element in her being able to go home. The doctors want them to be at 1000 when she leaves the hospital and antibiotics to go home; right now, she is 40. A long way to go, but when things start to go up, they go up very quickly. I figure they may come home by Sunday or Monday. At least I hope so, or the girls will be bumping into themselves as they go back in for the next consolidation!!

Chris

＊　＊　＊

5-30-09

Folks,

Anna has had everything that can be thrown at her today—
antibiotic vancomycin (the one that gives her the "Red Man
Syndrome" when not given without a good bit of caution ["Red
Man Syndrome" refers to an internal reaction to the antibiotic
vancomycin, which can make you feel as if you are burning inside,
as Anna did when she sustained the blister behind her ear during
the UAB chemotherapy treatments as a result of taking that
antibiotic]), 2 units of blood, 1 unit of platelets, Benadryl (as a
preparation for both blood products) and her vancomycin, and a
Neupogen shot (daily now) as well as getting potassium and magnesium drips today!

The good things are her fever has broken for most of the day, it has
remained normal or low grade for a short period of time. Also, the
pain associated with Neupogen shots has been minimal. The red
blood counts are very low, thus the need for blood and platelets,
but the white cell counts have stayed the same as yesterday, low but
beginning to inch upwards.

It looks as if she will be here into next week. Maybe by Monday
things will be lining up for her to get out of the hospital. I got to
give Pam a break at the hospital today as she took several hours to
leave and do other things, like cook something good!

We will survive this! But we will have to put in all the time
required. There is no time off for good behavior here.

Chris

* * *

5-31-09

Folks,

Anna has had a good day today having vancomycin (antibiotic) alternating with another kind, whose name I cannot remember now. She was [fever-]free for most of the day, but seems to have some chills this evening, indicating the return of fever even before the nurse comes in to do vitals. It has been a tough weekend and I will be glad to see it go as we rise in her counts in the next few days. Maybe she will be home by Tuesday!

Chris

* * *

6-01-09

Folks,

Anna has still had fever of 100 or more all day. This marks the 8th day of hospital confinement due to fever. Today the white counts are dramatically up indicating that she is now no longer neutropenic (or she has an immune system functioning now). At this point we usually go home, but they cannot yet identify the source of fever....hmmm...

[Anna and Pam] want to go home and be normal.

Chris

* * *

6-6-09

Folks,

I apologize that I have not written in three days, but it is because I was glad to return to normal for a few days and I only think to write an update when the girls are in the hospital. They came home on Tuesday to get in as many days as possible in a normal environ-ment before they must go back into the hospital for the next to last chemo treatment, which is scheduled for Monday, 6-08-09.

Also, I started back to teach this last week and I have been going at it for 15.5—to 16 hours a day trying to keep up with 4 separate classes that are doing the work of a 15-week semester in 5 weeks. So, I am as busy or more than are [Pam and Anna] having to do the same amount of teaching and preparation and grading. So, I let my mind relax as soon as they got packed and left the hospital, and I did not remember to write.

Anna has had a more difficult time this month recovering from the chemo's effects to her system than in the past. She had little energy for the longest time and some digestive issues, but she managed to feel better and better each day with better sleep at night at home in her own bed. Anna's 22nd birthday was on Friday, and she had a wonderful time hearing from family and friends, getting a new tag for her new car, eating lunch with her mom at Chili's, getting her nails done, going to the movies, and seeing UP, then on to the Iguana Grill for a Mexican fiesta before heading back home to open presents and eat some of Pam's homemade fresh strawberry birthday cake. All shared with a few of her close friends who have been supportive through all of this. She got presents for her new apartment life in Athens and she had another great night of sleep.

On Monday, they return to the hospital for the next to last round of chemotherapy and we expect to be there for 6 days. I am sure I will remember to write on Monday when they return and I get back into my habit.

Best,
Chris

*   *   *

6-08-09

Folks,

Anna and Pam went dutifully to the hospital at DCH to check in this morning and they were told by the nurse that they could not begin [Anna's] treatments today. Instead, she was to wait until next Monday and perhaps even as late as the next Monday. It, apparently, had been too little time since her last chemo treatment for her to take another, not the appropriate number of days in the interim. We had suspected all along that it was coming sooner than expected, but one of the three oncologists who take care of her in tandem had made a mistake in counting the number of days and had scheduled them to come today. Yet, the doctor could not count to 28, the requisite number of minimum days between treatments, and thus [Anna and Pam] found themselves psyched up to get going, packed up to move in, and nowhere to go. The good part of this foul-up is that Anna will have more days than expected this month to feel good! That is a good thing.

Pam and Anna took the opportunity to continue to shop for furniture for Anna's future apartment in Athens. She still needs bedroom furniture and a small eating area furniture and lamps, etc. Targets were made for future purchases. So, I will write when they do check into DCH—now scheduled for Friday of this week. 6-12-09.

More later.
Chris

* * *

6-12-09

Folks,

Anna and Pam checked into DCH at 9:30 this morning. By 12 noon they were in room 232, the finest room we have had at DCH so far. It is very spacious with many recliners and other chairs. They started IV fluids around 2:00 pm, pretreatments at 3 and the chemo started at 5. They will come in at 5:00 tomorrow morning for blood work—a daily routine, to monitor blood chemistry and counts. If things go according to previous form, [Anna] will get another treatment in the morning shortly thereafter and then be off for 30 hours or so before they go again.

Anna is in good spirits, having had a good week of freedom and productive activity in preparation for her move to Athens in August. Two more months to endure...

Chris

*   *   *

6-14-09

Folks,

Today was a difficult day for Anna. Physically it was a normal chemotherapy day, filled with its routines and familiar procedures and outcomes, just another in a line of 53. This is her 53rd day in the hospital. But emotionally it was a hard day. Stress, depression, anxiety, anger, sadness, all can be associated with cancer and any debilitating disease that impacts your life in a traumatic way and alters all plans, all habits, all comforts, all control. I experienced depression and deep feelings of sadness when I was first diagnosed with diabetes, as I love food and all things associated with it. My disease is for life, and it will impact my association with food each day for the rest of my life. I can only hope to win that private internal battle on most days. A struggle like that takes its toll and, on some days, you win and some days you lose.

Now, while my disease is not the same as Anna's in that my life was never in immediate danger when I was diagnosed, Pam (who also is diabetic) and I can both understand the feelings that trauma or a traumatic diagnosis can bring. We understand that the life of the emotions and the life of the mind that produces them have rules of their own, timetables only known to them, cycles that seem random and a process of adaptation and healing to a point of normalcy that only they and those well-schooled in their study can identify. All we know is that some days are harder to get through than others and this was one of those days. Tomorrow will be different; we hope it will also be better!

Peace is a real state of mind—BRING IT ON!

Chris

*   *   *

6-15-09

Folks,

Anna's day was better and worse today. Mentally and emotionally, I think she was more in control and more contemplative. She inquired about antidepressant medication, and [the doctor] agreed to begin her on some, thinking it would help. Physically, however, she had a miserable day, feeling very tired and sick. Sick is how she described it. Not nausea, although the stomach as a center was involved, but rather just a feeling of tired and low and yuck and bad. This is chemo at its best and this is precisely what her mind was revolting against when it reacted instinctively yesterday in the desire to revolt. There are physical realities with this treatment and each month the intensity of the physical reaction as the body gets incrementally weaker is more pronounced. No wonder the mind is trying to flee!

She/we take a corporate deep breath, knowing what is coming in the next several weeks as the poison does its work within her. It is like driving a car that is skidding on ice or hydroplaning on water and you know it will hit an obstacle soon and you take the breath, lock your arms on the wheel and brace for the impact that you know is coming.

Chris

*   *   *

6-16-09

Folks,

Today, Anna had stomach issues that were diagnosed as gastritis, due to the chemo's effect on the gastric lining. She was also told that [she and Pam] will go home tomorrow but return to the cancer center on Thursday for a shot of Neulasta which she understands is like the Neupogen shots she has had recently to stimulate the bone marrow, but this is higher powered and longer lasting. Apparently, the doctors do not want her counts to go down very low this time, and they are trying to prevent the chemo from bottoming out her counts due to its effects on her body. She will still be prone to [fever], etc. with this shot but she should not go down as far or as long. While that is a good thing, it does seem to confuse everyone. If they have the power to minimize the descent, then why have they allowed it in the past, and, the other side of the coin, if you do not want her to go down so far now, why give her the chemo to kill everything to begin with? Doctors do not explain anything. Go figure!

At least [Anna and Pam] should be home tomorrow.

Chris

* * *

6-17-09

Folks,

Anna and Pam are home again after the six-day stay in DCH for chemo. This one treated her body with disrespect, causing her to feel bad instantly from the first-hung bag on Friday. They are to return to the Cancer Center tomorrow to get blood counts and to get the high-powered Neulasta shot that is to stimulate her marrow at an increased rate and over a long period of time. They are trying to keep Anna's counts from descending to the bottom this time. Maybe they will tell her more information tomorrow when they see the doctor. At least tonight, everyone will have a good night's sleep for the first time in a week!

Rest!
Chris

*   *   *

6-26-09

Folks,

Anna and Pam and I went to the hospital last night around 9:30 after Anna's temperature rose to over 100.5, the benchmark for returning. We moved into the room about 11:00 pm and she received a unit of blood about 2:30 am. The blood finished about 4:00 am and then an hour of chills began, forcing Pam to pile on the blankets and even take out the hair dryer and blow hot air on Anna for 45 minutes! Our friend Nathan Smock got off his work shift at 11:00 pm and chose to stay with the girls until around 4:00 am! Now that is friendship!

Anna did not get to sleep until around 6:00 am and she slept virtually until 7:00 pm. They may be up all night again tonight! Such is our lives right now.

Peace,

Chris

*   *   *

6-28-09

Folks,

Today is the 60th day that the girls have been in the hospital since
March. Anna has had 2 more units of blood and 1 additional unit
of platelets, making 5 blood units in the last three days. As she says,
"Getting blood is not fun." It makes her feel very weak and generally
lousy, but it is designed to help raise her blood counts to a level that
is safe for her to go home. They say that she will go home tomorrow,
but [Anna's blood counts] will have to rise quickly and overnight for
that to occur. She wants to go home ASAP. Maybe tomorrow.

Chris

* * *

7-08-09

Folks,

Anna has enjoyed a normal week, one of feeling well and free of
disease-related trappings. We have done much work toward getting
prepared for her upcoming move to Athens and we have the end in
sight! She returns to the hospital on Monday, 7-13-09, for her final
regimen of chemotherapy!! The doctor is talking about final things
and the timing of them such as removal of the Hickman "port"
which has been used for all her treatments and must be surgically
removed and one last bone marrow biopsy—all of which will set her
up for her August 8th moving day, which is now being finalized. We
are getting excited to see the light at the end of this long tunnel!

I will begin writing in earnest when she returns to the hospital
on Monday.

Peace,
Chris

* * *

7-13-09

Folks,

Today marks the first day of the last 6-day round of chemotherapy for Anna. She and Pam went to the hospital this morning at 8:00 am, went to the Cancer Center of DCH to have blood drawn and checked before they were then admitted and placed in a room by 10:30. Anna immediately lay down on the bed and took a nap while [hospital staff] found another room to move the girls into because the first room had a lousy mattress, and another [room] was coming open momentarily. So, she got a chance to get in a good long nap while the other room became vacant and then cleaned before we moved them into to it by 11:30. I went home to walk the dog and when I returned many visitors began to come by, one after another, for good, much-needed distracting visits, causing one to focus on small talk and catch-up talk and career talk and humor. The chemo pretreatments began by 4:00 and the chemo itself started by 4:30, after the pharmacist created the magical alchemy and delivered it to the room for use. Pam and Anna had made extra effort to celebrate the beginning of the end by decorating the room with festive light strings on the walls and drip poles and pumps. Everyone was up, trying to endure the moment and celebrate its passage at the same time.

Then, as often happens, a chance meeting of a friend, whose son is also at DCH attempting to recover from a severe car accident, brought a different side of reality to our shared attention—that one where both friends are parents of children who knew each other in their smallest years and who now have undergone difficult personal trials and find themselves in the same place, them at DCH on day 11 and we on day 60+ of hospital stays. Anna had the opportunity to share her endurance process with him (the parent of the injured boy) for a bit and he, recognizing similar plateaus of the journey toward health that [our friends and their son] too will walk, was able to "get real" about discussing the journey they are on and his reaction to it. This is where the rubber meets the road, one person who has been there attempting to help another who finds himself there now, the exchange of secret strength [and] shared anxiety, an emotional compass passing between those who have been there to those just beginning, representing hope and encouragement even as the outcome is yet unclear for him [the newcomer]. This is powerful stuff, as real as it gets, things that have meaning and people remember even if the meaning is [as of] yet unexplained. Just the recognition of the moment is significant. Who knows the outcomes of our individual lives? Certainly not ourselves, that is what makes for the drama, and dramatic at times it can be. What you find in the hospital above all is courage—and the people who practice pursuing it!

Bless them all
Chris

* * *

7-14-09

Folks,

A normal day today for Anna and Pam. The second of six bags of chemo was begun at 5:00 am and ran until about 11:30. She slept through most all of it and then the early afternoon as well. Sleeping is a byproduct of the treatments since they make her tired, but it is also a coping technique. She had the rest of the day off and tomorrow as well before the next treatment begins on

Wednesday evening about 5:00 pm. We walked a little when she was up and talked, read, and played phone games.

We also thought about our friends down the hall who had a very tough day today. Bad things happen in this world, and we endure with as much optimism and grace as we can muster.

May peace come to those who need it.
Chris

*   *   *

7-15-09

Folks,

Anna had an off day on Wednesday until 4:30 pm or so when they began the pretreatment—then the first of the two middle bags of chemotherapy. We played cards and read, and she slept some as it makes her feel bad and run down. Mostly, we talked and kept up with the condition of our friends down the hall, which is deteriorating. I went back over to the dorm and completed the move-out of Anna's belongings, which needed to be done to repack and move to Athens soon. On Thursday she will get the second bag of chemo early in the morning—marking the midway point's passage in the treatment process. Almost done!

Chris

*   *   *

7-25-09

Folks,

On Monday the girls went to the Cancer Center for regular blood work and Anna received a Neulasta shot and tolerated it very well without incident. On Thursday, Anna and Pam went for their second scheduled Cancer Center visit and her counts were low to the point that she was given 2 units of blood and 1 unit of platelets which took all afternoon to receive. And as usually happens, about 24 hours after getting some blood, Anna began getting a fever at 11:00 pm on Friday evening. At 11 the temperature was 100.7 and by the time the doctor returned the call, and we went to the Emergency Room at DCH at midnight, her temp was up to 102.2. Even cancer patients wait in the Emergency Room and so we did from 12:00 am until finally receiving a room assignment at 4:00 am—now room #228. I hope that they were able to get [some] sleep, but I have not checked in with them to see, trying to not call until about noon today. But I doubt they were able to get a wink because of all the anticipated routines of getting medical histories, ordering and hanging antibiotics, etc., which takes a couple of hours before they can do any of the normal morning routines on the second floor.

We had hoped that this time Anna might not have to go to the hospital after her chemotherapy treatment, but nature stands up and goes on about her work. So, here we go on the back stretch, as race fans would say; we are trying to get [Anna's blood counts] low then get back up again [and get on through this process] so that Anna can move on schedule to Athens. The moving day is two weeks from yesterday!!! The clock is ticking...

Chris

* * *

7-26-09

Folks,

Friday night we went to the ER at DCH at midnight with Anna having a temperature of 102.2. We languished in the ER until 4:00

am before we finally got into the room (228), and [the girls] didn't get settled and to sleep until 6:00 am. Anna slept until 4:30 pm and had no temperature throughout the day until after her dinner at 5:00 of Indian food. We had just begun a card game after dinner when she spiked another temp of 102.1. She has begun a regimen of Tylenol and Motrin alternating every two hours and she is on IV antibiotics all day. Pam has put wet clothes on her for an hour as she has radiated heat from her skin (last night she was chilled—go figure.) We hope it breaks soon or they will begin to place her in ice packs to get the fever down. We will see as the night progresses.

Chris

*　*　*

7-27-09

Folks,

It amazes me how different every month's cycle of chemo treatment and the treatment's process can be. So far, no two months have been the same in [regard to] physical reactions. While there are some similarities of symptoms, fever, and the like, each has its own recurring pattern. This month she is spiking high fevers (101 or higher) lasting about 3-6 hours, then [the fever] will break for 6, then spike up 4 degrees in an instant. We have made the comment that each month there is a different roller coaster to ride with different lengths and size of curves. All in all, she is blah and has slept a lot. When she is not sleeping, we talk about theology and religious questions spawned by her discussions with the father of our friend whose son died this morning early at the West Alabama Hospice where they moved him yesterday. As you know, they were childhood friends and the same age and both have had unexpected experiences that have changed otherwise normal lives.

It is interesting how questions seem to have different answers when you see them [in] the glow of a different light, from a new side or perspective. What I am beginning to see is that faith is not static, able to fit neatly in a box, that never changes, so that people can become obnoxiously and dangerously pious. Life's experiences cause the perspective to shift, causing you to reassess, to re-question, to grow. You may even arrive at a new and unexplained point of view. I think it is interesting that life causes one to have to think and rethink. The result is tolerance and less sureness, not more! If you think you know all the answers—rethink, question, ask a different question!!!

Peace,
Chris

* * *

7-28-09

Folks,

Anna had a tough day today fighting fevers again in the morning hours and then the doctor comes in and, in the attempt to make the fevers go away, he put her on vancomycin, the antibiotic that gave Anna the "Red Man Syndrome" back during the original chemo process at UAB. In the afternoon, Anna received the "vanc" and again had a mild case of "Red Man Syndrome," saying it felt like the first day of a sunburn with mosquito bites all over it. This went on for several hours until around 7:00 pm when the fever seemed to have broken and Anna was able to eat her dinner in peace and visit with Pam and me and Tori and Nathan. We hope the white counts go up tomorrow and she gets to walk away from this before the walls close in.

Chris

* * *

7-29-09

Folks,

Yesterday, Anna almost fainted while walking, which has not happened since UAB days in March. Come to find out with the blood counts this morning, red blood counts were so low, she practically had no red blood count at all! No wonder she almost fainted! Whites are up a good bit however, which is a good sign the end is near, and her day will be spent pouring things into her body: Benadryl, vancomycin, two units of blood, one unit of platelets, Benadryl, vancomycin....We cannot wait to walk away from this, and God looks after those who cannot.

Chris

* * *

7-30-09

Folks,

Anna had a better day today, successfully negotiating the vanco-mycin antibiotic at twice the dosage!!! Both last night and today and tonight, she has received more antibiotics of the strongest [class of antibiotics available] than she has since the beginning of chemotherapy in March. I guess they do not want to take any chances with any other bug invasion right before we go home. Her blood counts were up today in every category from yesterday, but she still needs [the count] to come up during the night in the ANC, the actual immune system building cells. They were half this morning from what they need to be for her to go home. We hope that tomorrow's early morning blood count will be high enough to escape [back] to the rest of her life! Bring it on!!!

Chris

* * *

7-31-09

Folks,

Anna and Pam had to spend another day in the hospital today due to low platelets. Every other category of blood was up enough for her to go home but the doctor wanted her to get the platelets up before she leaves, so he ordered her another transfusion of platelets today along with two antibiotics. She has not had a significant fever in two days now and she is feeling much more energetic. She is very anxious to get out and get going! We trust that tomorrow morning [Anna and Pam] will get to leave, and if so, lunch at Iguana Grill is not far behind!

Chris

* * *

8-01-09

Folks,

At 12:10 pm August 1st, on the 75th day of captivity in the hospital, Anna and Pam broke out of prison and entered the world— without return, God willing! Like a condemned prisoner just paroled, we feel jubilant and hopeful about living the life ahead, but we are running forward into it [as fast as we can] just in case the parole board changes its mind! Monday, [Anna] should return to the Cancer Center for blood work and to schedule the removal of the "Hickman" port, which will mark the official closure of this chapter in this novel! On Thursday, the movers will pack her things into the truck and on Friday morning they will pull out toward Athens and a new life.

We thank you for your support, prayers, positive energy, good wishes, food, money, tears, handmade things, cards, books, balloons, etc. They have kept us constantly supported and uplifted, knowing that we have been on your minds. We hope to never return to this adventure after the last bone marrow biopsy which will be in about a month. We look forward to the day when we have trouble recalling facts about this nightmare. The one thing I know, when we do look back, the best memory I will recall from this is the faces of all the people who wanted to care and wanted to help, watch, pray, and wait—from Miami to Anchorage, from LA to NY, from Japan to Moscow. That memory will stay with us always.

Thank you and God bless us everyone!
Chris

*   *   *

8-14-09

Folks,

A bit more than a week has passed since last I wrote and much has transpired in the interim. Last Thursday, Anna and Pam met with the doctor and determined that it would be best if Anna delayed having her Hickman port removed until this week, even though it would cause her to miss one of her orientation sessions for her program, so Anna and Pam followed the moving van out of town toward Athens to be ready to begin moving into her apartment early Friday morning. The movers picked up all her new furniture on Thursday at various stores and finished the packing day by coming to the house and loaded her various things. On Friday morning, the guys quickly unloaded the truck, taking everything up to the second floor of her building and began to assemble furniture which needed to be put together. The movers assembled much more than they were required to and made our moving job much easier—thank you North American Van Lines crew out of Tuscaloosa!!! We recommend them for all your moving needs. Tori finished her math final exam at roughly 9:30—which she made an "A" on, and she and I left to join the girls in Athens, which we did by 3:30 that afternoon. We worked until about 11:00 that evening unpacking and doing all the things that are necessary before we stopped and went to bed, the girls at the apartment and Pam and I at the Country Inn down the road. On Saturday, we did some necessary shopping for last minute things and explored some, eating our way through Athens as best we could. Nathan arrived to join us by early evening, and he assembled the bookcase we acquired during the day and he and I installed the nice mirror we found, as well. By Sunday, we were able to finish the final touches and we returned home on Monday afternoon for Anna to finally have her "Hickman" port taken out.

On Tuesday, back in Tuscaloosa, we packed Tori's remaining things for her move to the dorm at the University of Alabama. Anna went to DCH to have the procedure and had it completed without major incident, by 11:00 am—although during the procedure, she heard them say that they had never removed her type of port before!!! We all met for lunch, and by that afternoon, the remaining hole in her chest was gushing blood, causing her to return to the hospital ASAP to get the bleeding stopped! After lots of pressure and some non-stitch type closure of the wound, she felt like it would remain [closed] without further incident.

On Wednesday of this week, Anna drove back to Athens, and just as she pulled out of the driveway, we were loading Tori up in the van along with all her bags, heading to the University campus here to move her into her new dormitory which she shares with three other roommates! After four or five hours, we had her things assembled and packed away nicely into their new resting places and Tori spent her first night as an official college freshman at UA!!! She is very excited and enjoys her new place immensely.

On Thursday, Pam and I collapsed as we were and are very sore with joints aching of old age and overuse. However, we were able to begin our usual three mile walk on campus again that evening late to avoid the day's heat! We discuss being empty nested often and are so far not unhappy with our new status! Mostly we are acknowledging the degree of stress that we have been living under for many months! Mostly, we want to rest and unwind, even as we immediately begin our new work schedule on Monday!!

We corporately say "Thank you" to all of you for your support, interest, prayers, and good wishes during our journey since March 2nd! Without your support, I am sure we would be in far worse shape at this point. physically, mentally, and emotionally. Yet because of it, we are remarkably calm, and dare I say it...*content* with how things are and where everyone is this day! No one knows what lies ahead for any of us in the future, but for the present, we are here, we are facing forward, and we are walking deliberately straight ahead...come go with us!

Chris

Chapter 6

ON MONDAY, AUGUST 17, 2009, BOTH PAM AND I
returned to the normal schedule of a new fall semester of college teaching—
Pam at the University of Alabama, and me at Bevill State Community College.
It was as if the summer of helping Anna heal and rejuvenate her health following her rounds of intensive chemotherapy left no time to exhale and relax
ourselves. But the normalcy of meeting a new set of students and beginning
to orient them to college life and immerse them in their class instruction
almost cloaked the reality of what we had just experienced over the course
of the previous five months. In addition, both Anna and Tori were going
through the same experience: they were both new students, though on two
different university campuses. Anna was a first-semester graduate student
at the University of Georgia, and Tori was an undergraduate freshman. Pam
relished the opportunity to see people again. Both colleagues and students
were a welcome sight from the never changing routine of the hospital. The
administration staff at her School of Music welcomed her back after having
covered her duties from the time she was forced to exit so unexpectedly on
March 2nd. Her students were ecstatic to see her return.

*   *   *

Pam taught courses in class piano and functioned as the coordinator of
accompanying for the university's School of Music. Class piano is a series of
four semesters of coursework that prepares music majors who do not play

piano, allowing these students to attain the skill level required to pass a juried piano proficiency examination. (All undergraduate music majors, regardless of instrument, were required to possess a certain level of performance skills on the piano.) As the primary instructor of class piano, Pam met or taught almost the entirety of the student body majoring in music. Additionally, because all music majors performed on some instrument (including voice), most students must perform on juries, or final exams in instrumental or vocal performance classes, or perform recitals for the public. Most literature performed in these setting require piano accompaniment to that solo instrument or voice. It was Pam's job to ensure that each student needing a pianist to accompany them during these performances was able to find one to rehearse with and then to perform with during their academic program's required juries and recitals. As coordinator of accompanying, Pam worked with and counseled nearly every music major at some point during their undergraduate career. She knew everyone—and, unlike some faculty, she worked with almost every student at some point during their time at the university.

Her personality was unique for a faculty member. She was open and approachable. She treated each student as a valuable person who possessed an individual gift. The students could easily talk to her about any subject without fear of ridicule or embarrassment. She could be trusted to keep personal information personal, and her students loved and responded to her ability to teach to high standards, encourage them to reach those standards, and successfully achieve their piano proficiency examination requirement goal. She slid easily into the role of playing the school's "mom" for the students, and they loved her for it.

*   *   *

Anna immersed herself into her new town, new school, new classmates. The University of Georgia's Master of Education in College Student Affairs Administering program called each year's entering group of students a "cohort." UGA accepted twenty "first-years" into each cohort. The nineteen colleagues Anna attended class with, studied with, researched with, tested with, and would graduate with became her support, her friends, and—soon enough—her chosen family.

UGA's cohort model was designed to keep the entire entering class of master's students together as they matriculated from course to course and semester to semester. They worked and learned together for the entirety of their degree requirements. Their faculty was of national caliber and included Dr. Richard Mullendore, Dr. Diane Cooper, Dr. Laura Dean, Dr. Merrily Dunn, and Dr. Michelle Espino Lira.

Anna was energized from the moment she arrived on campus. She was excited by her professors, by the tasks at hand, and by the atmosphere of learning within the subject she held most dear. The internal juices were flowing, and she could not wait to get deeply into everything. She threw herself into her studies as well as into the duties associated with her assistantship in the vice president's office. There was much to do, much to read, much to write: she was tasked with becoming familiar with the subject matter of her textbooks; the river of ever-expanding information relating current news and research found in professional journals, newspapers, and articles; and the body of information found in the mountains of articles previously published in those same sources. The students were taught to research, analyze, synthesize, compose, and present scholarly information in a professional manner. Anna loved it all. She had found her world and the people who inhabited it.

* * *

On the day we moved Anna into her apartment in Athens, the front door was ajar, having been left open by the movers who were constantly making trips to the moving van and returning with their arms full of boxes or furniture. We were unpacking boxes, washing dishes, placing items into their respective cabinets and storage locations when, during everyone's focused tasks, Anna's voice exclaimed, "Well, hello there!" I stuck my head up from what I was doing, expecting to see someone who I presumed had entered Anna's apartment in order to greet their new neighbor. Instead, what I saw sauntering around the living room rug was an orange-yellow tabby cat! Anna kneeled to stroke the cat, and he walked right up to her, sat on his haunches, and let Anna stroke his fur. He began to purr loudly. He had no fear of the new people moving into the building, and he acted as though he were accustomed to people in general. We assumed he must have belonged to a neighbor, and that he must generally have the run of the place. The cat stayed for about ten minutes, walked around observing and sniffing various boxes, and then, just as quickly as he arrived, he exited in the same manner, through the front door.

The day after Pam, Tori, Nathan, and I left to return to Tuscaloosa, Anna was exploring her apartment complex and met a neighbor, an older woman who introduced herself to Anna and explained several things to her regarding the way the complex was run, and the specifics regarding its amenities. She also fielded her questions. Anna asked the woman about the cat that had welcomed her to the complex. The woman told Anna that the cat did not belong to anyone in particular: he was a stray that lived around the apartment complex. She also explained that several residents left food out for him. Anna asked her if she could keep him. The lady concurred, saying that the other residents would be pleased to know that the cat had found his rescuer! So, that very day, Anna located the cat, took him to a local veterinarian to receive a checkup and shots, ensuring his clean bill of health. She adopted him on the spot! That night she called us at home and told us what she had done and that she had named the cat Edward.

Edward helped to make Anna's apartment a home. He was affectionate, yet still independent, and he was not offput by Anna's schedule, which often included her being away for hours on end. He was glad to share his life with her, and to have a regular supply of food and attention. She was adoring of her first pet. Athens was going to be a wonderful place for Anna to call home.

*   *   *

Pam and I were beginning to feel empty-nested. We were busy during our respective semesters of teaching. Both girls were thriving in their college lives, partaking of the fruits of the collegiate experience. They were happy and productive; every day, they increased their confidence in their abilities to function at a high level in regard to their coursework while still finding time to live a rich social life. Moreover, it was fall, and for the first time in our family's existence, we had two SEC powerhouse football teams to pull for! As we approached the close of the girls' first semesters, we could not help but feel that our collective futures were indeed bright again.

In fact, the first semester flew by. We began preparing for the upcoming holidays that marked the closing of the calendar year, always a joyous time filled with family celebration and gratitude, with Thanksgiving drawing ever closer. Pam and I were planning a large family gathering at our house, including both sets of grandparents and our siblings, as was our tradition. Menus were being planned and food was being purchased and stored away. Wine, conversation, pictures, and football on the television set were always regular activities during that time of year—and this year, the holiday season would be celebrated with even more gratitude and exuberance than usual. That familiar time of anticipation and exhaustion was upon us, and each night we crawled into bed desperate for the rest that sleep promised.

At 3:30 a.m. on the morning of Monday, November 16, the telephone rang out, splitting the darkness of our bedroom. I sprang up out of bed as if shot from the barrel of a gun, stumbling in the dark to get to the nightstand on Pam's side of the bed where the phone sat, hoping to reach it before she, too, was pulled awake by the ringing. But in the black of the night, just as my hand neared the receiver, I heard her voice answer, "Hello," before I could reach it. My heart was racing from the sudden exertion of getting up to answer the phone and the uncertainty as to what was happening. I heard Pam utter, "Yes…When?…Where?…We're on our way!"

Fifteen minutes later we were driving in the pre-dawn darkness, heading to Athens. Alex Miller, a friend and fellow member of Anna's cohort, had called from the hospital there to tell us that he, Anna, and cohort member Mark Torrez had been studying together that evening, preparing a presentation the three were to make in class, when Anna developed a fever and grew weak, not being able to walk properly. Alex had found Anna in the bathroom, lying on the floor, crying. They both lifted her off the floor and placed her in the car; then they took her to the hospital, not knowing what else to do. Alex and Mark brought Anna back to her apartment from the hospital when doctors released her after she explained to them her medical history, on the condition that she return home to see her oncologist immediately.

I drove as fast as I dared. We managed to arrive in three and a half hours at Anna's apartment, not knowing what we would find. We gathered clothes for Anna, then loaded her into the car along with her suitcase and Edward, the cat., We were back on the road again, headed for home, by 8:00 a.m. The ride home was tense with the uncertain quiet of it. No one knew what to say, and none of us wanted to speculate, lest we heighten the already palpable sense of dread. All we knew for certain was that the idyllic scene that was Anna's life for the previous three months had been inexplicably halted overnight.

*　*　*

We were working on our presentation at the last minute, which was typical for Mark and me, yet atypical for Anna. Sitting in that apartment, I remember feeling the weight of our project and the nerves stirring in my stomach. Anna wasn't feeling well, either. I kept telling her it was probably stress-related, or maybe the crushed red pepper flakes. She knew, though. It wasn't her stomach. It wasn't her nerves. It was something bigger.

I remember the fear in her eyes and feeling the fever in her forehead. She excused herself to go to the bathroom, but I followed her a few seconds later. I found Anna on the floor, next to the toilet...and she was crying.

At that moment, life became very real. My head was previously focused on CAS standards and PowerPoint slides. Yet, my heart led me to sit on the bathtub ledge next to her.

And there we were: an innocent, beautiful, young girl facing leukemia…and a clueless friend, scared out of his mind, who didn't know what to do.

There was nothing I could do to change what was happening. The only thing I could do was help her realize she wasn't alone. I placed my arm around her shoulder and sat there until she was done crying. That night changed everything. I may not have realized it then, but I certainly do now.

—Alex Miller, UGA CSAA 2011 Cohort, May 10, 2011
(excerpt from a Facebook Posting by Alex Miller)

＊　＊　＊

11-25-09

Folks,

I am pained to report that Anna went back to the Cancer Center for her monthly blood work on Tuesday and we were told that her leukemia has returned after three months of remission. At this point, she will have to begin again at the start of the treatment, receiving the original chemotherapy induction at UAB for a month or more of continuous stay. This time they will do the chemotherapy until she is in complete remission again and a donor of bone marrow can be found. At that point, they will kill her bone marrow completely and make ready to receive the transplanted marrow, allowing it to take hold and begin the process of replication, completely substituting a new blood system. The success rate of recovery is very high after transplant. Anna has requested that

the doctors put this into motion as soon as possible so that she might begin to get well as quickly as possible. Therefore, we anticipate returning to UAB as early as Saturday.

I know you all will join us again in keeping she and us all in your prayers and thoughts daily. As before, we hold to the idea that a repetitive focused thought of health, strength, peace, and confidence planted and reinforced by many will increase the power and speed of the manifestation of that request. I take comfort in the knowledge that you all have asked to be a part of that chain of people who have held us up and carried us through in the past. Please feel free to duplicate and pass these emails to whomever may want to know of our journey ahead.

For those of you who have already expressed interest, the donor/transplant bone marrow process has become much more humane in recent years. It was news to us to learn that donating marrow is like the process of receiving blood dialysis, where they filter the donor blood and isolate the marrow. The transplant, then, is like receiving a blood transfusion. The doctor has provided the following website address for me to pass on to interested people who desire to be tested as donors. http://www.marrow.org/

I will again write daily—or as close to that schedule as I can, and I will include more details as they arise. If you have email addresses of others who wish to receive this communication, please send me the addresses so that I may add them to the list.

We begin the journey again—thanks for going with us!

Chris

* * *

11-25-2009

Dear Friends,

It is with much sadness that I write to tell you that my leukemia has resurfaced. After a normal check-up on Tuesday, my oncologist confirmed today that my blood already contains 30% leukemic cells. If there is a bright side to this news, it is that we have caught it earlier than we did last time. The next step for me will be to start another month-long induction chemotherapy treatment at UAB hospital in Birmingham, AL, followed by consolidation treatments until a bone marrow donor can be found. I am planning to enjoy what I can of the Thanksgiving holiday with my family (ironic, I know) before traveling to UAB to get started with my treatment procedures on Saturday at the earliest. I will let you know my room number at UAB as soon as that information is communicated to me. I know many of you are already asking yourselves what you can do to help, so I have put together a list of ways that you can help me as well as others living with AML in this holiday season:

1. If you are interested in becoming a bone marrow donor, visit www.marrow.org for information on how to be tested. I recently learned that donating is a relatively easy process that does not involve surgery of any kind. It is, as I understand it, almost as simple as giving blood. The odds that you will match me are slim, but they are certainly better than not trying at all.

2. Give blood! Even if it can't help me directly, it will go to help someone, somewhere.

3. I know lots of people send flowers when friends are in the hospital, but I'm afraid I will not be able to enjoy them after about two weeks of chemo due to my compromised immune system.

Balloons, artificial flowers, funny cards, etc. are always good substitutes though ;-)

4. I also know that people like to send rich, chocolaty baked goods as comfort food as well, but again because of my chemo I can rarely enjoy them. I do, however, always need mild snack food like crackers, soups, mild cookies, teas, banana breads, etc. As you can imagine, eating is tough on a chemo diet. FYI, if you're thinking about cooking, I am not allowed to eat raw vegetables after about two weeks of chemo due to weak immunity as well. Everything I eat has to be cooked thoroughly to kill any bacteria that could enter my body (gross, I know).

5. Friends always ask me what I need in the hospital, and after my *extensive* experience I have found that the things I most enjoy are: pillows, blankets, socks/slippers, PJ's, hats/scarves (yes, I will lose my hair again), games, books, DVDs, music, magazines, bath products, pictures, and love letters (haha). I would also like to decorate my room for Christmas, since it looks like the hospital is where I will be for the holidays this year.

6. Visit/Call/Write. Don't be afraid! It's still me and I still love seeing and hearing from you!

7. Be happy. It makes me feel good to know that the people I love are happy, healthy, and doing the things that bring them joy (even when I can't).

8. Pray/Think happy thoughts. I never underestimate the power of love being sent my way in whatever form that may be.

I am sorry to pass on such sad news at this time of thanksgiving. Please know that I am thankful for all of you and that I will look to you for strength in the coming months. I am a tough

Georgia Bulldawg and I know I will beat this...again. In the words of coach Paul "Bear" Bryant, "I ain't never been nothin' but a winner."

Love and peace to you all,

~Anna

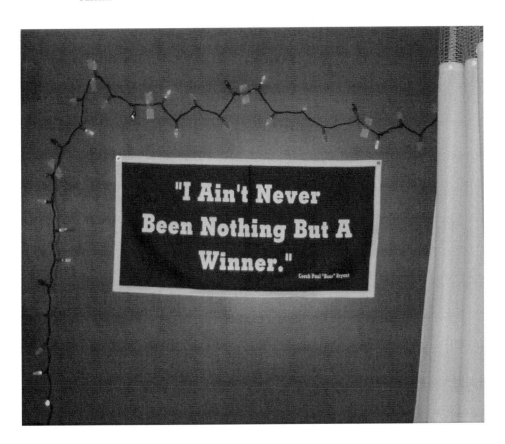

Chapter 7

11-27-09

Folks,

We have been preparing to return to the hospital in the short time since we learned that Anna will have to repeat her original induction of chemotherapy due to the return of her leukemic cells in her blood stream. Whereas we thought that she would return on Saturday to begin the treatment as quickly as possible, [we] will have to wait until the surgeons return from the weekend to, once again, implant her "Hickman" port surgically, through which they do all her intravenous work. So, we expect to check in on Monday to UAB Hospital rather than tomorrow. We have been gathering the things necessary to make her hospital room a home away from home for a month or more of continuous stay. Comfortable clothing, food, entertainments, bedding, etc. have been acquired and restocked, ready for packing and delivery. We will attack the hospital elevators with gurneys well stacked and balanced. We mean business!

I will report with addresses and room numbers as soon as I get them on Monday, and we encourage all types of mail. The reading of your letters and cards of encouragement were a large part of every day's routine in past visits. I welcome all the

Georgia friends into this email communication, and I appreciate your interest in Anna and her ordeal over the next many weeks. She has come to know and love all her new friends in Athens, and she wants you to be informed so you do not forget her interest in your lives there, in her absence from you. This will be an intense and vital battle for Anna's future health and well-being and we will need all of the help we can get as we take on this war against an unseen microscopic enemy. Together, we will see it through until the end!

Peace,
Chris

* * *

11-28-09

Folks,

This is how my day started...

"Chris, I am a regional Community Relations Mgr. for H & R Block, and in that position can direct our activities. I would like to have a Nation-Wide Bone Marrow Registration Drive and would like to have Anna as a spokesperson for this. Please share with me your thoughts on this. I will contact the appropriate people on Monday but would love to put a face on this project that would help so many. Let me know if this would be a positive thing for you folks, and we will hit it hard! My love to you all!...."

Of course, Anna agreed, and I responded immediately. I also discovered a local drive in Winfield has been created and is being advertised to promote bone marrow registration, thanks to Janie Hillis and friends, and there are already campaigns being organized at the University of Alabama and in Georgia. By the end of the day, we had received a text message from a friend in Taiwan saying that Tzu Chi Hospital, where he is, has Asia's largest database of marrow donors and [Asia's largest] marrow bank, and he forwarded their information to hold for future use!—I can only say that word has been out for only four days, and I have only sent two previous emails and we are amazed at how quickly information travels and how much faster personal concern manifests itself into generous and useful actions.

Anna went to have additional blood testing done at DCH in Tuscaloosa today and it determined that she is without infections and her blood levels are ok but indicating a 14% leukemia cell content in the blood, down from the 30% found on Tuesday. Things change I guess, but it is better to start out with fewer enemy cells than first thought. For those of you who have inquired as to what you can do and send, etc., Anna has decided that she has head covering and scarves from the first wave, but she will likely be spending Christmas in the hospital. She wants us to decorate her hospital room for the holidays so she can enjoy as much festivity as possible. Therefore, if you must send her something in the hospital or bring it when you visit, she says she would like to receive Christmas ornaments! In this way, she can begin to build her own set of ornaments for use all her life, but in so doing, she can remember each person who shared it during this trying time. We think that is a terrific idea!

The cars are ready to be packed and we will drive off when the phone rings on Monday saying a room is available. Keep us in your daily meditations!

Peace,
Chris

* * *

11-30-09

Folks,

Anna and Pam got moved into UAB today. Her address is...

Anna Gordon
UAB Hospital
1802 6th Avenue South
Room W 942
Birmingham, AL 35249

Her room is decorated for Christmas, complete with small tree with small ornaments and lights, Christmas bedding, colored lights around the room's ceiling perimeter and snowflake lights in the window. DVD is hooked up to the TV, and pantry materials including teas, coffee machine, snacks, games are arranged. It is a small room, W-942, but we are on the list for a bigger one as soon as one becomes available. It was nice to see some familiar nurses' faces from back in March and they helped make our arrival smooth and more welcoming.

They will perform the surgery necessary to implant the "Hickman" port into her tomorrow. The port will be the highway into her bloodstream for all meds and chemo as well as blood taking, etc. When I left the hospital at 5:00, we had not seen the doctor yet.

There is some movement on the national marrow promotion that H&R Block is planning. I received this earlier this morning.

"I have a Commercial Web Designer coming in today to build a website, I was able to call in a favor, this guy is AWESOME, his clients include Hershey's and American Airlines, so I'm sure he'll do a great job! In addition, another IT guy I know (oddly enough he's

originally from Maine) has donated the web hosting and will put the site on a server that will support 50,000 hits a day!!"

The domain name that they are going to use may be...www. annasarmy.com or some such name. I will let you know more as it happens.

Peace,
Chris

*   *   *

On November 30th, the day we moved Anna and Pam back onto the ninth floor of UAB's Wallace Spain Building to receive the chemotherapy that would kill her bone marrow so that a bone marrow transplant could be given, a most familiar face showed up in the doorway of her room.

*   *   *

She [Anna] went on [after leaving the hospital in remission], matriculating at the University of Georgia for graduate work in higher education. After she left, I contacted her via Facebook, as is done these days, to tell her that I was glad she had done so well, and that if I could ever do anything to help, to let me know.

Time passed and chapter two began with a message from Anna: 'My cancer is back.' I went to the room where Anna was going to be at UAB, and found Pam in a rare moment...standing, alone in the room, holding back tears and fear...signs that evaporated when I walked in after knocking. I could see her, in that moment, steeling herself.

—Dr. Rob McDonald, May, 2011 (excerpt from a speech)

* * *

Rob McDonald, the medical intern at UAB who was on his oncology rotation when Anna received chemotherapy to get her leukemia to go into remission during her first chapter with the cancer, was indeed a welcomed sight. He and Anna had become friends after his rotation finished, and he moved on to another area of specialization for a period. After learning that Anna's cancer had returned, he was often there to offer support, field medical questions, and to encourage us all in our new journey. He came by Anna's room whenever he had a moment to spare, knowing that even late-night hours would not be an unwelcome distraction or a burden on Anna and Pam.

If at some point a confusing procedure or comment by a physician left us with anxiety or concern, Rob explained in better terms what the procedure entailed and why it was being performed. If he did not know the answers to these questions, he would leave the room to investigate, asking other physicians who knew what the prognoses or outcomes of a procedure would be and what the procedure was for, and he quickly returned with those reassuring answers. Rob was kind to us all. He helped us enormously through the days that followed, and his and Anna's relationship grew, even in the unlikely situation that encircled her.

Anna lived in the hospital room. She breathed the same air, stared at the same walls, saw the same faces, every day for hours on end. When she was up for it, a welcome visit from Rob led to a walk through the hallways and corridors of the hospital together, talking, exercising Anna's body for a short while, providing her mind with a pleasant distraction. During these excursions, Pam felt like she could take a break, too, knowing that Anna was not only with someone supportive and interesting, but someone who was a physician, who had Anna's immediate medical needs, limitations, and interests at heart. He would also know what to do if, while out of the room, something occurred that required specific action and appropriate attention. Nothing could be more comforting to us all.

*　*　*

I've known Anna and her family since I was a medical student, since Anna was first diagnosed by Dr. Phillip Bobo. There wasn't much to those first encounters at UAB. Anna was a bright, athletic young woman, who had developed a blood cancer. She received treatment, sailing through chemotherapy in a relatively easy manner, if losing her hair and staying in hospital for weeks on end can be called 'easy.' Her room had Christmas lights in it, and there were always snacks there, readily shared with those of us working there.

And there was the sign:
'I ain't never been nothin' but a winner.'

—*Paul 'Bear' Bryant*

*   ⋆   ⋆   ⋆*

And there were the cards covering the walls, tended by Pam and Anna, gestures of love, humor, compassion, sympathy, and camaraderie.

Anna was a proud graduate of the University of Alabama. Have you ever met a graduate of Alabama who wasn't proud?

We went for a walk, breaking unreasoned rules, and by virtue of indoor corridors, made our way to the Children's Hospital. They have a place called Safe Harbor, with games and…a basketball court! We played H-O-R-S-E. Now I love basketball. And I don't like to lose. I don't like to lose no matter how pretty my opponent is. You hear me?

Anna, however, also does not like to lose. And a little cancer and a large, new catheter under the collar bone on her shooting arm…these inconveniences were not going to get in the way of this. And I mean I tried. This was not even a little letting up to show sympathy for 'the cancer girl.' She wouldn't have any of that, and neither would I. And God bless it if she didn't beat me.

OK…three times.

Pissed me off…not in a bad way…in a way that you couldn't help but be completely, utterly admiring of her. And all the time with that smile, that lights up a room. With those looks that have turned heads everywhere she goes. With that quick, sharp wit that was characteristically hers.

—*Dr. Rob McDonald, May, 2011 (excerpt from a speech)*

* * *

12-01-09

Folks,

A hard day today. Anna had a bone marrow biopsy done first thing today, then an echocardiogram, then the surgery to implant the "Hickman" catheter. The biopsy is done to confirm her leukemia return (which it did) and to determine what type of treatment to do on the cancer. We met the new doctor, a new leukemia expert,

Dr. Foran, who explained that the leukemia will be more difficult to get back into remission the second time around and it will be more difficult on Anna. [The doctors] are likely to use a different chemotherapy [regimen] this time, [which] the biopsy report will determine, [and] which [Dr. Foran] will order. Priority one is to get [Anna] back into remission, and as such, we should prioritize our thoughts and prayers. One step at a time. This week will be vital in that the chemo will be infused…and then it will do its work throughout the month. [The doctors] may start tonight, or it may be in the morning.

Despite her long day, when they rolled her back into the room at 3:25, Anna was remarkably pleasant but hungry. She was not allowed to eat anything since last night, and I called Surin West to order her favorite dinner, and they were closed for two more hours. So, soup was ordered to tie her over until Surin opens and she can get what she wants.

The night was ok, but they came in to draw blood at 4:30 am and weighed her at 6:00 am. We will see what tonight brings.

Peace,
Chris

* * *

12-02-09

Folks,

Anna started her chemo today. It will be for 6 days, and [the doctors] will use 3 different drugs. It will be infused into her body for these 6 days then take the next 4 weeks to work, ridding her of leukemia cells in her bloodstream. This is our hope, and this is our prayer. At the end of this time, the doctor will perform another bone marrow biopsy to judge if, indeed, she reaches remission. This is our focused goal—to reestablish remission during this first month. Her mood is up, and she was up walking around some this evening after having a day with several visitors.

More tomorrow.
Chris

* * *

12-03-09

Folks,

Anna was moved into a larger corner room, almost twice the size as the first one, today! This is a good thing, and the nurses are looking out for us, attempting to make her stay as pleasant as possible. The new room number is W-926. The address is the same as before, and yes, even with the first incorrect address that I gave to you early on, mail has found her! She has received many cards and packages already!

Today marks the second day of chemotherapy. She has three different medicines infused into her arm. The first bag takes an hour, the second takes six hours, and the third, another hour. They start her in midafternoon and finish around midnight! So far, she has had only a little nausea and we are hoping that it will stay that way. She walked a good while this evening before and after dinner, around the hospital and explored the Camellia Suites (the section of rooms built for rich and famous clients in years past, but now just another wing). Those rooms have refrigerators, leather sofas, raised beds with mahogany headboards, recliners, and massive bathrooms! I guess they once treated high-dollar folks well. Anyway, the wooden floors make for a good walking surface and nice scenery!

We hope for a restful evening so we can do the same thing all over again.

Peace
Chris

＊   ＊   ＊

12-04-09

Folks,

Anna got good news today from the doctor as he made rounds. The blood sample that they run every day had no cancer cells in it. This means that the sample that was taken this morning showed no cancer cells; however, it is only a sample that was caught "floating by." We will see what tomorrow and the next day's samples say, but we are headed in the right direction. That is the good news, the bad news is that the drugs made her feel "yucky" today. When asked to describe how she felt, she said..."I feel like I'm on chemo." I guess only someone who has felt that knows what that feels like. Since she did not feel perky today, she slept most of the day, especially because the chemo treatments don't get finished until midnight or so and one of the drugs to "pre-treat her against negative reactions" is a stimulant. We explored DeVinci's in Homewood for dinner with takeout and discovered a terrific mom and pop restaurant! We highly recommend it. She received many cards in the mail and Tori came with Christmas stockings filled with stuff—movies, candy, ornaments, snowman decoration, etc.

Tomorrow Anna is looking forward to a visit from several of her UGA friends who are coming from Athens to spend two days with her, right in time for the Alabama–Florida Game tomorrow!!!—I hope the nurses don't find us screaming too loudly, but they may have to put up with us or let her go!

Anyway—Roll Tide Roll!!!
Chris

* * *

12-05-09

Folks,

While Anna didn't feel well today, at all, due to chemo effects making her have another "yucky" day, she was visited by seven of her University of Georgia graduate student colleagues who are friends in the same program as Anna there at UGA. They arrived with gifts and laughter and smiles, and it lifted Anna tremendously! Then, all of these "Bulldawg" followers raised cane as they all watched Alabama beat the Florida Gators into submission and tears!! A great time was had by all!! Needless to say, we thank those wonderful students for coming to UAB on an overnight stay to brighten up Anna's day and we thank our University of Alabama players for giving us so much of which to be proud as the world watched. It was a memorable day!

Roll Tide!
Chris

* * *

12-06-09

Folks,

Anna had a good day today! Her friends from the University of Georgia returned to her room for more time to visit before they had to return to Athens mid-day. It meant so much for Anna to see them and spend time in their company again. There is nothing like the camaraderie of a peer group, and when 20 new first-year graduate students enter a program of study together, it is an intense and permanent bonding. Pam and I thank them for the sharing of themselves with us at considerable sacrifice given this time of final exams. They are welcome at any time to return again and again! Now she rests and gets ready to finish this chemotherapy treatment in the next day or so before it begins to do its work within her body. This afternoon was spent reading newspapers, both *Tuscaloosa News* and Birmingham papers, to relish the sports page articles and photographs of our boys! I would only wish Anna to feel well enough to go to Pasadena in January! What a glorious trip that would be...

Peace, and Roll Tide
Chris

* * *

12-07-09

Folks,

Today marks the sixth and last day of the chemotherapy treatment
that the doctors have created for Anna's disease. She will receive
the last of the three daily drugs tonight at 1:00 AM. Already the
blood counts are descending, causing Anna to receive her first
treatment of blood platelets. Her white and red cell counts will
descend over the next two weeks, her platelets will decline, and
her immune system will be nonexistent before the month is out.
The cycle usually takes two weeks after the week of chemo, before
the blood begins to rebuild itself to the level it can stand alone and
sustain itself. Tomorrow, she is likely to receive a blood transfusion with one or two units of blood.

Not until Anna became ill with this disease did I realize just how
important the people who donate blood are to so many people's
lives. Those who volunteer and regularly give a unit at local blood
drives rarely see who receives their gift, but know if you have ever
donated, you are vital to the health and well-being of so many people! Continue to give if you can. Already in the 82 days that Anna
has been in the hospital, and even in the days without, she has had
untold dozens of blood transfusions, and each was donated by an
unseen person—thank you!

Peace,
Chris

* * *

12-08-09

Folks,

Anna had a good morning and a terrible afternoon. She slept
well and had several visitors in the morning, but by lunch she was
feeling queasy, and she asked for anti-nausea medicines. She was
given, as we later learned, one that she has a reaction to, and the
hospital was told about it when she checked in, rather than the
one that works well for her. She spent the afternoon in a twilight
drugged-up state half between conscious and unconsciousness—
and still QUEASY! Only later did the nurse discover that she could
not have that [anti-nausea medication] and that the doctors had
not put the appropriate medications on her chart! It is the responsibility of the patient to be in charge of his/her care. Note to the
public: question everything, every time, without apology! I hope
it's a better night than it was a day.

Chris

＊　＊　＊

12-10-09

Folks,

Anna is in the pattern of surviving the dropping of her blood
counts. Yesterday, she received a unit of platelets and potassium.
During the evening, she felt very unsettled in her stomach. I guess
this recipe of drugs affects her more this time. Also, they said it
would be harder on her this time, so I assume the increased nausea
is an indication of that. She had less stomach unease today and
felt like getting out of the room to hear members of the Alabama
Symphony Orchestra's brass section play at the hospital today. She
and Pam are friends with two of the musicians and they asked the

girls to come by and listen if they felt like it. She "skyped" with her cat here at home later this evening, getting a connection made with "Edward" every few days so that he will remember his "mommy" while she is away. He and I are getting to be much better friends in [Anna's] absence. Nothing much to report. I will write when there is more to tell.

Chris

*   *   *

12-11-09

Folks,

Anna received a unit of platelets and a unit of blood today. The pretreatment for the blood products made her sleep most of the early part of the day, but the afternoon and evening found her feeling fairly perky, actually. Anna's friend Trey came over from Athens for a visit today, and Anna enjoyed seeing him a great deal as well. Other than those highlights, not much is going on. But the doctors are pleased that during her blood count descent, she has not yet spiked a fever, as is expected. We hope for another good day tomorrow.

Peace,
Chris

*   *   *

12-12-09

Folks,

This is day 4 after chemo stopped and as expected, Anna began to have fever today. When I left the hospital at 8:15, her fever was 99.8 or so. When it gets to 100.5, they begin antibiotics to ward off any infections that may be present in her unprotected body due to a low immune system caused by the chemo. With the antibiotics come pretreatments of anti-nausea meds and potential blood units. This will be the course of the next several days as this daily drama plays itself out. However, we all watched the Heisman presentation, and we were overjoyed to see Mark Ingram Jr. be rewarded for his efforts. Anna squealed as his name was announced and Mark made the yuck of a fevered body feel better.

Roll Tide
Chris

*   *   *

12-13-09

Folks,

And so, the fevers begin...as expected about four days after chemo, it started last night with a low-grade fever of 99. During dinner and during the Heisman the low lingering fever kept hanging on. Today it went full bore hanging around the 101-102 area. As of 5:00 this evening it still has not broken. While the nurses have given Tylenol, the antibiotics have not yet made their way to her IV, waiting on the doctor on the weekend to get the word and call it in and then the pharmacist to get here and make it up and send it to the room. Still waiting...I guess this is what the week ahead will be like. She has already had platelets and a unit of blood today. Bring on the antibiotics and sleep!

Peace
Chris

*   *   *

12-14-09

Folks,

As I signed off about 5:00 pm yesterday the fever was 99 and holding over the past 24 hours. She had been given blood and platelets, then around 7:00 it all went bad. Fever went to 102, they started antibiotics and Tylenol, then fever spiked to 104 and she had some pain in her legs. They gave her some oxycodone and she reacted negatively shortly thereafter, beginning with violent shaking and convulsions alternating with chills! All of this happened right at the [nurses'] shift change, so everyone was in a meeting getting assignments when Pam had to make a large enough deal to get someone's reaction. Then they all came running and took over—getting Anna back together with fluids and oxygen and other IVs. Chest X-rays were done as well as several other tests to see what the reaction was to exactly. Finally, the shaking stopped, and the fever broke around 10:30.

Poor Pam was scared and shaken, as would anyone be, and the girls managed to endure the worst medical event of this new season. Thankfully, the evening was quiet and more restful for Anna, and so far, today, Monday, 2:30 pm, there has been little drama.

"A little less noise, please..."

Chris

*   *   *

12-15-09

Folks,

This morning, the doctors informed us that Anna has a "Graham negative" blood infection which caused her convulsions and high temperatures. Probably originating in her mouth, from sores caused by the chemo or from her GI bacteria, it, nevertheless, has settled in her blood. Now this is a serious condition but one that the doctors feel will be taken care of with the use of specific antibiotics targeted to the specific culture that was grown in a dish from her tests. During each cycle of chemo treatments, Anna has always been open to infections during her [immune system's down time]. This is the first actual infection that she has encountered, however, during the entire 6 months of chemotherapy. We are concerned, but optimistic that all will be well. Currently there is no more fever and she had units of blood and platelets today in addition to antibiotics all day. She did sleep most of the day because the infection took its toll on her the night before.

We are appreciative of all the concerns, prayers, well wishes, and positive energy being sent Anna's way and to us as well. We feel it and we feel your thoughts and energy. We are lucky indeed!

Peace,
Chris

* * *

Even before Anna's leukemia, it had been our family's tradition to send Christmas cards to family and friends whom we rarely got to see, but whom we enjoyed keeping up with, rekindling old friendships. Somewhere along the way, Pam asked me to compose a Christmas greeting, have it copied, usually on holiday stationery, so she could then insert it into the Christmas cards as she signed and mailed them. I was glad to write the greeting as long as she would stuff the envelopes. It turned out to be a fair deal for us both. And so the Christmas newsletter, as it came to be called, became an annual tradition as well. Here is the newsletter from the fateful year of 2009.

* * *

12-17-09

Christmas 2009

    This is the year of extremes for the Gordon Family, of beginnings and endings, of highs and lows, of joy and pain, but not despair. It also afforded each of us the opportunity to experience visible grace, active in our world, to an extent never before known by us, reminding us of the fruits of a life spent interacting with others.

    The spring saw final preparations being made for graduations for both girls, Anna from the University of Alabama, and Tori from Paul W. Bryant High School. Both girls were set to be honored with inductions into multiple honor societies and honor rolls, including, for Anna, Phi Beta Kappa, and both girls were finishing with perfect grades, 4.0 or higher. There is no higher positive extreme that the girls could have attained with regard to their academic experience and performance.

    The negative extreme was also experienced by us all when, on March 2nd, at 21 years old, Anna was diagnosed with Acute Myeloid Leukemia, AML. Our world, very predictable and productive as always, immediately stopped, as if a stick were thrust into the spinning spokes of a bicycle tire. All external activity and plans ceased! Everyone had their daily existence changed and their stable and predictable futures forever altered.

    Pam and Anna packed and moved into UAB hospital within 48 hours and doctors began the long process of chemotherapy treatments. Anna's academic future was in doubt; within 8 weeks of graduation and in the middle of research designed by her and attached to a faculty member's grant with assurance of publication as an undergraduate in Psychology, she was forced to walk away and focus on reestablishing her health, leaving graduation uncertain. Pam, too, walked away from her job and provided intense care as a vital partner in Anna's recovery on a 24-hours-a-day basis. Chris had to continue working at all his jobs and maintain all aspects of the household while the family was fractured, and Tori was left to continue her life virtually alone and isolated for many hours at a time. All of these circumstances, for each individual, had within them the potential for disaster as the family dynamic was forcibly altered.

Yet, in the midst of uncertainty, almost at every turn and with each circumstance, we watched grace pour over us in the form of people, coming as if from out of the blue, helping ease and straighten every bump, curve, and difficulty. The University of Alabama faculty and administration immediately gathered and voted to [certify the completion of] Anna's graduation requirements, deciding she had done more than enough to not only complete the courses necessary for graduation, but officially maintain her status of highest honors, graduating her summa cum laude! Pam's School of Music rallied and distributed her workload amongst themselves, finishing out the semester for her many classes. People from across our lives, both near and far, present, and past, from Alaska to Miami, Los Angeles to New York, and Japan to Russia, bound themselves with us to daily pray, chant, meditate, or send positive energy and thoughts toward Anna's immediate benefit and recovery. Like never before, we watched a parade of people march as an army of support in word and deed. Even people we do not know became involved.

Anna did go into remission and she, as well as we, were able to reclaim a sense of normality in our daily lives. In August, after the last chemo treatment cycle arrived, she was able to, yet again, pack and move, within 48 hours, to a new academic situation in Athens, Georgia, where she was accepted to begin a master's degree in Higher Education, Student Affairs Administering. One of the top schools in the country in her field wanted her and offered a full scholarship as well as a graduate assistantship in the Vice President for Student Affairs' Assessment Office. We moved her into a new apartment, and a new life began, making new friends, learning what she most enjoyed and wished to pursue, and living a reclaimed life.

Tori began school as a freshman at the University of Alabama, where she would become, from the first day, immersed in her new life and her interest in photography. She took a job as Staff Photographer for the Crimson White, the official student newspaper of the University, where she attended football practice on her first day of college and took photographs of the players practicing for the upcoming season that would make the front page the next day—what a beginning! She would move into her dorm, meet new friends by the hundreds, and establish herself as a presence and personality of consequence on campus within the first few months. She met with Chip Cooper, the famous official photographer for the University of Alabama, who is teaching and mentoring her in her newly designed degree in Photography through New College. She would also become deeply and personally involved in "UnAshamed," a large gathering of students on campus for the purpose of ministry to fellow students. Pam and I both returned to our daily lives in music and teaching, reclaiming our professions and our careers, doing what we do.

Then in late November, Anna's cancer returned, taking her out of remission after only three months and forcing her to immediately interrupt her very productive and enjoyable new life and begin che-motherapy treatments again from the beginning! The goal is to put her back into remission and acquire a bone marrow transplant, which should give her the best opportunity for permanent recovery from one of the most devastating of cancers. Again, she and Pam have had to walk away and refocus their daily efforts. Chris maintains life as necessary for the entire family and Tori continues forth virtually alone for much of each week, self-directed and self-focused without the usual support of family in normal ways. Again, devastation and derailment could be the outcome for all of us and, in addition, we must endure the insult of spending Christmas in the hospital, altering time-honored and time-built holiday traditions for our family and extended family.

But it is the Christmas season after all, and ultimately the participating and celebrating of Christmas in each of our lives is the embracing of hope—hope for our individual futures in the New Year, but also hope for our family's endurance and success, as well as the hope for a happy, healthy, and peaceful New Year for all. Christ came as hope to the world. Now as we celebrate the season with all of you, we grab hold of it with extreme vigor, never letting go—HOPE!

Merry Christmas from the Gordons...
Chris, Pam, Anna, and Tori

*   *   *

12-17-09

Folks,

Today, Anna lost her hair for the second time. It began to come out on her pillow and clothes yesterday, and today she had a nurse shave it off to not have it come out in clumps and get in/ on everything. She had it shaved the first time, also, after a while, but this time she planned on shaving it as soon as it let go. So, by evening, she was in a scarf and completely relaxed, not living through the anxiety of the first time. It comes and it goes, and it will come again. No fever for two full days now and antibiotics seems to be working. Routine and waiting seems to be the tasks at hand.

Peace
Chris

*   *   *

12-18-09

Folks,

Not much to report today, she has slept most of the day. She and Pam were up long into the night. Foggy, gray, wet, December day!

Chris

* * *

12-19-09

Folks,

Anna had the most interesting day. All kinds of activities of diverse origins made the day memorable. No fever and a quiet morning, with one visitor, turned into nausea by early afternoon, calling for anti-nausea meds. By the time the nurse was able to get into the room and hang the bag of medication, more visitors started to arrive including an unexpected friend from Anna's undergraduate school. During her visit, another high school friend came. During that visit, a male quartet of two physicians and two insurance agents, who all attended Birmingham Southern College and sang in the choir program there, knocked on the door and entered for a concert of Christmas music, gospel, and barber shop music. Just as they were doing their third piece, yet another couple entered the room, making a total of twelve [who] enjoyed the concert for another 20 minutes or so. After they all departed, Tori arrived for dinner!

Such is [Anna's] life at the hospital these days, I am sure she has the most interesting room on the floor if not the whole building! I would love to hear the stories the nurses tell about the goings-on in our room when they go home each day... :)

Peace
Chris

* * *

12-20-09

Folks,

Sunshine is a good healer! It was nice to see the sun for the first time in a week or more. Pam got out for lunch for the first time in the last 21 days. Anna was brought lunch from Dr. Rob McDonald: Indian food, one of her favorites, and no fever, no blood, and no platelets again today!

Chris

* * *

12-21-09

Folks,

It has been a quiet day. We are grateful for the sun this morning. Her blood counts are beginning to rise, making Anna anxious and hopeful to go home before Christmas. I know the counts will go up quickly once they begin [rising], but I do hope that she is realistic if we have to stay put for a day or two more. We will see. She slept most of the day because neither she nor Pam slept very well [last night]. Day 22 in the hospital so far this stretch, wears on a body, both patient and caregiver. Just antibiotics today. More as it/if it happens.

Peace,
Chris

* * *

12-22-09

Folks,

[During] every hospital stay for us, there has been a hard day, one horrific, can't-wait-to-get-past kind of day; well, today was the day!! For reasons [including] emotional endurance reaching its end, physical endurances being challenged, reasons such as the holiday arriving, which [had been] emotionally held at bay but then there comes the realization that it must be addressed and dealt with and endured even when it is wished away...and for reasons like well-meaning but insensitive doctors who frighten their patients with discussion of procedures and possibilities that are not present and actually rare but that get discussed when another member of a rotating team comes in and hasn't read the chart [closely] enough to know the state of the patient and then talks out loud in unneeded speculations—all these and more made it a tearful, despondent, and emotionally stressful day, a day to release and let go, a day to get over and climb your way out of tomorrow. It was a day so bad that visitors were turned away, deflected, or altogether canceled.

It is a tough thing to be seriously sick. It requires adapting many skills and graces to navigate a sustained hospital stay with many nurses, doctors, visitors, well-wishers, relatives, and interested parties. Some days are not graceful. We will attempt to be graceful again when the time comes back around for it, maybe!

Sigh...
Chris

*   *   *

12-23-09

Folks,

Today was a better day than the disaster of yesterday. The blood counts, however, are still hanging around the bottom of the spectrum so blood was ordered again today. She had blood units yesterday and today. Apparently different recipes of chemotherapy have different patterns of blood count rising. [The current] recipe seems to linger on the bottom longer than the original induction recipe; therefore, the expected results have been different and that is one of the reasons Anna expected to be home by Christmas. This time it is different, and we will have to play it out to the end. But we were told that she should be home by Monday, December 28. They will then schedule a bone marrow biopsy to see if [Anna] has achieved remission status again, and we hope to do the biopsy in Tuscaloosa. They have also scheduled the first transplant doctor's appointment for Monday, January 4 to explore that whole realm. They have told her that the transplant process will be a long one, taking potentially another 100 days. Let's just hope we get there. Remission first!

Anna wrote a new set of words for the Twelve Days of Christmas, from a cancer perspective...

On the 12th day of Christmas my true love gave to me...12 different nurses, 11 pills for popping, 10 pairs of PJs, 9 hats to choose from, 8 bags of platelets, 7 days of chemo, 6 blood transfusions... 5 mouth washes...4 weeks as a patient, 3 IVs, 2 Hickman lines, and a bone marrow biopsy!

Humor is important!
Chris

* * *

12-26-09

Folks,

Christmas Eve and Christmas Day saw her counts go down and then rebound up to half the amount that is needed for her to go home. By today she was expecting to go home, but her counts went back down again this morning forcing her to stay probably until Monday. This recipe of chemo is new to us, and we are surprised to not be able to predict its behavior time and again.

This Christmas season marked the first time that the Gordon family was apart, and Pam and I for the first time in 28 years. It was different for everyone, forcing us to improvise and to make do with whatever came along. We ended up having a huge amount of company [including] family, extended family, and friends from near and far, expected and surprise visits from friends passing through town who made a special effort to stop by on the way to their destinations. We were exhausted but smiling and surrounded by love of family, of nursing staff and friends—all who came together to make their and our holiday brighter.

We never cease to be amazed by people, and during this season of hope and love, it is pouring all over each of us!

"God bless us everyone..."

Chris

* * *

12-27-09

Folks,

Blood counts went up today, about halfway to what they need to be [for Anna] to go home. We have been here before, several times in the last week, only to fall back down yet again. Tomorrow morning may find her [counts] down again, but we hope they will be up, up enough to go home. The doctors had said Monday a week ago, we want it to be Monday. The girls need it to be soon!

Hopefully...

Chris

*   *   *

12-28-09

Folks,

We're Home!!!!

As of 8:56 pm we are back home and the fire has been lit in the fireplace, the first since before they went into the hospital. Half of the cars are unpacked, we needed three cars to get all the Christmas and regular stuff back home. The girls are in their rooms going over their Christmas gifts, and for the first time in 29 days the entire family is under one roof again! Anna and Pam go to get blood work done in the morning here at DCH and see the oncologist here. January 4 is the scheduled bone marrow transplant team meeting at Kirklin Clinic, and a biopsy will have to be scheduled within the week. I don't think it will be long that we get to spend [time] all together, but for right now, it is enough!

Peace,
Chris

Chapter 8

1-1-10

Folks,

Happy New Year!!!

I hope this year will be much better for us and for most everyone I know than last year. There is nothing much to report because we are doing very little other than hibernating! We watch football and scream at the TV and eat and nap, pet animals, and nap and eat and enjoy time together. We are likely to have about 2-3 weeks at home before we take Anna back for more chemo. The girls went back to the oncologist at DCH yesterday for blood work and Anna is now fully recovered. Monday is the first transplant team meeting with us at Kirklin Clinic in Birmingham, and Tuesday will be the bone marrow biopsy to determine if she is back in remission. Remember that it will take 2-3 days to get the results back on that so we may know by next weekend. So, we are officially in "maintain" mode with monthly chemo treatments to keep her at this point until remission has been determined and a donor has been identified. We circle the wagons and wait.

Football has been good medicine for now and we enjoy each other while we can.

Roll Tide!

Chris

*   *   *

1-4-10

Folks,

While I do not yet know a lot as we have not had adequate time to debrief from the transplant team meeting today, the high points of the road ahead seem to be...

1. One consolidation chemo treatment. This is like the four consolidations of the summer after the one-month initial induction in March. These tend to be just to keep her in remission while time passes. These usually take 4-5 days of chemo then go home, which usually ends in an expected fever and return to the hospital for a week. So, roughly, 14 days in the hospital in the next month.

2. One month of intensive chemo designed to remove her native marrow system and ready her for transplant.

3. Transplant, one month in hospital.

4. 70 to 100 more days of daily Kirklin Clinic visits of 8 hours a day, so lodging near Kirklin will need to be identified.

All the above is best case scenario, and it also supposes remission status, which is not yet determined but presumed at this point. Remission will have to be specifically determined by biopsy expected soon with results, potentially by the week's end. Again, we were told to expect 6 months to a year from this point.

One day at a time...

Chris

* * *

1-5-10

Folks,

Yesterday was the initial meeting with the transplant team at the Kirklin Clinic for Anna. It was a day of straight talk and listening to hard words. Every detail was described including all possibilities, regardless of [their] rarity. This seems to be routine at the beginning of a fork in the road, where physicians want to make sure that patients are made aware of what does and can go on, so that the patient has time to fully prepare for what lies ahead. Much of it was sobering and difficult to hear and it is still taking us time to comprehend. The highlights seem to be ...

The bad news first:

1. Anna has a 60% survival rate.

2. At some point she will have a pain pump attached with morphine for pain.

3. Since the gastric system is so involved in the effects of chemotherapy, food will become much more of a problem, and she is likely to require some type of alternate feeding for a while.

The good news:

1. [The hospital has] already run a preliminary search through the donor database and 513 potential matches have been identified already. This is more than excellent.

2. Anna has a 99% chance of finding a match, again above excellent!

3. Her age and physical condition weighs the coin toss in her favor.

Today, Anna has the bone marrow biopsy done in Tuscaloosa to determine the remission status of her leukemia, which usually takes 2-3 days to process completely. We should know by the weekend if remission has been achieved, so the calendar I outlined for you in yesterday's note can begin.

Indeed, these are sobering things to think about; but they are like other situations in life that people face. I am sure that soldiers must undergird themselves emotionally before going into battle, especially when casualties are predicted to be high. Each one musters their courage and prays their prayers, turns the situation over to God and grabs his rifle anyway to storm the Normandy beaches in the face of incoming fire. Anna is not made of Teflon, and we are not immune to fear, but there comes a time when you must take a deep breath, grit your teeth, and go....

That is where we are.

Chris

                               * * *

Anna had many doctors. The journey started with Dr. Phillip Bobo in Tuscaloosa, the physician who initially diagnosed her condition. He then immediately referred her to Dr. Dubay, an oncologist on staff at DCH in Tuscaloosa. Each time we used a medical facility in Tuscaloosa, it was Dr. Dubay who supervised her case, writing her prescriptions, pharmacy orders, and release orders, either through the hospital or through the DCH Cancer Center, which is associated with the University of Texas MD Anderson Cancer Center. When Dr. Dubay sent Anna to UAB for treatment, Dr. Baird, a staff oncologist, supervised her initial chemotherapy treatment, aimed at putting Anna's cancer into remission. All the physicians were empathetic to Anna's status as a cancer patient—and as a young woman. They were efficient, caring, and productive in regard to the results they obtained and in the treatment of her care. It was not until we were introduced to the four physicians that comprised the team who supervised the care of patients in the UAB Bone Marrow Transplant unit that Anna, as a patient, and ourselves, as Anna's family of caregivers, experienced any form of negativity, doubt, or lack of empathy for Anna as a person, not seeming to be cognizant of the emotions and uncertainties of a patient experiencing new and dangerous situations with no knowledge of what they were going to face.

Our first introduction to the physicians at the BMT unit took place when Anna and Pam met with Dr. #1 to receive the overview of the bone marrow transplant process and to sign consent forms. During this exercise, physicians inform the patient of every negative aspect of the upcoming procedure, listing facts regarding survival rates and describing complications other patients have faced. In Anna's case, the conversation seemed unduly mean-spirited, with little regard for the emotional fallout of the prognosis and the danger that potentially lay ahead of her. It seemed as if Dr. #1 were presenting the facts of the disease—and the transplant's role in potentially halting the disease's progression—while lecturing a classroom filled with first-year medical students. There was absolutely no part of the doctor's rather conversational tone that indicated the information she was presenting to Anna, who was a 22-year-old woman after all, had life or death consequences! There was no apparent sensitivity on the doctor's part, and no recognition of the overwhelming amount of information that Dr. #1 had just dispensed. I am sure she felt she had done her job well in presenting the facts as required by her unit's policy. We saw right away that this group of doctors were different.

The second disturbing encounter with the BMT physicians occurred after Anna underwent testing (following her chemotherapy treatments) to determine whether her leukemia was in remission. This time, Dr. #2, the physician on call for that period, entered the room and announced that although the tests indicated that Anna was clear of cancer cells in her blood and that her leukemia was in remission, she suspected that cancer cells remained in Anna's body. She matter-of-factly announced that the transplant would be worthless, in her opinion, and that we should consider leaving and calling in hospice! Then she made an about-face and exited.

Anna, Pam, and I were left in despair, feeling all must be lost and that Anna's battle would be over before it had even begun. Looking for hope, we appealed to Dr. #3, the head of the BMT, for clarification of Dr. #2's comments. He declared that we should dismiss Dr. #2's suggestion and pronounced that we would "of course go ahead with the transplant." We were getting emotionally whiplashed!

*　*　*

The events that transpired in 2010 showed me a force in life with which I was unfamiliar. Of course, I knew about love, about charity, about empathy. But everything I knew of these forces derived from a spectator's point of view: I was outside of the forces' spheres of influence. At that point, I had never experienced love demonstrated through people other than family. But I also had never experienced a tsunami of disaster…a situation in which a health crisis could be so consuming and so dangerous that the threat of death, financial ruin, the loss of house and home, was likely. I had good health insurance, and I realized a lot of people could not say that, but expenses were multiplying. The hospital and doctors' bills were arriving, they would eventually total $4.5 million dollars, with twenty percent of that coming from my pocket. An apartment in Birmingham was necessary for Anna's treatment: I was in my car driving to and from work and driving to and from the hospital in another city, and driving twenty-seven hours a week to perform my duties as both college faculty and church staff. The gasoline bill was adding up as well.

Anxiety over my daughter's health and future combined with the stress of work-related obligations melded with financial worries, even though Pam's employer graciously paid her in full for each semester of teaching she had to walk away from to care for Anna when lengthy chemotherapy treatments, followed by a bone marrow transplant, became a reality. But during those semesters in which she did not begin to teach, she drew no salary for months.

The family budget was unrecognizable. That is when I became the focal point and recipient of light and love, love from friends, colleagues, family, church congregations, even perfect strangers, in the form of money.

Debbie Watson, who at that time was vice president for private banking at the Bank of Tuscaloosa, is a dear and treasured friend. She and her husband, Sammy Watson, were our neighbors for many years, living only two houses down from us. Almost immediately after we moved into the neighborhood, we met Debbie and Sammy in the street, which was the social center of my circle. The girls were small, Anna nine and Tori five. The Watson's cocker spaniel and their beautiful swimming pool became an instant attraction. We spent many hours at their house, talking, swimming. We even used their basement as a tornado shelter when necessary. Pam and I joined their church, the Covenant Presbyterian Church, not long after we moved into the neighborhood. When the girls were young, the church held a ceremony celebrating the youths who had recently become church members, formally marking their graduation from child to church member. Becoming a member of the church required a time commitment on the youth's part: finding a mentor to instruct them on the meaning of church membership, learning the information, and ultimately agreeing they possessed the desire to join the church as a full member. Anna asked Debbie to serve as her mentor; a few years later, Tori asked Debbie the same thing. Graciously accepting, and regularly keeping appointments with each girl, Debbie steered Anna and Tori through the process. Confirmation Day ceremonies were significant events in family life. Debbie and Sammy Watson were right there in the middle of it.

In response to her own anxiety caused by reading my updates each day, I suppose, and uncomfortable with the thought that there was nothing significant she could do to tangibly help Anna in her cancer battle, Debbie asked me for the email addresses I used when sending my updates. When I looked around my inbox after a few days, I saw that Debbie had created a letter and sent it to each person following Anna's journey; the list of followers had now reached into the hundreds. In the days before GoFundMe and PayPal, this is the way it was done.

* * *

1-8-10

Dear Friends,

Several days ago, Chris Gordon shared some sobering facts to ponder in regard to what Anna is facing. He compared her situation to that of a soldier. What she is going through is…

"… similar to other situations in life that people face. I am sure that soldiers must undergird themselves emotionally before going into battle, especially when casualties are predicted to be high. Each one musters their courage and prays their prayers, turns the situation over to God, and grabs his rifle anyway to storm the Normandy beaches in the face of incoming fire. Anna is not made of Teflon, and we are not immune to fear, but there comes a time when you have to take a deep breath, grit your teeth, and go...."

Anna Gordon is a beautiful, 22-year-old with her whole life ahead of her. One of the things that makes Anna different from other University of Alabama honor graduates is she has leukemia.

The Gordons have held to the idea that repetitive and focused prayers for health, strength, peace, and confidence, lifted up and reinforced by many, will increase the power and speed of the manifestation of those requests. They have also taken comfort in the knowledge that so many friends and strangers are part of the chain.

Throughout the whole process so many of you have asked, "What can I do to help?" Until this point, prayer has been the one thing on the list. Also, cards, visits, and gifts of food, clothing and many other things have been a tremendous help. The road ahead is going to be an expensive one. Here is a list of future needs:

1. Bills not covered by insurance.

2. Moving Anna's things back from Athens and into storage.

3. At a minimum, 20% cost of her bone marrow donor's expenses, not covered by insurance.

4. Expensive drugs.

5. Daily living expenses for two separate households for several months.

If you feel moved to contribute financial support, an account has been established at The Bank of Tuscaloosa to help Anna along this journey. If you would like to make a donation, please feel free to send a check, payable to "The Anna Gordon Fund," or if you would like to make an anonymous donation, please send a check to Bank of Tuscaloosa, Attn: Debbie Watson, P.O. Box 2508, Tuscaloosa, AL 35403.

I thank you for your support of Anna in the past several months, in the present, and in the months ahead yet to come.

Debbie Watson
Vice President, Private Banking
Bank of Tuscaloosa

* * *

We had not asked for money, we never talked about money outside of family, but this unexpected and unheard-of letter became the breaking of a dam containing the pent-up emotions of hundreds of families and friends, acquaintances, and strangers alike, all of whom were waiting on every daily update email of mine, hoping for good news but praying when there was none.

These people now saw something tangible they could offer their energy to, their ideas to, and into which they could invest their love. Other elaborate fundraisers sprang up at different times, in different towns, involving different churches and workplaces, all creating ways to harness the fundraisers' skills or talents, transforming them into an event by which money could be raised and donated to us to relieve burdens, provide us peace, and reflect their love of Anna—and us—while we all walked the same path together.

In addition to individuals writing checks to "The Anna Gordon Fund" at Debbie's bank, my Sunday School class at Fayette First United Methodist Church organized a spaghetti lunch in the church's cafeteria area. After the eleven o'clock service on Sunday, congregation members could buy plates of food, stay, and eat together or get a boxed lunch to go, to eat at home later. The faculty at the University of Alabama School of Music held its own fundraiser: concerned faculty donated cash from their wallets, or wrote checks, giving the entire collection to Pam on the day she walked away from the church for the first time, when Anna was initially diagnosed.

Bevill State Community College, the Fayette Civic Center and Art Museum, and friends and actors of Tuscaloosa Community Theater also came together to create and sponsor an event called "Anna's Night Out":

> On Friday evening, May 21, there will be a Dinner Theatre/ Silent Auction held in the Earl McDonald Auditorium on the Fayette Campus of Bevill State. "Anna's Night Out" will feature a wonderful homemade meal along with a performance of "Love Letters" by Kathy Wilson and Gary Wise of Theatre Tuscaloosa. The Fayette Art Museum is sponsoring the Silent Auction that will include selections from local artists, autographed books from Alabama authors, college sports memorabilia (UA, AU, MSU), a signed autographed hat from Tony Stewart, and much, much more.
>
> Tickets are available for purchase at $20 a person or $35 a couple. If you would like tickets, please call Glenda Robertson at the Civic Center, 932-8727, or Betty Crowley at Bevill, 932-3221, ext. 5677.

The evening's event was huge and spectacular. Small southern towns have traditions that collectively make up its social life, and the tradition of individuals signing up to host a table seating six or eight guests obligated them to invite their friends or family to purchase tickets for those seats. The host of the table would then develop a theme for that table and then decorate the table with items conveying that theme, using their own fine china tableware, silver, crystalware, cloth napkins, centerpiece, even party favors! There was a competition, official or unofficial, for the best themed and decorated table. This made it fun for the guests and the table hosts alike. The dinner was catered, and our family friends Kathy Wilson and Gary Wise, long-time actors in the Theatre Tuscaloosa organization, volunteered to come and perform the play "Love Letters" as entertainment.

In addition, a committee of members organized a silent auction. They approached businesses for donations of food, gifts, prizes, vacations, or services, to be displayed on exhibit tables so the evening's guests could view them and then write their bids for purchasing the items they most favored. The committee came to me one day at work and told me that part of the auction was to be sports memorabilia. The part of the auction was designed to motivate men to submit bids, as they usually left the bidding to their female partners. The committee members asked if I knew anyone associated with athletics at the University of Alabama who might be able to supply donated items, such as a signed football from Nick Saban, perhaps. Indeed, I did. Our friend Rita Martin was an office manager for women's gymnastics; she worked daily with coaches Sarah and David Patterson. I called Rita to inquire about the event committee's request for items, and she agreed to look around to see what donations she could round up. Not long after my request, a day or two prior to the night of the event, a large box was delivered to the committee. In it were treasures that far surpassed the committee's wildest hopes. Rita had personally approached everyone in her office, and she had contacted all of the other team sports, whether a men's team or a women's team. She delivered eye-popping items from the majority of those she approached.

There were game and match tickets, autographed sports gear (including footballs!), baseballs, hats, helmets, and posters from many famous coaches. There were catered box seats, jerseys (new and game worn). David Patterson, a supreme wood-working hobbyist, hand-crafted a fountain pen. In addition, there were items collected from other area college and university campuses as no institution wanted to be left out of the memorabilia competition. The evening's bounty for auction was impressive for any sports fan.

I arrived with my mother-in-law and brother-in-law, and sister-in-law, John and Kay Daughtry, along with Tori. A table was set for us up front, directly beneath the stage, so we could enjoy the best view of the night's entertainment. Upon entering the auditorium on the campus of Bevill State Community in Fayette, where the event was held, the first thing I noticed was the TV cameras. A producer for a local television station was there to film the event for all to see. This was an area in West Alabama whose population was truly engrossed in the drama of Anna's cancer journey. At the conclusion of the evening, the committee chairperson presented me with a check and asked me to say a few words. She came to my table and handed me the microphone, and for the first time, I turned around behind me to look at the crowd seated at table after table. I saw familiar faces, one after another, as I scanned the room. I was standing with microphone in hand looking into the faces of colleagues, friends, former students whom I had taught during the course of the last twenty years, area clergy and politicians….The crowd came not only from the city of Fayette, but from cities across the region, like Gordo, Tuscaloosa, Reform, Northport, Aliceville, and even Birmingham. The faces of so many people who populated my life in so many different ways was overwhelming. As I began to speak words of thanks to so many people who were responsible for assembling such a complex event for the benefit of only my family, my voice began to crack. Humble tears started to flow down my cheeks, and I was barely able to finish a comprehensive thank you. I will remember the feeling of pure love washing over me, being witnessed by the other members of my family who were seated at my table, for the rest of my life.

"A Night Out for Anna", presented by
The Fayette Art Museum
May 21, 2010

LOF Productions photo file # 10322
jdaughtry@LOFproductions.com
704.375.8892

People in West Alabama circled Anna and our entire family, providing words of encouragement, prayers, financial gifts, offering to employ any talent or skill they possessed that might be of tangible use. One of these offers caught me off guard. I was scheduled to perform with the group I cofounded, the Tuscaloosa Horns, who had decades of experience playing with nationally and internationally known music bands that required an accompanying group of professional horn players when they performed in the southeastern United States. The city of Tuscaloosa had just constructed its first amphitheater, and The O'Jays were scheduled to provide the opening night's concert. The Tuscaloosa Horns had a multiple-decades association with The O'Jays, and of course they wanted to use us on the gig in our hometown. It was an exciting event for the city and people of Tuscaloosa, who finally had its own concert venue, and I was humbled to be a part of the opening event. However, a local band in Fayette named the C Plus Band decided to create a fundraising concert for Anna and my family on the same night as the O'Jays concert. Of course I chose to be present at the event designed for Anna. I backed out of playing at The O'Jays concert and attended the C Plus Band fundraiser instead. The C Plus Band was comprised of local Fayette citizen musicians who performed popular rock 'n' roll and R&B tunes at the local country club and other venues. They played for wedding receptions and various event and festival dates across the area. I knew many of the band's personnel very well, and it was an honor to be the recipient of their gift to our family. That night, the same auditorium at Bevill State Community College in Fayette where Anna's Night Out had been held was filled to capacity when I arrived. Hundreds of people bought tickets to hear the C Plus Band perform, and again I was overwhelmed with the love and generous capacity of small-town America. While I missed a concert of rock 'n' roll Hall of Famers performing to a capacity crowd in a first-rate performance venue in my hometown, nothing compared to the feeling I received from the C Plus Band members and those who attended the concert, held in the unassuming venue of a community college auditorium in a small town in West Alabama.

Two additional gifts that I can still recall as representing a caliber of generosity I had never experienced came from individuals who, at the time, could not be more different. The first came from a full professor in the School of Music at the University of Alabama, where Pam taught. When Anna was initially diagnosed with AML in March of 2009, she was in the final few years of her teaching career. From the moment the news broke that Pam's daughter had cancer, this senior faculty member contacted her financial adviser and asked that a $100 check be mailed to our address. Her gift was not a one-time gift; rather, a $100 check arrived in our mailbox each month until I begged the professor to stop—which was dozens of months later! In fact, the checks stopped temporarily after I implored her to cease and desist, believing her generosity to be above and beyond what may be asked of anyone. But as soon as Anna relapsed, the checks returned to their monthly schedule.

The second gift of generosity and empathy we received still makes my breath quicken and my eyes water whenever I think of it. Pam taught piano to the university students, but she also maintained a slate of private piano students ranging in skill levels from beginners to those who were on a level with pre-college performance majors. It was common for Pam to teach piano to two or more children within the same family. Families interested in acquiring high quality instruction from a reputable and experienced instructor of private piano for their children would have each child begin instruction at an appropriate age. As older siblings continued to progress, younger children would learn to development fundamental skills. Thus it was that Pam became a beloved teacher to a family in Gordo, Alabama, who drove the one-hour commute to and from their home to have each of their five children take lessons from my wife. This continued over many years.

Soon after Anna was diagnosed, the mother of the family began to prepare entire home cooked meals at the kitchen in their home. They would pack the meals fastidiously into a picnic basket, thoughtfully including eating and serving utensils, plates, and drinks, then load the picnic basket and some of their children into their van and drive to UAB Hospital to hand deliver the meal to Anna's room. She and her children would stay only briefly, then return to their van and drive back home again. The delivery of the home cooked meals happened many times over Anna's cancer journey. While the generosity displayed by the effort of planning, cooking, and delivering the meal was remarkable, and while the skill to pull off the feat was equally impressive, it is the creativity, effort, and empathy displayed by the family's twelve-year-old daughter that will be burned most indelibly into my heart for the rest of my life.

Witnessing her mother's many acts of generosity to our family, their daughter Kate began to desire to follow in her mother's footsteps: she wanted to raise money for our family. She took stock of her skills and decided there was indeed one thing she could do: she began to sell her own crocheted creations. Her "Anna Bags" were small, crocheted coin purses, large enough to carry folded cash and credit cards. There was enough room left for a tube of lipstick and a package of gum. A crocheted strap was attached to the body of the purse and could be hung on a woman's shoulder. When Katie announced to her family that she would begin to make the purses, she asked her family to help get the word out to friends and other family members, so she would have a ready supply of customers. One evening, when her mother was going to deliver another picnic basket with a complete homemade dinner to the hospital, Kate decided to come along. She brought a check for the amount of money she had raised. When Katie gave the check to Pam in the hospital, it totaled more than one thousand dollars! The level of empathy, and the effort and time invested by a twelve-year-old young lady to raise over one thousand dollars by selling homemade purses for twenty dollars each, boggles my mind and touches my heart to this day. But her act merely exemplifies the degree of love that flowed in our direction, streaming in from all around us, during this time. I still shake my head in astonishment and humility.

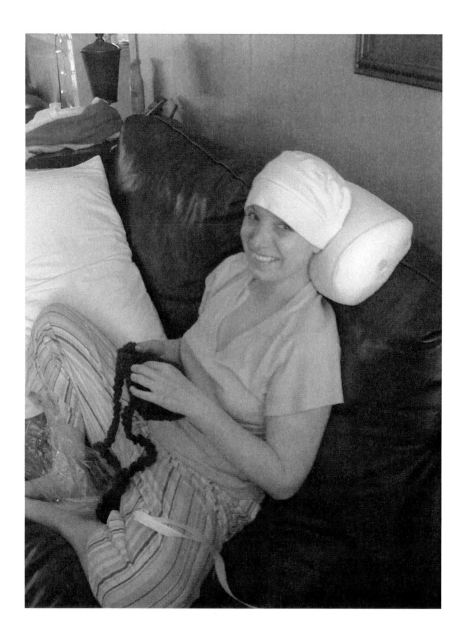

* * *

1-6-10

Folks,

The expected bone marrow biopsy scheduled for yesterday did not happen because Anna's platelet count was lower than the doctor wanted. He put off the biopsy until Friday of this week to give her time to improve that number for fear of bleeding during and following the procedure. So, today we sit and wait until Friday.

More later,
Chris

* * *

1-8-10

Folks,

Today Anna did have the bone marrow biopsy that had been scheduled since Monday of this week. As you know, lower counts than the doctor wanted to see delayed the biopsy until today. Anna went to the Cancer Center at DCH to have [the procedure] done at 10:30. It all went well, except that in the middle of the procedure, the needle malfunctioned, causing the attempt[ed] biopsy to be stopped, a second needle retrieved, and a second biopsy [performed]. So. Anna had to endure the procedure twice today! It was not the doctor's fault, he is very good, actually, creating as little discomfort as possible. But the second insertion did cause him to [prescribe] antibiotics for Anna to take over the next 5 days just in case the double bone penetration [introduced] unexpected bacteria into her [system]. The results will not be back until the middle of next week at the earliest, but the doctor was encouraged that all looked good because of the speed in which her counts have recovered.

We are encouraged and we are inspired to continue our very own "process," as Nick calls it, having watched the Tuscaloosa teamwork all year, to overcome adversity. We are tremendously proud to know them, teach them, and be fans.

Roll Tide,
Chris

* * *

1-11-10

Folks,

We heard from Anna's physician today regarding the results of the bone marrow biopsy done Friday. While they still await one small portion of the test, they have declared Anna to be in remission! We are thankful for positive results and for your efforts in praying and well-wishing for this result for the last month. The doctor does not think that the remaining test information will change the status one bit when it comes.

While this is wonderful news, it also means that we are set firmly on the transplant path, from which there will be no return. She will undergo a consolidation chemo to keep her in remission soon while they seriously, actively, do an in-depth donor search beginning now, from among the 500+ indicated so far.

Here we go...

Chris

* * *

1-19-10

Folks,

Anna and Pam left the house at 5:45 this morning, heading to the Kirklin Clinic for an echocardiogram, then a visit with her primary oncologist in Birmingham, and finally they checked into the hospital at UAB. Pam could not sleep and stayed up all night the night before packing and organizing for the return trip, then after the morning at Kirklin Clinic, the girls had to wait several hours before a room became available for their [stay]. Finally, around 4:30 or 5:00 pm, they were given room W950, probably one of the worst rooms possible, very small and right across from the nurse's station, which is loud and active 24 hours a day. In addition, Pam had to unload the completely packed car by herself, taking each load over 5 blocks and 9 stories from the car to the room, and there were 4-5 loads! All of this led to a very frustrating and stressful day, completed with no sleep for 36-40 hours, ending in constantly interrupted sleep every day for days [on end while sleeping] in a CHAIR! A mother's love is often immeasurable!! She is my hero.

They enter this week [scheduled] for a consolidation chemo to keep the remission status intact while they narrow the search for a bone marrow donor. They are likely to stay for four or five days before they return home. Then we await [the] fevers that usually come [while they are] at home, forcing them back to the hospital for days of antibiotics to fight the fevers. [The doctors] tell us we may have two or more months of these consolidations before the transplant process begins. We will see…

Anna has created a CaringBridge site, and I will post both emails and copies of these emails on the CaringBridge site to accommodate the increased demand for information regarding Anna's progress through the transplant process. You may access the site by typing the following address…

www.CaringBridge.org

Click "Visit A Website" and enter the name…annagordon

You will be required to register your name and email address for future log ins, and then you may visit her site, read her journal entries, and sign her guest book. I will also put up more pictures from time to time.

Thanks for keeping up and for supporting us as we travel this winding road toward health and sustained life for Anna for many years to come!

Peace,
Chris

*   *   *

1-20-10

Folks,

Pam and Anna slept some last evening and [Anna] has been receiving the consolidation chemo treatments designed to keep her in remission while the donor process continues. Today there seems to be some movement on finding a donor and things seem to have speeded up some, indicating a reduction of [names on the donor list] toward a useful selection. We hope they arrive at a perfect match who is also still willing to donate as soon as possible.

Pam included a note she wanted forwarded to all of you this evening…

Thanks everyone for all the messages and offers of help. Yesterday unfolded slowly and we really did not realize that it was going to be a nightmare until we were in the middle of the day, I didn't call for any help. Anna and I were just bouncing around like unleashed balloons for a while until we got a room.

Today has been better. We have received more news about the bone marrow donor process and Anna feels pretty good...just tired. Chris is a much better writer so I will let him fill you in on the specifics. Just know how much we appreciate everything you are all doing for Anna and our family. We read every message and card. It is very overwhelming, but in a good way.

Much love,

Pam

I want to thank all of you who wished me a Happy 50th Birthday today!! I do not feel old, just look it!! You all have made it much more memorable, and I thank you for all you do to support us in this journey.

Peace,
Chris

* * *

1-21-10

Folks,

Not much to say today other than the girls had a good day. The chemo is going normally with no adverse reactions. They expect to go home possibly on Saturday. I went to UAB for the first time this week and I took Pam out for dinner at a small excellent family-owned Italian spot in Homewood called DeVinci's—yes, I know he spells it DaVinci, but they don't! We ate a wonderful meal, where I go get takeout for Anna often, and we talked about all of you.

You who read this and react to these meanderings and overwhelm us with your kindnesses and actions of love in various ways dominated our discussion and we tried to come to terms with your cards and letters, your gifts of baskets and food and games and entertainments—and now your resources. For two parents who just try to work hard and do quality work as often as they can, it is a difficult and unusual thing to open up and accept the love of others. It is easier to deal with individuals, but when there are so many coming from all over at such a rate that you can barely remember who did what yesterday much less a week ago...the light of your generosity is so bright it is hard to see sometimes.

We cannot express enough gratitude or adequately and appropriately respond to so broad an outpouring of concern. I beg for you to not feel thwarted if, and when, we fail to show how much we are grateful, individually, and adequately. We can spend the rest of our lifetimes and still not do what is required. I only attempt to honor your thought, your prayers, your hopes, and your shared grasping for a long-term positive result from this struggle. Thank you for walking with us and for holding our hands. That is all we can offer.

Peace,
Chris

* * *

1-22-10
Folks,

A good day and a routine one, the girls do indeed come home tomorrow. Many decisions to make in the next few days regarding the Birmingham post-transplant stay. Anna's Athens apartment will be packed and returned to Tuscaloosa next weekend. I closed the arrangements for that today. I entrusted the task to the people who moved her over there in the first place. They did such a good and thorough job, it made them the obvious and appropriate choice to close that chapter, for now. So many things rushing to a head, I feel it getting closer to game time. This week may be one of the last of rest for us all before the rush of the approaching storm arrives.

Peace to you and to us,
Chris

*　*　*

1-23-10

Folks,

The girls left the hospital today and we continued the tradition of eating somewhere before we go home. It seems as if the regular choice when we leave DCH is Iguana Grill and when we leave UAB, it is to go to PF Chang's! Again, it was wonderful. The doctor told us that they are very close now in the donor search and that they could have a single donor identified by Monday!! If, and when, that becomes true, and the donor search is completed, and the single willing person secured, then the second step in this process will have been accomplished. We will know more by next week. For now, we enjoy being at home for a few days before the chemo begins its work on the bloodstream and the counts begin their tumble, leading to the inevitable return to the hospital for antibiotics. For now, we enjoy the familiar…home.

Peace,
Chris

*　*　*

1-29-10

Folks,

The girls have been home for several days now and they have had
to go to the DCH Cancer Center for blood tests and discovered
that [Anna's] blood counts are now at zero. The chemotherapy in
the hospital has done its work and she has reached the bottom.
She now must climb back out of the familiar trough in which
she finds herself. To help that process along, she will receive four
Neupogen shots, one a day for the next four days. These are the
ones that are designed to increase the amount of new blood cells
that the bone marrow makes, causing her to reach the top quicker,
thus keeping her immune system exposed to outer infections for
less time. The shots also cause her physical pain because the new
cells are churned out of the marrow at such a rate that Anna can
feel the bones working, squeezing, and ringing out every new cell
as quickly as possible. This is felt [as] a moving pain that rotates
around the skeleton and can be excruciating.

In a visit to the cancer center yesterday, more information was
given regarding the transplant process. We do not know any more
specifics of whether the final donor has been determined, but
[that determination] is close and [the search is] in the final stages.
Rather, what was discussed was more about the timing of the
process when it comes. Without going into the specifics of the discussion, it was frightening to learn, once again, that the process is
one that "plays for keeps" and it can have a very negative outcome.
We have heard that before, but each time we hear it the time grows
shorter until it will be upon us and upon her. It is a hard thing to
contemplate your mortality when the game that determines it is
imminent and growing closer every day. As I have said before,
Anna is not made of Teflon, and we are not immune to fear. Fear is

a real thing for all of us, but it can be overwhelming for a 22-year-old who should have all her life left to unfold. We broke last night under the weight of it. Most days it can be kept at bay and under the surface, but on occasion, it emerges and paralyzes everything it touches, until it can be re-collected and stuffed back into the duffle bag from which it poured.

I remember once in my youth that I traveled with a church youth group for an afternoon of fun at Pointe Mallard in North Alabama. At the time [the area was] famous for [its] then new water park whose main attraction was an Olympic size diving platform! Of course, all of us had to go and demonstrate our mettle by jumping off the tower. I took my turn waiting in line and climbing the steps up to the 30-meter platform. All during the wait the lifeguards kept hollering "Dive at your own risk!! If you go up to the tower you must go off. No one is coming back down these steps!!!" I remember finally climbing up the last steps to the platform, and what I was not expecting was the view. You could see for miles from 100 feet up in the air. I looked all around me and then I went to the edge and looked down.

The pool at the bottom looked to be the size of a postage stamp! I was so high up I had all manner of thoughts as to where I might land. It might be on the concrete, or the parking lot, and it was going to hurt!! The boy that jumped before me landed funny and splattered all on the surface of the water causing the lifeguards to have to jump in the pool and pull him out. That took a long time and I had to wait up on the platform thinking my fearful thoughts that were raging into panic. I was going to have to jump off that platform and I remember looking over the edge staring at the water...

That is where we are now. It is getting real; there is no possible turning back. Anna will have to jump, and us with her, soon......

Sigh.

Chris

* * *

1-29-10

Friends,

For those of you that might not know, Mary Ann is the agent for Vladislav Lavrik and the Russian National Orchestra. She is also my friend. Our connection was Vlad, because of the recitals I played with him two years ago. She is a special person and understands what we are going through because her husband had leukemia. He lived a good life. She understands the challenges we are facing. I thought you all might be encouraged by her letter and the ability of one life...Anna Gordon's...to bring the world together. It's pretty amazing. I found pictures of the cathedral and Madonna to which she refers, and I have posted them on the photos portion of this site.

Love,
Pam

Subject: Happy Birthday

Dear Pam!
Hello from Russia! I will return to the US tomorrow, and I know that you celebrate your birthday during the last week in January (not sure which day). I remember this because I celebrate my birthday during the first week in January. We are "Januarians" and I have been thinking of you in rather special ways. First of all, Vlad had five concerts during the past week. In all of them he was brilliant. I have some photos to send you, but

as usual I am rather behind the curve in getting through my to-do list. My reason for being here is to organize an 18-day tour of the US Army Brass Quintet in April-May commemorating the end of WW II. Vlad is a big part of this project. While here I had the great pleasure to meet his family—parents, wife, and daughter. They are all as marvelous as Vlad—a wonderful family. In St. Petersburg, my friends have begun to pray for Anna at the biggest orthodox cathedral in the city, Kazan Cathedral. I was present today when the priest began the service for Anna in which prayers and songs were offered, candles lit in front of various historic icons (including a Madonna with child framed in silver with pearls and gems) symbolizing the power of faith. I know you have many people who are strangers praying for Anna and now there are many praying in [the] Russian language. They began their vigil today, actively seeking to give you miraculous strength to endure the next phase of treatment. Russian Orthodox believers include among their saints many who have experienced miracles. They asked me to pass along these stories to buttress your faith. One friend will translate a few stories to make them accessible. Pam, you and Chris are doing a marvelous, amazing job with communications that hold together your family and friends through a very difficult period. I want you to know that this process, however painful for you and Anna, is helping us understand the meaning of life, friendship, sacrifice, and faith. Thank you for finding time to include all of us in your journey, the ups and downs, and even a few ordinary days such as a birthday.

Love you,
Mary Ann

P. S. When I get home, I will send you something from Vlad.

Mary Ann Allin
Swashbuckler Enterprises, Inc. and
American Council of the Russian National Orchestra

* * *

2-2-10

Folks,

As many of you may not know because I have been too busy to write, Anna developed a fever spiking to 103.6 on Saturday evening at 9:00. She was placed in a room, DCH 228, by 9:30 and has been there virtually asleep almost 18 hours a day since. Her blood counts have been on the bottom, 0 as of Friday's lab work, and it has really wiped her out and caused her to bruise terribly this time. She has received one unit of platelets, on Saturday night after admittance, and 2 units of blood on Sunday. All the blood prep work is Benadryl, and it causes her to sleep. She has now received 6 Neupogen shots, one a day for six days, and she has received antibiotics each day while working hard to bring up the counts, but it is a slow go. These are the days that are trying and methodical. Here is where you pay for any time [you previously spent] away from the hospital during each monthly chemo cycle.

I left Sunday afternoon to go to Athens to meet the movers who packed up Anna's apartment on Monday and moved [her belongings] back to Tuscaloosa on Tuesday. I cleaned out the refrigerator, mopped and vacuumed floors, and cleaned bathrooms, preparing for inspection by the property management. The movers packed for six hours after having driven for six on Monday and loaded the truck. They chose to sleep in Atlanta and drive the rest of the way today where I met them to deliver the goods for storage. Sadly, and unwillingly, we close the current chapter on life in Athens at the University of Georgia. Anna so enjoyed her time there and will always cherish the friends she made there. The future will compose another chapter when it is time.

Thank you for being on this journey with us. We are amazed daily by the expressions of love and concern and by the actions of love and help. Empathy, grace, love, self-sacrifice, all positive thoughts, and prayers are real. They bear witness to the finest heights that people can reach. When we receive your thoughts and actions, gifts, and resources, each one of us is helped in the process and made better. I believe it was designed that way!

Blessings to you all,
Chris

* * *

2-3-10

Folks,

Not much to report today. Anna slept most all day due to her low counts but also because of 4 interruptions during the evening by workers in the hallway doing floor polishing and stripping with loud buffer machines and nurses wanting to take vitals at 2:00, etc. When she did wake up near 8:00 pm, she was hurting in her bones from the shots making the marrow work hard and a fever began. All in all, it was a yucky day. The doctor came in and said, "I wish I could lie in bed all day instead of standing on my feet all day and working long hours." Anna replied, "Let's swap!!" He left.

Chris

* * *

2-7-10

Folks,

Anna is receiving blood and platelets today to counter the low red blood cell count which has declined in the last few days. The good white count has improved some yesterday and today. Anna has now achieved 20% of the white cell count necessary for her to leave the hospital; the other blood levels have declined, however. Progress is being made, but it is slow and methodical, causing her a good deal of low-grade fevers and the yucky feeling that comes with them.

We are humbled and grateful for the people of Fayette First United Methodist Church and the people of Fayette who have so openly and willingly supported our family from day one with prayers, encouragement, and now time, effort, and money. Today my Sunday school class hosted a fund-raising spaghetti lunch for the church and community members, providing an opportunity for donations of financial support to help offset the additional expenses associated with a bone marrow transplant. We are not accustomed to receiving such support or such open love and affection directed our way. We are thankful and honored to be a part of your lives and you become more a part of ours.

Peace,
Chris

*   *   *

2-8-10

Folks,

Today Anna's neutrophil count, the white blood cells that fight infections, was significantly higher, reaching 300 of the 500 necessary to go home and not be at risk of outside infections. That means the end of this hospital visit is within sight. Maybe tomorrow or Wednesday will see the girls returning home. Also, we heard from the bone marrow people and they have whittled the 10 [potential donors] down to 4 that they are working on. The 10 that were possible matches were the ones they were going to begin calling and double-checking to see if they were still willing and able to donate. Some were no longer able to because their own health conditions [were] changing, and some could not be available at this time. So, of those that would and could, [the staff is] doing detailed testing at this time. The nurse indicated that we may know the final donor within 2 weeks or so. All in all, it is good to see the light at the end of this tunnel.

Peace,
Chris

* * *

2-10-10

Folks,

Yesterday I forgot to send a note saying, officially, Anna and Pam got home! It took a while, however. The doctor told them they could go home at 8:30 am but recommended a platelet transfusion first, since [Anna] was bound to need one in a day or so anyway. So, [the doctors] ordered the platelets and 5 hours later [the platelets] arrived in the room after [the doctors had first discovered that the platelets] had been canceled and [Anna's] platelets given to a heart patient on another floor. [Anna] had been taken out of the system by someone thinking that she had already left that morning. They had to reorder the platelets and by that time the stock was depleted, forcing someone to drive to Birmingham [to] get a bag! It was a regular clown car fiasco, but Anna's diligent nurse investigated, found out what happened and kept on the powers that be until platelets were delivered and transfused at 3:00 pm, letting her go by 3:30.

We then went to eat at Iguana Grill for a celebration, which served as breakfast for the girls since they had not eaten all day!

Home Sweet Home!

Chris

* * *

2-12-10

Folks,

Today marks the successful completion of step number two in Anna's complete recovery. As you remember, the first step was to reach remission and, unfortunately, we had to do that step twice. But the second step is to find an appropriate donor, and we were notified that one has been found and is willing to donate!! We now begin the accelerated laps leading up to the transplant process.

The transplant team will tell us about the schedule for moving forward next week. What we know now is that they are going to look for a second donor as a standby, which we highly endorse, and they are going to have to put Anna through a battery of tests in preparation for the transplant. We do not know how long this will take.

We are thankful for the donor who stepped forward and was willing to say yes to the idea and the process. Literally that person will save our daughter's life! "There is no greater love…"

Peace,
Chris

* * *

2-20-10

Folks,

We received word regarding the upcoming schedule for Anna's transplant. While not fully detailed, it does hit the highlights of when we can expect to be doing various things.

March 1st—Anna will have a bone marrow biopsy to determine if remission is still intact before she can move through the process ahead; and she will have a spinal tap in the lumbar region to make sure that leukemia has not spread to other regions of the body. We have little information on this procedure or [why it is needed], but we know it must be done at this time. It has not yet been determined if [the two procedures] will be done in Tuscaloosa or in Birmingham.

March 3rd—Anna will report to Birmingham for a full day of tests determining her overall health with regard to heart and lung and other organs. These tests will determine a baseline, we suppose, [against which the team can compare] later when the heavy doses of chemo run their course.

March 22nd—The week of the 22nd, Anna will have to sign consent forms giving permission for the procedure to begin and for Blue Cross to give consent to cover the procedure. While signing, she will also begin taking a drug, palifermin, to help prevent mouth sores that will come in the next week.

March 29th—Anna will be admitted to the 3rd floor Bone Marrow Transplant ICU to begin treatment that will compromise and eliminate her native bone marrow system and prepare for reception of the donor's marrow which will take place 11 days afterward.

April—and potentially [longer] will be spent in the ICU adapting and recovering from the procedure.

Now we have an idea. Maybe with the coming of spring, all good things will grow, 'tis the season!

Peace,
Chris

*   *   *

2-27-10

Folks,

[The transplant team has] identified another perfect match for Anna, giving her a backup and alternatives for the month of March. The newest is a girl and the former is a guy. From what we know, the guy is having some difficulty with his schedule and [needs] to delay until late in April. The girl donor is being consulted at present to determine if she is available closer in March. We think she will be and there may be a tweak in the schedule for when the transplant will take place, and thus when Anna must begin her "chemo of preparation." [The team] should tell us by Monday, maybe. Nevertheless, Monday will see Anna getting a spinal tap for a test at DCH in Tuscaloosa. On Tuesday, she will go to Birmingham for the bone marrow biopsy to determine if she is still in remission to begin the transplant process. Tuesday also marks her/our one year "cancerversary." Thursday, she will have other organs tested in Birmingham. We will then know the remainder of the month's schedule, hopefully.

We wait, plan as best we can, but we are anxious. Things will pick up soon.

Peace,
Chris

*   *   *

3-1-10

Folks,

Anna and Pam arrived at DCH for the spinal tap this morning at 9:00. The procedure went well, [the doctors] took four vials of spinal fluid for testing to see if the cancer is in the central nervous system, a predetermining precaution to the transplant, as is all this week's testing. We don't know when we will hear of the results, but I assume it will be this week. [Anna] came home for rest and took a pain pill, and we will watch for headaches and soreness for the rest of the day. Tomorrow, she and Pam will go to the Bone Marrow Transplant ICU on the 3rd floor of the Wallace Spain Building at UAB to have a bone marrow biopsy. They want to do this one since they will be looking at the results instead of [having the procedure done] at DCH and the results shipped. I assume this is [because we will have the results faster], but I would rather [Anna and Pam] not have to be on the roads tomorrow with the expected rain/snow [that is predicted]. [Anna] will meet the new case manager for the remainder of the transplant—[the case manager] who will be administering the biopsy—tomorrow.

One test down this week and several more to go. She is brave and takes it all in stride saying, "I don't have much choice, do I?" I suppose not, but grace is in the choosing of your attitude. Today she was graceful!

Peace
Chris

* * *

3-2-10

Folks,

One year ago today, around 11:00 am, Anna was told by Dr.
Phillip Bobo that she had cancer. It was confirmed by oncologist
Dr. Dubay at 1:00 pm and we were being admitted to UAB for
treatment by the next day. What a year it has been for her, for us,
and for all of you, who have volunteered to travel this journey
with us. Yesterday Anna received a spinal tap, investigating the
central nervous system for leukemia. Today, she and Pam went to
Birmingham to UAB to have her 6th bone marrow biopsy in one
year, to recheck for remission status. These, and the organ scans
that are to come on Thursday, are designed to establish that she is
cancer free and ready to begin the transplant process.

She was given meds today to help with the pain and discomfort
of the procedure, but Pam reported to me that [the procedure]
still hurt her. It seems to become more painful and with higher
degrees of discomfort each time [the doctors] perform the procedure—injury now to insult. Anna remarked that she has a "Devil's
Triangle" on her back and upper pelvis where the holes form a
triangular area, from the spinal tap and previous marrow biopsies.
We now wait for the results, hoping merely for the opportunity
to begin yet a more dangerous journey that lies ahead for us in a
few days.

We had it confirmed that she will begin the transplant process by
entering UAB on March 30, [when she will] begin receiving the
chemo that will compromise her native marrow system. She will
receive transplanted marrow on April 9 or 10. We hope for the
10th because Tori's birthday is on the 9th. We wait and are anxious. Apologies to all ahead of time if we are short tempered or

slow to respond or late to clue into normal life and conversation. Our minds are busy, and our stomachs are running in other directions. We hope you understand…

Peace, and soon…
Chris

*　*　*

3-3-10

Folks,

It was a hard day today, full of anxiety and fear and flowing of tears. We got a phone call this morning saying that cancer cells have been found in Anna's spinal fluid. What this means in total we are not yet sure. It is too soon, and we have not yet talked to doctors enough to know the significance of this news. Instead, our own imaginations have had their turn to play in our minds. But [at] the end of the day what we seem to know is as follows.

[The doctors] are not wildly concerned about this. Apparently, for a test [to show cancer cells in a patient's spinal fluid during] the regular pre-transplant protocols happens often enough. The initial bone marrow results also look good, but a more thorough result will be available tomorrow. It seems that the spinal and cranial system and the marrow system are separated by a membrane that does not let things easily through it. Therefore, results [for each system] can be different. It seems that the cancer cells that they found were few in number and may be residual cancer cells from the previous year rather than newly created, indicating growth. This is especially [likely] if the marrow is still clean.

The action that is required at this point is for Anna to continue tomorrow to UAB for the organ scans and then to return on Friday to UAB to redo the spinal tap to check for reader error or more in-depth information. While they are there, however, [the doctors] are going to inject a directed chemo treatment into the central nervous system itself. They will then have her come back for four additional treatments of spinal chemo, on an outpatient basis at UAB, next Tuesday and Friday and the next Tuesday and Friday. The plans for the upcoming major chemo are still in place with the same entry date, March 30.

This adds stress and uncertainty to the mix of an already stressful month. Our nervous systems seem to react as if having been punched in the stomach, having yet another mountain to climb on the road to complete health. I am sure this will pass, and things will return to being optimistic and hopeful. It's just not every day that you feel that way.

Maybe tomorrow,
Chris

* * *

3-4-10

Folks,

The girls have returned from their long day in Birmingham with only a bad headache as semi-permanent damage. It seems like [Anna] has had several headaches this week. Mostly, all her organs, one after another, were poked, prodded, measured, dyed, photographed, and most of her blood removed for testing (somewhat in jest.) She said she felt like a cow at an auction, referring to the very impersonal way of laboratories and their staffs. People get so desensitized to the fact that the person in front of them has ears and feelings and is not a lab rat. They made it through the day and made it home with no major issues. Tomorrow is coming and they need to relax and sleep before then.

More as it comes,
Chris

* * *

3-5-10

Folks,

Today the girls went back to UAB to have the spinal tap redone and while they were there, to have the first spinal chemo inserted. They were scheduled to be there at 11:15 and [the team] got started about 11:45. They had Anna on morphine and some other meds, but they still managed to hurt her. This is the second day in a row where she has been made very uncomfortable. In addition, she became nauseated and got sick several times, causing them to have to put an IV of anti-nausea meds into her line. She felt weak and lightheaded, as if faint, and sick, and in pain until 5:30 when she finally felt well enough to leave the hospital. Anna had excruciating headaches all week from the spinal tap last Tuesday, head holding, pounding headaches. If she must endure that every day for the next two weeks while they do four more of these spinal chemo treatments, she will be a zombie. It was a difficult and stressful day.

The bright spot—the bone marrow showed no cancer cells— COMPLETE REMISSION! So now, we must get through these spinal experiences and then on to the big one March 30.

Pray for headache relief!!

Chris

* * *

3-8-10

Folks,

Today Anna and Pam returned to the UAB Bone Marrow
Transplant unit on the third floor of the Wallace Spain Building to
receive the second installment of the five spinal chemo treatments.
A new doctor did the procedure this time, [she] said she had "done
this a couple of times." She managed to do a pretty fair job, however, and there was not a great deal of discomfort this time. They
also pretreated Anna with anti-nausea meds before the procedure,
like they do in a traditional blood chemo treatment, and this
seemed to minimize the amount of post-chemo nausea, enabling
the girls to return home with much less fanfare and sickness than
Friday's adventure.

The results of the spinal fluid test of last Friday did indeed confirm
the presence of some leukemic cells in the fluid. Therefore, they
will be doing all five of the designated treatments. Other than that,
the day seemed to be more routine. That is a good thing!

Peace,
Chris

*　*　*

3-12-10

Folks,

Today, Anna had her third spinal chemo at UAB. It was by far
the one that made her most sick. She received the spinal tap at
12:30 pm and was sick until 6:30 pm. We didn't get her home until
almost 8:30. The day started well, however. We found an apartment in Birmingham for Anna and Pam to stay when they come
out of the hospital. We signed a lease, and we will move into it in

the next few days. It is a perfect spot that is the perfect circumstance for our needs. We are very grateful that this has been made possible, in so many ways.

Peace,
Chris

*   *   *

3-16-10

Folks,

Today was the fourth of five chemo treatments for Anna, and counting the preliminary testing spinal tap, the sixth spinal lumbar puncture. The attempt to get fluid out ([to test it] for leukemia cells) was virtually unsuccessful today, yielding very little fluid. In the attempt to get fluid out and eventually to get the chemo treatment dose in, [the team was] inside her spinal column for 50 minutes, poking, prodding, and readjusting the needle. Almost barbaric, even to describe, Anna said very little and tried to cooperate with the doctor. At one point, the attending physician came in to offer "coaching." The only positive from the day was learning that the four previous treatments have brought the leukemia count in the spinal fluid down to almost "0" and by Friday, the last treatment day, we expect it to be gone completely.

She repeated the previous pattern of nausea and sickness which lasted until we got home at 8:30 pm from a 12:30 PM appointment! We will be eternally grateful to leave this chapter of the story far behind. Now we have three days of headaches to look forward to before the next appointment. This is no fun for anyone!

Chris

*   *   *

3-19-10

Folks,

Today was a hard day. Anna, Pam, and I went to UAB to receive the last of the spinal chemo treatments that [Anna] has had to endure in the last two weeks. Anna woke up with such a headache that she barely made it downstairs, staggering and weeping in pain, the greatest pain she has experienced yet. It was the type of pain that forces the body to sway back and forth, attempting to find a place in your posture where it hurts the least but finding no relief. It was the type of pain that causes one to weep in despair, knowing that this cannot go on and you have no idea how to make it stop. After making her take every pain relief pill that we have in the medicine cabinet and after Pam and I had the discussion as to whether we should keep our appointment at UAB or not, we finally bypassed the idea of going to DCH for pain relief and we decided that going on as quickly as we could to UAB so that they might see what type of suffering she has had to endure, [because] maybe they can fix it, was the wisest course. So off to the car with Anna lying in the backseat we went. Mercifully, the pain subsided enough to travel as soon as the meds distributed through her bloodstream.

I dropped the girls off at the side entrance of the building and temporarily parked so I could get a wheelchair to escort the girls up to the 3rd floor bone marrow transplant ICU where we have been going for these spinal treatments. As soon as we departed the elevator, we noticed a group of people congregated just outside the ICU door. As we navigated [Anna's wheelchair through] the people, I noticed the face of Mr. Sprinkle standing there, whom we had met last Friday by accident through Lana Langley's visit with him and Pam Sprinkle. As you may remember, Lana introduced us last week when Pam Sprinkle had been transferred to the ICU. I recognized him and was going to say my "Hellos" and "Hope y'all are doing bet-ters," when he said "… She passed away 30 minutes ago." I breathed in quickly in shock and continued walking to get the girls into the ICU entrance. As soon as I had delivered them into the room to await the doctor, I went back outside to say I was sorry. He walked to the elevator with me, and I told him that we (our church) had been praying this week for them and that I could not believe that she could have passed so quickly. I looked him in the eye and asked him if there was anything I could do for him. He immediately said, "Take care of your daughter." Our eyes filled and our voices cracked as we recognized within each other's face the monster we both have been battling. It is real, it is scary and does not play around, but rather, it plays for keeps. Even in his deepest and most immediate grief, having lost his wife only 30 minutes before from the same disease that our daughter is struggling to overcome, he wanted me to hang on and keep going and he hoped for a different outcome for us! Now that is compassion, he [offering it] more than I on this morning.

It is a monster we fight, indeed. Anna had doctors begin working on her back, attempting to draw off spinal fluid first, then refill that space with chemo [drugs] afterward. Three separate doctors punctured her spine over and over again for most of three hours with no success!! Each one giving up and calling in another. Fluid must be drawn for testing and if [the doctors] get none, they cannot put in any chemo; otherwise, the balance of the fluids and pressures is off, causing even more pain. So, the head doctor on the floor finally said, "Enough!" Instead of today being the final day of spinal chemo, yet another one is scheduled for Monday.

God bless the Sprinkle family tonight and all those who battle the monster called cancer!

Chris

* * *

3-22-10

Folks,

Today Anna and Pam went by themselves to UAB to have the
seventh spinal tab. The head physician in the Bone Marrow ICU
did the procedure. Pam insisted that they go to radiology and use
imaging systems to guide the procedure this time and the doctor
agreed that he would try only once and if he did not get in, he
would send them to Radiology. What I say now, I have not yet confirmed because I was not there, and I have not yet talked to Pam
regarding the details. She won't talk about it yet, I don't think she
can, but what I do know is from text messages that she provided
from time to time, in short bursts, from inside the procedure
room and a few phone calls.

She said, "It was awful and horrific." [She also reported that] Anna
declared that [the procedure] was hurting her, and that Anna
cried. Pam said the doctor said that the spinal column and nerves
were inflamed, and I imagine that after the two and a half hours on
Friday they were. Nevertheless, he went ahead and took out fluid
and replaced the space with the last chemo treatment, which burns
its way down already "inflamed" nerves. Insult to injury I say!

These two weeks have been the worst experience by far in this
whole year-long ordeal. Anna is in constant mind-numbing pain
and neither she nor Pam has slept at night since early last week.
One of the previous medications that were given was caffeine pills,
which help with the pain of headaches. It also keeps Anna up at
night, all night on 200 mg worth. When she is on her feet, it is only
to bathe or go to the bathroom, and she walks hunched over with

stooped shoulders and neck held up tight, close to the body to not cause pain from the movement of the body. This is and has been torture for her and for us to watch.

I am glad it is over, and I pray that the pain ends soon, although reports from other patients on the internet indicate that this can go on for weeks afterward. We just want her to feel good again, just in time for them to have to bring her down with the scheduled chemo that compromises her native bone marrow system before transplant. We do not want them to have laid her low just in time to endure the most severe chemo of all coming soon without time to adequately recover!

At this point what will be will be…it is nearing game time where the outcome is for real!

Peace, please…
Chris

*   *   *

3-23-10

Folks,

Today has been quiet, very quiet, and that is a good thing for now. While Anna is not out of pain, the new medications [the doctors] have given her are at least making her sleep, for hours on end, almost continuously. While it is drugged sleep, it does allow her time to rest, and when she is asleep, she is not in pain!! She slept all night except to wake and take more medications, and thus Pam did as well. Today, she has been asleep all day, and she is likely to continue, getting up only to eat a bowl of oatmeal and take more medication.

For the first day after, I will take quiet and be grateful…

Thanks to all of you who prayed for it!

Chris

* * *

3-25-10

Folks,

I did not have time to write Wednesday because I was in Birmingham all day moving Anna's things into her new apartment. I was not able to unpack everything, but furniture is placed, and most boxes unloaded, just not yet put away. Pam and Anna have spent both Wednesday and Thursday going to DCH where Anna has received IV fluids, two bags a day, and IV steroids designed to reduce inflammation in her spine. I am happy to say it is working, almost miraculously so!!! As soon as these [treatments] were administered Anna felt immediately better, able to walk and move some. After two days, she is moving at ease and even having some "attitude" return to her nature and body motions. She will go [to DCH] yet again tomorrow. We are grateful that someone took the trouble to [show] her some concern and begin to treat her previously debilitating symptoms.

While she is not running marathons yet, returning to some type of normal is terrific and we hope that it continues to progress throughout the weekend and into next week.

Peace,
Chris

* * *

3-30-10

Folks,

Today begins the countdown for Anna['s transplant], nineteen days and counting. She and Pam went to UAB today for five hours of "education," which is the code word for reminding you about everything that could happen to you in the next few days that is not pleasant and unallowable for me to report here. It was also a day for Anna to sign consent forms, many consent forms, including forms to use her body and blood for research purposes, and finally the consent form that "clears them" to do the procedure.

It is the time we have been anticipating and dreading with every fiber of our being, the descent into the unknown. We have been surrounded by love on every side [from] people we know and people we know nothing about. The irony is that we stand alone to endure this, we want everyone, and we want no one, we need everything, and we want to be left alone and be normal. This has changed our lives forever and none of us will be the same when this is over, we can only pray that we are better in the end and still useful. We will begin the march with heads held high and chins firm, eyes fixed on the prize, even when they are filled to overflowing, we will walk on.

Tomorrow Anna will have surgery to implant a second Hickman port, a twin to the one she has on the other side [of her chest]. On Thursday and Friday, [the team] will begin giving her IV medicine treatments to combat the inevitable mouth sores that will come from the chemo. Monday will last ten hours, and they will give her a test dosage of the chemo, monitoring her responses to it. In this manner they will determine the final dosages that will kill her native marrow system without killing her. On Tuesday, she will be admitted to the Bone Marrow

Transplant ICU on the 3rd floor of the Wallace Spain Building and on Wednesday, they will begin the drip.

The girls are staying in the apartment tonight and for much of this week to be at UAB early in the day for appointments. Now is the time to pray, now more than ever. Let the vigil begin.

God help us all.
Chris

*   *   *

3-31-10

Folks,

Anna had a second Hickman port implanted on the other side of her neck and chest today, giving her two stereo ports for the delivery of medicine and blood. A frustrating day of waiting, she was to go in at 10:00 am for the surgery. She was not called back until 1:00 after not having eaten since before midnight the day before and she was not able to leave until close to 7:00 pm. She had her first meal of the day at about 8:00 pm.

Tomorrow, she will receive medicines through those ports that will combat the expected mouth sores to come. She will receive them tomorrow and Friday. I hope sleep comes quickly tonight for all.

Peace
Chris

*   *   *

4-1-10

Folks,

Today was a good day; sunshine always makes you feel better. Anna and Pam had a good day, too, sleeping late at their apartment then going to UAB for thirty minutes of IV meds to help prevent mouth sores. Anna is cooking dinner tonight in her kitchen, chicken divan, claiming her new apartment for herself. It is a good thing that she is chipper enough to enjoy and do things she loves in the last few days before [she and Pam] enter the hospital for the extended stay.

Bon appetite
Chris

*   *   *

4-4-10

Folks,

Pam and Anna packed the car and drove away to Birmingham today after lunch, they must be at UAB at 8:00 am. Anna will spend ten hours there, where she will receive a test dosage of the chemo that will be used to compromise her native marrow system, and she will be monitored during the process. The results will determine the correct and final dosage, which [Anna] will begin on Wednesday after [she and Pam] check in on Tuesday.

It was a lovely weekend doing things we like to do, but also, it was semi-sweet in that much thought went into what was going to be needed over the next several months. Packing was paramount in anticipation of the longest stretch of continuous hospital stay so far. We are anxious, no doubt, but we are also expectant of overcoming this chapter in our lives, even though it will be hard and drawn out. We are also profoundly grateful.

It is not lost on me that on this Easter Day where we celebrate sacrifice and love given for us all, our family is celebrating the sacrifice and gift of love from a stranger to our daughter in the form of bone marrow. This person knows none of us and she is not allowed to know us for at least a year, but she chooses to sacrifice for Anna's benefit in an example of modern-day hope and purest love, not for personal gain or glory, but no less [meaningful than] the grander examples with which we are more familiar. It still fulfills the pattern presented to us all, long ago: "Greater love hath no man that he lay down his life for a friend." While we trust it won't cost the donor her life, she is [nonetheless] laying herself down and giving to another.

I am preparing a letter to our donor of thanks and encouragement, of gratitude and respect for what she does, because we think it is important to say thank you before she does what she must do. I want to give all of you who are on this journey with us the opportunity to express what you wish as well, if you so desire. The bone marrow transplant coordinator for Anna's case provides this service to families in our situation. It is allowed with certain restrictions, and you should know those up front if you wish to send a message.

You cannot mention your name or your region or state or community.

You cannot mention Anna's name or the Gordon family name.

Your message may be subject to editing.

You may do some of the following suggested items.

Express your gratitude for what [the donor] is about to do.

Offer encouragement.

If you would like to write a message, I will be more than happy to include it in a package to give to the bone marrow coordinator to edit and forward to the donor. Please get the message to me in an email or snail mail me. I must have these in hand by Sunday evening, April 11th, next Sunday.

You may email me or mail it to the house. Thank you for your support physically, emotionally, and financially during these days. The hard part begins!

Peace,
Chris

*   *   *

4-5-10

Folks,

Anna and Pam started at 8:30 am this morning at the Bone Marrow ICU and [Anna] received a test dosage of the chemo she will receive over the next 12 days. Roughly every two hours, the nurses took blood samples for testing, looking for whatever reactions they deem important to make adjustments that will lead to the final dosage specifically for Anna's body. They finished earlier than expected and the girls left the hospital and returned to the apartment at 4:00 pm.

Tomorrow, the girls go to the hospital and check in with the computer people in admissions, then leave for lunch and last-minute errands, before they return midafternoon to begin preliminary tasks in the ICU. On Wednesday, the chemo begins.

Many of you have begun to send letters or statements designed for Anna's donor. I encourage as many as who want to say something to please write a brief note. I have already begun to cut and paste them in a continuing document, like a "Guestbook," which will be given to the donor. If you are planning to write, please observe the parameters I laid out in my update yesterday.

I am honored and humbled and deeply moved as I read what you write. Our hearts overflow.

May you all be blessed for choosing to participate.

Peace,
Chris

* * *

4-6-10

Folks,

The girls entered the hospital today. For the first time, in all the past year's 150+ days in the hospital, the experience has never been what they experienced today. The bone marrow unit was stifling with a thick pall of negativity and institutionalization amongst its staff. All afternoon practically every doctor and nurse who came in to deal with Anna at all talked about death and mortality rates in fearful rigid prose. They would allow Anna to have practically no personal items intended to give the room personality or brightness, no cheerful lights, no personal sheets of color, no anything, practically, that would give Anna a sense of individuality and control in a foreign environment. The hall is very rigid in their rules and initially, at least, seemingly inflexible in allowing anything that would contribute an aesthetic value or indicate an enhanced quality of life for the patient.

Immediately, with the taking away of any freedom of movement or freedom in expression, Anna descended into despair, institutional despair, and no one seemed to be sympathetic toward her acclamation and assimilation to the new "home" at all. Tears flowed, anxiety reached out and spilled over the edges for several hours. Finally, around dinner time of 8:00 or so, she began to adjust and acquiesce to what is no doubt going to be a harrowing experience for the next many days.

This will be very hard, physically, mentally, and emotionally on Anna and on all of us surrounding and reacting to this. When they say the first hurdle is to keep her alive for the next several weeks, they are not kidding, and they expect everyone associated to strap it on and get prepared. So, like it or not, this is what must be done and here we go.

Chris

*   *   *

4-7-10

Folks,

Today has been a nightmare of the worst kind. After having gotten no sleep from the evening before, due to anxiety and interruptions (and for Pam, no bed, only a recliner), Pam and Anna were told that the doctors see blast leukemia cells in the previous two blood samples and that Anna has likely relapsed, making the transplant useless. All this by 8:00 am, the doctor now continues with a conversation that includes words such as "experimental treatments," "research projects" and "hospice."

But just to be sure, they do a bone marrow biopsy at 8:30 and say that they can tell in twenty minutes whether the marrow is clear. Four hours pass, while the girls try to comprehend the concept of these being the last days, until the main transplant physician comes in and declares her marrow clean, no leukemia! As if it were a bad "April Fool's Joke," we immediately begin to celebrate that everything is back to normal, and the nurse comes in to hang the chemo bags and begin the treatment.

At 5:30 the doctor comes in again and says, "I am still concerned that we are seeing these premature blasts, but we will go ahead with the transplant process because that presents the best possible option for Anna's treatment, and we will see where we are a month after." So, we were down on the floor, then up and grateful to have dodged a cruel bullet and finished the day with tarnished optimism. We never want to live through another day like today.

I pray everyone in that room gets some sleep tonight and tomorrow is a better day!

Chris

*　*　*

4-8-10

Folks,

How things change in an ICU, today Anna did not have chemo, it was a rest day on the schedule. She will resume tomorrow. The girls had a very good night's sleep, and today they were moved to the largest room on the floor, moving from the smallest where we started on Tuesday. If you want to send mail, here is her address: Anna Gordon, UAB Hospital BMT, 3rd Floor, WP, room p350, 619 19th Street South, Birmingham, AL 35249.

Also, today, the head transplant doctor assured us that he felt everything was fine and Anna's chances of having a successful transplant are very good. He even showed Anna how they do some of the complex blood cell readings, including her in her treatment. He realized quickly that he was dealing with a formidable young woman when she caught him in a miscalculation. I think they are bonding! The mood is much better today! Things change quickly up here.

We are in much brighter spirits, more like polished optimism rather than last night's tarnished optimism. We thank you for all the concern from our supporters. We could not go through this without that support.

Peace,
Chris

*   *   *

4-9-10

Folks,

Today is Tori's 19th birthday and she has had a nice day spending it with friends by the pool. I am grateful they have organized a "Tori Day" on her birthday. We celebrated it with her before Anna and Pam went into the hospital last week, so I am glad the actual day was special as well.

Anna resumed receiving chemo today and she has spent it doing crossword puzzles and the like, napping, and visiting with family. It is unfortunate that she will not be able to have visitors in the ICU like she sometimes did in the past hospital stays. None are allowed due to infection possibilities and her physical condition, [which] she wants to not to have to [bear the physical burden of having to talk to visitors] as she progresses [down this road].

Another day down, one at a time...

Chris

*   *   *

4-10-10

Folks,

Today was a good day. Anna had her fourth chemo treatment, and she still feels pretty normal, so she did normal things, or as normal as you can get in an ICU. She walked the halls, twice, played backgammon, watched movies, ate a tuna fish sandwich and dill pickle chips for lunch, and Chinese food for dinner.

If she still feels normal, we will try to provide as much normal enjoyment as possible. Soon enough, it will all change. We are grateful for days like today!

Peace,
Chris

*   *   *

4-11-10
Folks,

Anna spent the day resting, sleeping much of it, due to drugs used for pretreatments so that the chemo is well tolerated. She received the first dose of a second type of chemo, apparently there is a recipe of three, and she will receive this for the next few days. She is beginning to feel mildly "yucky," but still well enough to want to eat while she can. She ordered a quarter pounder with cheese and a large fries for lunch, nothing like a dose of "All American" junk food for a good comfort experience.

Tori and I, both, got to visit most of the day before we had to get back for her to attend a school event. We visited at the apartment, very handy for out-of-hospital down time, and Pam cooked dinner and is taking it to the hospital, more comfort food from the Gordon family recipe cabinet!

This week will be more involved as we progress, I am sure. It is lovely to think that so many friends will be remembering Anna and her donor in prayer on Thursday as we head into the transplant event this weekend. As I mentioned, I took the donor comments that have been sent to the Transplant Coordinator for editing and for delivery. She tells me that there are several [levels] of people [in various national offices] whose eyes pass over the comments, so it will take a few days and likely be delivered after the transplant "harvesting" event. I hope that she feels as loved as we do when I read your comments.

If you are interested, I am attaching the donor comments document to this email. It is anonymous as far as people's names who wrote [the comments], and it includes only the digital entries that were sent to me. The other entries, snail mail, and there were a few, have been given [to the Transplant Coordinator] to be included in the package as well, they are just not included here, in the event you don't see yours. Thanks to each one who wanted to express a comment. Through these, you can easily see the magnitude and power of an individual's choice to personally become involved in a situation and how many people are affected by the ripple effect surrounding that choice. Every individual [carries] a powerful potential for positive action in the world.

Would that we learn to choose well, every day...

Chris

Comments to Donor:

To whom it may concern:

I am challenged every day to try to do the best I can to walk a walk favorable to my fellow man and to God. Sometimes I get discouraged and rationalize my inaction. Then someone like you comes along, unselfish, willing, caring, and loving, and willing to get out of the boat and try to walk on water for someone whom you don't even know. May God bless you and the recipient in a special way as you set the example of what it means to love your fellow man, even as He has loved us. I thank you.

Hello friend!

I know you are a friend because of your willingness to sacrifice for our friend. :) During the past year of the roller coaster of sickness and wellness, we all have prayed and tried to help the best we can, but we recognize fully that YOUR sacrifice is the one that will make the difference here...the difference of a lifetime. Now all thoughts and prayers turn to the upcoming days for you and our friend. We pray that the upcoming procedure will be as painless as possible for you and that it will lead to a successful outcome for our dear friend. We cannot express our thankfulness for your courage and willingness to put a stranger's life before your own comfort.

Please rest assured that you are sacrificing for not only a person very much in need, but that you are making the investment of a lifetime. This individual is one of sterling character who has always been a loving daughter and sister, a hard-worker, and a winner. She has so much to give to the world in her future. She will, no doubt, multiply the blessing you have bestowed on her to many, many others in the upcoming years. You are not only giving a huge gift to an individual, but an immeasurable gift to her wonderful family and to all of us who sit on the sidelines and pray and cheer. YOU are making the difference here. YOU are saving a life. YOU are a fine example to all of us...of a silent, unrecognized act of kindness...

of doing unto others as you would have them do unto you...of loving one another.

God bless you and your family as much as you are blessing our dear friends.

I would like to say a big thank you to the donor for helping to heal someone in our family who is so important to all of us. Heaven has a special place for people like this donor.

You are giving a wonderful young adult an incredible gift! Thank you for your selflessness and your willingness to go on this journey. Your gift is priceless.

Dear Precious Donor,

It is with my deepest respect and heart-felt gratitude I write on behalf of a person who is much loved by our community.

Thank you so much for your personal sacrifice as this is a level of commitment of a higher calling.

No words could ever express how thankful and grateful the world should be for a person so giving as yourself.

May the blessings of my Lord and Savior be with you forever! Both of you are truly champions!

Peace.

I would like to express my gratitude for the bone marrow that you are giving freely to my friend's daughter, to offer her a renewed body. I want you to know that I will be praying for you and for her to find the courage and strength for this procedure. The Love you are showing, for someone you don't even know, is the LOVE that all of us must find in order to live our lives to the fullest. Thank you and may God Bless You.

If someone posed the question "What would you be willing to do for a complete stranger?" I'm not sure what my answer would be. I am sure I'd give money, food, clothing, my time, prayers, blood. I can't think of much else. But here you are donating something that is lifegiving, it is bigger than I can imagine. What a special and gracious human being you are; what a great deposit you are making in the karma bank. May your selfless act be rewarded so nothing that is awful will ever befall you. May your life be as gratifying as you can dream because your selfless act will give the recipient the chance to live a complete, full life full of wonder and accomplishment. Thank you for your gift.

Dear Good Samaritan-

I will likely never meet you. Yet, this process has taught me that amazing things happen every day...things that change the world and intertwine all our lives. Your sacrifice illuminates just how beautiful it is to live, helping one another and those in need. My friend is so blessed to have your gift. Also, I am equally blessed because your grace gives me great hope for my friend, humanity, and the power of one. I am thinking of you often during this time and hoping that you do not forget what you are doing...bringing a smile to the faces of hundreds and allowing one smile to keep shining for many days to come. Blessings to you and your family!

—Full of Hope

The term hero comes to mind to describe you. (But not the media-hyped, sensationalized kind of hero our society worships today and forgets tomorrow.) You are the real deal. You are making a sacrifice in complete anonymity to save the life of a person who is very dear to us. I can think of nothing more noble, and we thank you from the bottom of our hearts.

Dear Donor:

Each of us can give in a unique way, if only we will see our calling. You have been richly blessed to see. There is a community beyond your knowing that is praying for you with profound gratefulness for your gift.

I have always been touched by acts of courage. What you are about to do for the beautiful daughter of my friends is beyond an act of courage. It is an act of love for humanity. The gift you are giving reaffirms my own belief in the goodness of others and offers this exceptional young woman a chance at the life she deserves.

You are an inspiration to all of us who are on this journey of support for our friends.

God bless you.

DEAR PRECIOUS PERSON,

I AM VERY TOUCHED BY YOUR INCREDIBLE ACT OF KINDESS!!!!!

IT IS HARD TO IMAGINE THAT MANY PEOPLE WOULD BE AS KIND AS YOU ARE BY GIVING ANOTHER PERSON THAT YOU DON'T EVEN KNOW A GIFT OF LIFE.

YOUR GENEROSITY IS SO SPECIAL, AND I KNOW THAT YOUR FAMILY MUST BE SO PROUD OF YOU TO GIVE OF YOURSELF IN SUCH A LOVELY MANNER.

THANK YOU FOR GIVING THIS REMARKABLE GIFT!!! THE PERSON YOU ARE GIVING IT TO COULD NOT BE A MORE SPECIAL PERSON.

THANK YOU FOR MAKING A HUGE DIFFERENCE IN THIS PERSON'S LIFE.

GRATEFULLY,

A FRIEND OF YOUR RECIPIENT

Love and kindness are never wasted. They always make a difference. They bless the one who receives them, and they bless you, the giver.

Dear Donor,

It is obvious to say we are grateful for your willingness to give of yourself to our daughter. You are providing our best hope for her life to reach a plateau of health for years to come. It will allow her life to flower and provide her the opportunity to give back to a future world yet to see her gifts mature.

What is less obvious is that because you are stepping forward to give unselfishly to a stranger, you are inspiring hundreds upon hundreds who are watching and who are intimately involved, following, praying, hoping, and cheering for the grandest of outcomes for you and for our daughter. You are serving as an example of the best of human potential, being realized in a world much more accustomed to ignoring humanity's needs.

Your gift of selflessness is breathing life and hope into not only our daughter, but hundreds and hundreds of people whom you may never know. They know you, however. I can only hope to be counted on to act in the same way when that opportunity comes. Until then, I can only say thank you, what you are doing is more important and more significant than you know.

God speed and God's peace be with you, forever.

Many people, like me, care deeply about the recipient of your donation, but we can only perform tangential acts to try to make things better. You have the gratitude of all of us, because *you* are the one who will make the real difference. Your selflessness makes me humble. Thank you so much. Keeping you all in my heart,

---

Dear Donor,

First let me start by saying that you have been in my prayers for months. I don't know who you are, and when my prayers first started it was not known that you would be the donor. Thank you for your willingness to make this sacrifice for a complete stranger. I know this family is very grateful to you for what you are doing. Please know that there are a lot of people praying for you and thanking God for you, and we will continue to pray for you throughout this process. Specifically, I will be praying that God will strengthen your body and keep you healthy, that the procedure will go smoothly, and that God will be with you and your family before, during and after the procedure. Thanks again for what you are doing.

May God bless you and keep you close to Him.

Thank you so much for donating your bone marrow. What an amazing, unselfish gift of love and life! May God bless you.

While I too have offered my DNA for a potential match, I haven't been called. I want to say thank you for what you are about to do…help others in need in one of the most critical times in their life. You are helping them directly and untold family, acquaintances, and friends indirectly, [those] who love and cherish the individual you are now matched with. I don't know how I will feel if I am called, but I hope I will have the opportunity you have now been presented and accepted.

Thank you is not enough, but it is heartfelt. Thank you.

Your compassion, generosity, and courage will be sustaining a life created by God. I cannot envision an act that he would look upon more favorably. You are in my prayers.

To whom it may concern:

I would like to tell you how wonderful I think you are to offer yourself as a donor and to be placed on the National Bone Marrow Registry to help a complete stranger. To offer life-giving marrow to someone suffering with a possible "death sentence" speaks so highly of your Christian heart and spirit. As you undergo the transfer procedure, I will be praying for your well-being as well as for the recipient of your life-saving marrow. Please know that everyone who knows your recipient will forever hold you in a special place for helping. I wish you a speedy recovery and that our Lord and Savior will be beside you and the recipient when the time comes for the transfer of marrow. In Christ,

Dear Donor,

Thank you so much for the sacrifice you are making for my friend. She is such a special person, and I know that she would be thanking you herself right now if she could. The person you are donating to is strong, funny, beautiful, and has so much promise. I knew long before her diagnosis that she would be one of those people I look up to, even though we are peers. She's got a great self-confidence and carries herself so gracefully through the good and hard times. Please know that the gift you're giving her is so precious, and that she and all her family and friends will be forever grateful to you. Please also know that I'm praying for you as you go through this process. Thank you and God bless.

We are touched by your selfless and courageous decision to donate bone marrow to a person you don't even know. Your kindness will give this special person a chance to live a happy and fulfilling life. We pray the procedure goes smoothly for you both. You have our sincere gratitude, and may God richly bless you for your compassion.

May God bless you and keep you for passing on the gift of life to someone that I love. I am lifting you up in prayer along with our church family member and pray that you are blessed exponentially for giving anonymously. THANK YOU! How encouraging that Good Samaritans are alive and well today!

Dear Donor,

I am one of so many friends who has followed the illness and challenges which you have come forward to alleviate. Thank you for your courage and generosity. You have graciously offered and have been chosen and accepted. We are so grateful!

God bless you.

Dear Donor,

I would like to express my thanks and gratitude to you for the unselfish gift you are offering. You will be helping a beautiful, cherished young woman who is fighting for her life. You are a stranger to us, but you offer the gift she needs the most. Those who know and love her can only wish we could do as much.

Through your willingness to give, you bring hope, life, and encouragement. Others may now be encouraged to follow your example, step up and offer to help another by registering as a donor. Thank you.

To us you are the answer to prayers. We now include you in our prayers. We pray prayers of gratitude and prayers for your well-being. May the Lord bless you and keep you always.

With admiration and gratitude,

Dear Donor,

Heroes come to us in such surprising and unexpected ways. You will now wear that badge always. Our thanks do not adequately express our deeply felt gratitude to you.

Please know that you are being lifted in prayer.

"I thank my God every time I remember you, constantly praying with joy in every one of my prayers for you"—Philippians 1:3-4

Dear Hero,

You may not see yourself as a cape-wearing Superhero, however, in my musings that is exactly what I imagine! Just as a Superhero swoops in to save the day at the last moment, you are saving the day today. I can't imagine what your reasoning is to save the day. But, just like a Superhero, you don't really need a reason! You may have a significant motive, perhaps a family member or friend has been affected by an illness that required a hero. I pray that your hero was found. Perhaps you heard of this specific need and went to be tested. Regardless of the reason, I'm so thankful that you are the miraculously brave individual who will stand up to save another person's life.

In this high-speed, always-urgent time when our own priorities cloud the needs of others, I am thankful that you have chosen to take the time to save a life. I pray that the blessing you are giving today will be richly rewarded.

I don't know who you are, but I know you are brave, you are kind, you are altruistic. You are a Superhero! Thank you!

To our dear Angel of Mercy,

It is hard to imagine such an act of loving generosity. Were it for a family member or a beloved old friend perhaps, it would be somewhat understandable, but for a complete stranger? You may have no concept of how many people have you on a pedestal because the lovely person you are helping has so many people who are devoted to her. And by the way, she and her family are handling this crisis with enormous courage. She is setting an example for all of us.

We know that we are not allowed to mention anything personal about the young lady you are extending this life-saving help to, and we are not permitted to know anything about you. However, we can't help but hope you are allowed to mention your gift of life in such a way that others might be encouraged to follow your example. Your wonderful story should inspire others to respond to the need for donors. We wish we could trumpet your gift of love far and wide.

You are daily in our prayers, as is the young lady whom you have befriended. You probably already have stars in the crown reserved for you, but if not, we are sure you do now.

—From very grateful family friends

Dear Donor:

Just another thank you for your unselfish gift of yourself to an extremely talented young person, one anyone would be happy to claim as his or her own. What you are doing is very brave. You have my deepest gratitude and appreciation.

Peace be with you, Another appreciative follower of this tumultuous saga

---

Dear Donor,

I am so grateful to you for giving our friend the chance to live. I have known this patient and the family for 2 generations and can say that they are truly what we call the "salt of the earth." When we found out that a transplant was needed, our entire family signed up to be potential donors. We weren't selected for our friend, but perhaps one day we will be called upon to make the sacrifice that you are making. Thank you for your gift. May you receive many blessings in return.

*　*　*

4-12-10

Folks,

Again, today was uneventful, filled with chemo, rest, and anti-boredom activities, whatever can make the time pass. Pam made dinner at the apartment, again at Anna's request, and brought it back to the hospital. Claustrophobia is a real problem in the hospital, especially when you feel fairly well. Cards and letters arrived today as well.

One more day down...

Chris

* * *

4-13-10

Folks,

It has begun...Much like listening to James Spann (local weatherman for those who do not know) predict thunderstorms and tornados in an all-night vigil, the much-forewarned predictions of physical frailties finally came over Anna at 8:30 pm or so. Today she started a regimen of ATG, something designed to "kill her immune system." She will take IVs of ATG through Friday. She now has extensive body pain, chills...and [the doctors] have identified a specific bacterial infection, forcing Pam and Rob, also Tori and me, to wear protective yellow gowns when in her room.

Since this began just fifteen minutes before I write this letter, the extent to which she will be uncomfortable and the form that it will take will be discovered during the night and tomorrow morning. We have been waiting, and the warning siren just went off, indicating a funnel is on the ground. But like with James Spann, it will take the morning light to determine if it is an F-1 or F-5!

And so, it begins…

God help us,
Chris

*   *   *

4-14-10

Folks,

The morning light revealed an F-3 storm, with multiple layers of attack to fight. Last night, she experienced severe bone pain as the chemo kills her marrow, which lives in the bones; the pain is like receiving a bone marrow biopsy. She was given morphine and Decadron for the pain. She experienced a fever of 103 because [the doctors] have discovered that she has VRE bacterial infection in her digestive system, an infection usually picked up in the hospital by cancer patients and others with immune deficiencies who endure long hospital stays. She has been receiving antibiotics, magnesium, potassium, phosphorus, and anti-nausea meds of various types because she was sick most of the evening with nausea.

This is bad, but it is not abnormal when the ATG is given. Unfortunately, she will receive ATG through Friday. We hope that with each installment, the physical reactions will lessen somewhat. Another main difficulty is the lack of sleep, first caused by the reactions themselves, and then due to new [sensitive] pumps going off every five minutes all through the night and day today. So, when you can fall asleep because you are not ill, which Anna and Pam finally did at 4:30 am, you are awakened by sirens going off that require the nurse, so you must get up and call and have someone enter and work with it for 10 minutes then leave, to have five minutes of rest and just about drop off when it goes off again—madness! These are new and improved pumps just off the truck with [the doctors using] Anna [to experiment] with them. We were also told that the BMT unit will be using Anna to break in a new computer patient records software program. I can only imagine how that will go.

The girls need sleep and patience and a break from the anxiety, but I am afraid it is just the first storm of the season.

Chris

* * *

4-15-10

Folks,

Today was more of the same. Anna received another round of ATG as well as pretreatment drugs, antibiotics, pain killers, magnesium, potassium, and even a unit of blood platelets. She responded well throughout the day but may experience a return of the reactions of Tuesday night and Wednesday. She did have a round of chills today but managed to stay upbeat and relaxed. I hope the night is less violent than was the night on her first exposure to ATG. Anna drew a picture of the bunny that produced the serum she takes to kill her immune system. Drawing is a form of therapy for her, and it is relaxing.

Tomorrow is the day the donor will give her gift of marrow. I pray for her safety and comfort, and we celebrate her choice! Saturday is the transplant day that Anna will receive her gift.

Godspeed
Chris

*   *   *

4-16-10

Folks,

While there is some sickness and uncomfortableness associated with this period, Anna is remarkably "up" and positive and optimistic regarding tomorrow's transplant. The donor reported to the hospital where she was to undergo the harvesting procedure and her marrow is to be delivered to UAB around 10:00 pm tonight. They will process and prepare the material and begin giving it to Anna via IV pump around 1:00 pm tomorrow. Thank you to our donor, we are forever grateful for your gift!

This week has been a week of uplifting love and generosity like I have rarely seen. So many people have stopped what they were doing and held us all up to the heavens in local churches in Fayette, Aliceville, Tuscaloosa, and in Russia. People have gathered in homes, in places of work, and even in schools in Alabama, Texas, North Carolina, and Japan and these are just the people that I personally know about.

People have given their time, their resources, and their talents to support all of us on this journey. We are still here, we have not withered from the task at hand, and we will continue forward into the next phase. Tomorrow will be a small party with cake and signage and laughter and prayers, a "rebirth" party. While there will only be five of us there in body, we know and feel the presence of hundreds celebrating right along with us! Come join in our celebration, you have earned a right to be in the party! Have one where you are, too!

Much love and optimism,
Chris

*   *   *

4-17-10

Folks,

What a day! We had a little of everything today—a transplant which got under way by 2:00 pm after a lot of pretreatments; we had a small reaction to the transplant that occurred around 4:00 pm with chest pains and anxiety, which the doctors addressed right away with morphine and antibiotics and oxygen and steroids; and after [Anna] got resettled, we had a party with cake all around, celebrating rebirth, even including the singing of the "Happy Birthday Song!" It is now officially Anna's Rebirthday!!

I know there will soon be negatives to report that will be expected by next week, but today, we only celebrate. We even had some football today, and we won!

Peace,
Chris

* * *

4-18-10

Folks,

Today we come back to reality from the euphoria of yesterday. While
we celebrated, as much as we were able, the completion of the step
which ended in [a] successful transplant, today we remember that
the next and far harder step begins—to live through the next two
weeks! During these next two or more weeks all the effects of the
chemo that she has endured for the last 12 days (the chemo which
is ten times stronger than anything she has ever experienced) will
begin to evidence itself in her body. Even as the new marrow tries to
find a new home among her bones, the body itself will crash during
the next several days and then must rebuild itself over a long-pro-
tracted year to achieve the desired quality of life that the marrow
promises to give her. These next two weeks are critical, and therefore
she is in an ICU.

She will experience fevers, sores in her mouth and entire GI tract,
she may require an IV feeding tube because [the] compromised
GI tract will lose its ability to process and move food. She may
require a ventilator if her lungs get overcome with mucus caused
by an inability to swallow. This is the time we have been cautioned
about from the very beginning of [the] discussion of bone marrow
transplant, this is the fight that will determine if she survives, this
is our "valley of the shadow of death."

I wish, like the psalmist, that we could say we "will fear no evil,"
but that is exactly what we fear and just because we pray and hope
and persevere, the fear remains. I suppose that is why it is said that
"courage is not the absence of fear, but the ability to keep going in
spite of it." Well, Anna must keep going, she has no choice, and we,

too, have no choice. I think that this may be the hardest thing we have ever had to work through…

Anna began to feel bad this afternoon, and she descends. Chills have begun. God help her come out on the other side!!

Chris

* * *

4-19-10

Folks,

Today, Anna experienced intense nausea during the night and some in the morning. She met a new physician who will take over the day-to-day hospital visits; [he] takes over from the exiting "fellow." He gave her several new medicines designed to reduce nausea and prevent marrow rejection. The doctor discussed the feeding tube with Anna and investigated her mouth condition. He suggested that she may require the IV feeding soon, but she could try to continue to eat today. He also discussed the morphine pump, and he is preparing her to request it when she feels she needs it. It, too, may be needed soon.

Anxiety is high, but we walk on. We're still here.

Chris

* * *

4-20-10

Folks,

Pam and Anna had a very good night of rest last night, the best Pam has had since she checked into the ICU, but by morning wave after wave of sickness came to Anna. She endured so much sickness and pain in her mouth (now beginning its decline) that during the morning the doctor started her on the morphine pump that we have heard so much about. It did provide some degree of comfort and allowed her to sleep all afternoon. She ate a popsicle and requested some pudding, but Pam says the nurses will start the IV feeding tube tonight. She will still be able to eat when she feels like food, but she will more than likely get most of her nourishment via IV for the foreseeable future. (You know she has four IV lines, two on each side, and they are constantly filled with all manner of fluids that are pumped into her by three different pumps now.)

Much mail has arrived, but [it is] not yet opened because Anna is sleeping so much now. There are many things to explore when she feels like it. Also, Tori and I attended the University Singers Concert, conducted by Dr. John Ratledge, last evening at the Moody Music Building on the UA campus, where we were delighted to hear the students sing a masterful concert in Anna and Pam's honor. I must admit that I was deeply moved by the music, the students' passionate performance, and the connection that our family feels with the students, faculty, and staff of the University of Alabama. Much of our life has been spent and invested there and it was over- whelming to me personally to see that labor bear fruit in such rich soil—we are grateful for their efforts and for their many kindnesses as we travel the road we walk. I cannot speak about the University without also acknowledging the unwavering compassion of its President, Dr. Bob Witt, who keeps an eye on Anna's journey, send- ing encouragement from time to time, as his relationship with Anna goes back to her recruitment to the University five years ago. We are grateful and honored by so many who walk with us, it seems to grow daily, exponentially.

We keep watch, and we keep faithful to see this through…

Peace,
Chris

*   *   *

Part of Pam's responsibilities at the University of Alabama was to function as the piano accompanist for the University Singers, the school's premiere student choral ensemble. The director of the ensemble was Dr. John Ratledge. Every day, Pam would rehearse with the singers, and they became very close working together in this way. When Anna first got sick, one way that John kept the singers aware of how their missing colleague was faring was to give the singers a report on Anna's condition based on my regular emails updates. Their collective concern grew as the journey became more difficult.

John Ratledge has the longest, kinkiest, tight, curly hair I have ever seen. The tightness of the curls masks its actual length. One time, when things with Anna got stressful for all concerned over an extended period of time, John came up with the idea of doing some good while distracting the students from the discouraging events occurring at the hospital. He offered to straighten his hair if the students raised enough money. Of course, the students were motivated to make him straighten his hair, first, because they thought he would look ridiculous, and second, to see if he would, actually, do it. Obviously, John's offer was a high-risk proposal, at least for him. Nevertheless, he boldly announced the challenge, and he was willing to go through with it. He gave the students a week to deliver the money necessary to get him to perform his hair-straightening boast, and they did it!

John entered rehearsal with a hair stylist, who sat him in a chair in front of all the students. The stylist washed and straightened John's hair, then dried it straight, the length reaching down to the middle of his back. Of course, pictures were taken to document the event, preserve the laughter of the students, preserve a sacrifice for Pam and Anna to see and to share with all of us, as he brought pictures to the hospital for us to look at. He then proudly delivered the check from his students to Pam: they missed her presence, musicianship, and humor!

*   *   *

4-21-10

Folks,

Today was calm and quiet and predictable, in other words, it was a good day! Anna is comfortable, with pain relief and nausea relief, keeping [the nausea and pain] at bay. She sleeps well and often and still she can get up and shower and walk some and even eat soup and pudding and the like. Her hurt tongue is swollen, making it difficult and I imagine painful to talk, but we are no worse today!

The girls have had two very good nights and we hope for a third, so far so good.

Peace,
Chris

* * *

4-22-10

Folks,

The night and day saw much sleep and calm. The pain level did rise again, and the doctors responded [by] raising the morphine push dosage in the pump that Anna manipulates when she needs relief. This evening, fever sneaked into the scenario for the first time. It was expected and the nurses were amazed that it had not arrived by this time; but by dinner time, it was hovering around 100 degrees.

That will be the main concern of the evening, watching to see how high it will go and being ready to attack it when the time comes. They treat fevers with antibiotics when it reaches 103. With the rise in fever and pain, Anna is now in the early stages of seeing the full effects of the chemo and how it will attack her body. The next many days will be spent rallying her body to endure [the effects] until [they] subside.

We begin to get serious. I hope she sleeps through most of it.

Chris

* * *

4-23-10

Folks,

Anna had a difficult day. She was in a good bit of pain during the early morning because there were difficulties getting the morphine pump settings correct and the keys to the narcotics cabinet were misplaced, causing her to be in unnecessary pain for two hours while the keys were retrieved. She has run a low-grade fever for two days and the doctor wanted to ward off a fever spike by calling for vancomycin, a powerful antibiotic—the one that causes "Red Man Syndrome" which Anna had last year. Anna can take this antibiotic, but with specific pretreatments and pump speeds. This floor of doctors and nurses has not been trained to know her body yet and the pump speed for the vancomycin was too high, causing her to react with skin itching and a slight but uncomfortable burning sensation.

She is weak and can barely stand enough to walk to the restroom and take a shower, falling back into the bed with muscles almost shaking. Between the fever, the Benadryl pretreatments for the antibiotics making her sleepy, and the rising pain levels due to the chemo effects, she is miserable.

I hope that she does not spike a fever tonight, even though the doctors predict it.

Peace,
Chris

* * *

4-24-10

Folks,

It was a stormy day outside and a stormy day inside as well. This was by far the worst pain control day ever. The pain levels have reached the upper strata of morphine's ability to control it. While there is the ability to push an extra dosage once an hour if she needs it, Anna had to receive a unit of platelets today, and with it, Benadryl pretreatments, which impede the amount of pain reliever she can have because [the combination of the two drugs can] cause her to be too sleepy and too drugged to breathe properly. [The team] wants to avoid [using] the ventilator, so Anna had to endure some excruciating pain throughout the day. The pain was so much that she just collapsed and wept. There was nothing anyone could do to help. It was a nightmare for Pam emotionally who had to bear witness to the day.

These are the bad days; the ugly days that you hope to endure and get through so that better ones can replace the memory. The nurse confirmed that she is nearing the bottom in blood counts, in pain, and in stamina. Mercifully, the fevers that have been predicted have stayed away from spiking to high levels, so far. The only thing to make life worse would be for them to begin while these continue.

She cannot eat or speak at this point—I pray she sleeps…

Peace—please,
Chris

＊　＊　＊

4-25-10

Folks,

Today Anna was still struggling with pain, with nausea, with fever (now going to 100.4, the first level of spiking, as it is called, [which] they treat [by means of pre-established] protocols), and with no energy, body shakes, and some chills. She can barely swallow, making pills very painful and difficult to take, even water is excruciating. These are the dark days, and she must endure these for another week. By the end of this coming week, she should begin to see rising blood levels and a returning white cell count which means [her body has begun to establish] more of an immune system. That would help a good bit with the pain and fever issues.

She is doing and progressing very well. The doctors are pleased with how she is handling everything. This is a hard and expected process. It is very difficult on the individual and [Anna's] body and there is an expected pattern of behavior, and she is right in the middle of it. We will have to grit teeth and get through this to come out on the other side.

Anna's fellow graduate students participated in the Relay for Life in Athens in Anna's honor over the last few days. I thought I would include some pictures of their activities and antics. We appreciate their efforts and dedication to Anna and her recovery.

Peace,
Chris

*   *   *

4-26-10

Folks,

Anna had another trying day. First, she choked and gagged on
some liquid medicine that she could not swallow, and Pam had to
run and call for help from the staff. They had to give Anna more
morphine and Ativan to calm her down. At this point she can
swallow practically nothing, and she has mucositis, [which is]
associated with the chemo treatments [and which] is now a growing problem, coming from her sinuses. Dealing with the pain and
the lack of ability to swallow makes for a difficult balancing act.

She is still trying to move around by walking as much as she can,
[but given] the weakness that she has [walking] is of limited effectiveness. Today's choking was disturbing for all concerned, but the
girls will try to put it behind them and continue to try and find a
positive attitude. As I have said before, this is hard, it is ugly, and
we must push through it—one hard day at a time.

Peace—"Now would be nice…"
Chris

*   *   *

4-27-10

Folks,

This morning, after no sleep all through the night, Anna cleared an
intestinal blockage the doctor has been worried about. This allowed
her mind to relax from the stress and concern of it, and she and Pam
slept most of the morning and some this afternoon. She still maintains a low-grade fever which the doctors attend to with vancomycin
and other meds. She is still in great pain, but somehow today she

seemed to have more energy and more desire to talk, being chatty for about fifteen minutes this evening. Usually, it has been too painful to talk and swallow, so either there was less pain or more energy and desire to participate in conversation. I take it as a good sign.

Anna began to lose her hair in earnest today, the third time she has done so because of the chemotherapy. It began to come out in sections and so Pam used the nurses' clippers and buzzed it off right before her shower this evening. Tomorrow, she gets the last round of the chemo that is used to battle, delay, and impede the severity of the "graft versus host disease" (GVHD) that is a concern after the transplanted marrow takes root and begins to produce. While it is useful in that area, the chemo is the one that does most of the mouth and throat damage, and thus [causes the most] pain. Often doctors forego the final dosage to save the patient some pain, but in doing so, they open [Anna] up to [greater] risk in regard to the GVHD disease. This is a classic example of Anna choosing to take on more pain and discomfort to better battle her cancer and attempt to ensure herself a better result. It is heroic when you consider she has endured so much already.

The blood counts are inching their way up, four straight days of white cell increase. It is only miniscule increments of improvement, but it has been four straight days. Hopefully, the new marrow is planting and producing in its new home. Anna said tonight that she had some bone pain this evening, which is indicative of the bones producing cells, so again there seems to be progress. The doctor said he thinks she will be here another two or three weeks if all goes well. So far, he is pleased; she is right where she should be. Well, of course, it's Anna Gordon, I could have told him that…

Peace,
Chris

*   *   *

4-28-10

Folks,

Things change quickly in an ICU. I have said it before, but I am still amazed when it occurs. We took a step forward yesterday and two steps backward today, the white blood cell count plummeted back down to the bottom of the basement, undoing any glee established in the earlier upward migration. In addition, we have come to learn that Anna's liver is not working properly, filling her bloodstream with bilirubin, and causing her skin and eyes to be jaundiced. Tests are being run this evening and we will soon see if it is a condition known as VOD where blood vessels in the liver are blocked by degrading tissue caused by the chemotherapy, or the onset of GVHD, graft versus host disease, which I mentioned last night. It could be either and both conditions could range from extremely mild to severe. What we know now is that her liver is swollen, it is painful, and her skin is jaundiced.

In addition, Anna had another choking incident this evening causing her to become agitated and anxious, the second such episode in the same number of days; furthermore, by evening when I left, she spiked a fever of 100.5 and rising, the highest so far. I am afraid that we are still languishing in the pit of transplant hell, where the body is deciding how it will react to all that has been heaped upon it, trying out various options, uncertain of which way to go and how to react.

I thought her body had rallied and now it has been derailed for a while longer. As I have said before, this is hard, this is very hard for and on Anna, and on all of us as we react to her [ever-changing condition]. What changes tomorrow…?

Chris

*　*　*

4-29-10

Folks,

Anna had tests today to determine the condition of her liver and blood culture tests as well, looking for infections. It seems that the liver has seen increased blood flow today, indicating [there is] hope that Anna's liver has just been stressed [by] the effects of chemo rather than the onset of VOD or GVHD diseases. That is good news, and the doctor tells us that he hopes [the liver] will cease to be a problem in a few days. We hope he is correct.

On the other hand, [Anna's] blood cultures show that bacteria have been growing in her blood and it is the VRE or vancomycin resistant enterococci infection. Since this infection is resistant to the best of antibiotics, vancomycin, [the team] will have to alter the antibiotics to something that still works on this bacterium. Also, tests show that Anna has an infection of the throat, by the name of Candidiasis. . This is caused by high use of antibiotics and is treated with anti-fungal medicines. So, [Anna's] liver problems, her throat problems, and her blood infection are caused by what [the team has] had to do to combat her cancer. I cannot keep from remembering a line from a film a patient speaks when she tells her son she is diagnosed with cancer. "I'm going to beat this thing. You know, I was doing fine before they started curing me!" We know the truth in this statement. Fever is up and down; white counts are up a minuscule amount today.

One step forward, two steps back—we are doing the hokey pokey! "That's what it's all about."

Chris

*   *   *

4-30-10

Folks,

Today is a mixed blessing in that there is still fever, ranging in the 100-degree range, and there is still pain. The doctor says that the liver damage is correctable and that he believes [Anna's liver] will be back to acceptable conditions in four or five days. Anna's intestinal blockage is completely gone now and her throat, while painful, is working. She was able to swallow three separate medicines by mouth this evening without difficulty. Before, the muscles would not work in the way they were designed to work while swallowing, as well as being inflamed and painful. Her white counts also rose a slight bit. The doctor says that her blood counts should begin to respond within the next fifteen days if the transplant was successful. Finally, Anna can talk a little more regularly now, bringing emotion and personality back into her body. We take that as a good sign.

Peace through sleep,
Chris

*   *   *

5-1-10

Folks,

Anna has seen her throat get much improved. She can both swallow and drink, things she was not able to do for the last seven to ten days. She still has pain in her mouth and throat but those things, as well as speaking, are much easier. [[The team is] filling her with ridiculous amounts of fluids.

Pam writes on her Facebook,

"...getting platelets, Phenergan, TPN, fluids, morphine, antifungal, cyclosporine, acyclovir, daptomycin, Actigall, lactulose, Benadryl, you name it—and those are just a few...spelling I'm sure is not correct but you get the picture."

I can attest that this list is only partial. When they told us that Anna would need two Hickman ports, with a total of four portals each, in which you can run eight different things at one time, they were not kidding!

The blood counts remained the same today and we wait for them to begin to go up. That is the goal here, to get new, fresh, healthy blood—the kind you don't have to pump in!

Peace,
Chris

*   *   *

5-2-10

Folks,

Anna is progressing! The doctor told us that her liver counts (the bilirubin amounts in the blood) are beginning to go down, meaning he was [justified] in his hope that her liver damage was temporary [due to] chemo-induced trauma. He says it will correct itself in a few more days. [Anna's] white counts went up slightly today; those are the ones we are looking at to indicate marrow is engaging and producing new blood. She still maintains a fever and she is having muscle pains all over, but she is getting antibiotics by the truckload, and potassium, and two units of platelets today, as well as the regular boat load of fluids and meds that she receives daily.

The doctor said that "today she turned a corner." Let's hope his GPS is full of battery and the newest installment of information is paid up!

Peace,
Chris

* * *

5-3-10

Folks,

I am amazed at how quickly things change! Anna's white counts doubled today! Last night she ate some soup, and she is talking practically nonstop. There is less pain now and the doctor said today that they could be out of the BMT ICU and into the apartment by the weekend!!!!!!!!!

Wow, this is hard to believe but they say she has done really well. "So be it"—isn't that what Amen means, after all?

Smiling for the first time in a long time,
Chris

* * *

5-4-10

Folks,

Today, Anna continued to progress. She was taken off the feeding tube and she ate some macaroni and cheese as well as a hamburger. She was also taken off the morphine pump and she reported no pain this evening. She walked several laps around the ICU halls and had no mouth pain to speak of. Somehow though, she has begun to have vivid nightmarish dreams that cause her to awaken in a panic with high blood pressure and high breathing rates. The doctor says that this is normal for many cancer patients, especially those who have had traumatic treatments. These have hindered her sleep for the last several days and [the team is] giving her something to sleep and to negate her traumatic dreams tonight.

They did a CT scan this evening on her chest looking for explanations of a cloud in her upper right chest area. The doctor said that when new white cells are created, they go to where infections have been first, and the cloud is likely white cell activity working on past infections of a few days ago, but he wants to be sure. [Anna] continues to have some upper body swelling that concerns them slightly. The doctor said while she may be on the fast track to getting out, he is not so sure that it will be this weekend as another doctor predicted. We are hopeful but we will see. Soon is good enough.

The power of hope...

Chris

* * *

5-5-10

Folks,

The results of the CT scan of last night showed that Anna has had some pneumonia in the bottom lobe of her left lung. Apparently, she has had it for several days, but it was only discovered when they did some X-rays looking for possible blood clots when they saw something cloudy in her chest. That is what [triggered] the CT scan and thus the pneumonia [diagnosis]. The white blood cells have been working on [the pneumonia], however, and [the doctors] are treating it with antibiotics. They are also giving her more meds to help in her sleeping difficulties. They took her completely off liver medications today, so the liver is deemed restored.

She is still uncomfortable and feels generally lousy, but this is on a scale of normal. It is much better to feel lousy when compared to feeling normal than it is to feel good in comparison to feeling near dead...which was the case five days ago.

We're making progress!
Chris

*   *   *

5-6-10

Folks,

As I entered the hospital room this afternoon, I entered to laughter! Anna and Pam were already engaged in conversation and for the next 45 minutes to an hour we animatedly talked and laughed about silly things; my daughter, who has tremendous wit, had returned to me. A personality that we have been working hard to protect has reemerged and come back to us. This is someone I recognize, not the person whose body was occupying the bed in the room all month who borrowed my daughter's face and who was mostly mute for many weeks trying hard just to breathe; no, this was someone who like Lazarus was returning to her former place in the conversation.

This reanimation is real and is made possible through another's sacrifice, a gift offered in a hope of help. The help has been claimed and she is emerging slowly from the cocoon. Soon the promise will be even more evident, but I can see it today, coming, building, ready to reclaim its place in the conversation of life.

There was some discussion of leaving on Sunday, but they want to wean her off antibiotics before she leaves and they want to give her more time with her blood counts way up, so Sunday, Monday, Tuesday ... it almost doesn't matter—I've already seen what I need to see!

Peace,
Chris

* * *

5-7-10

Folks,

Not much to report today other than Anna is feeling much better, sitting up in a chair out of the bed, reading, etc. Her white cell counts are up a little more, but reds are down some, this is normal flopping around. They did a chest X-ray to see if the pneumonia has gone, but there has been no report as the day closes. The girls did sleep well last night, the first such night since they came to UAB a month ago. Anna dreamed, but dreamed of food, nothing scary. Mostly the girls are bored at this point and ready to leave. We just must wait for the word to come down. I like boring at this point.

Peace,
Chris

* * *

5-8-10

Folks,

Dr. #3, the main bone marrow transplant physician, has declared that the girls can leave the BMT unit on Sunday afternoon!! The

X-rays indicate the pneumonia is gone, and he has ordered the operating room to remove one of her Hickman ports today! Sunday will be Mother's Day and our thirty-fourth day in the BMT and our 159th day in the hospital since March 2nd, 2009.

The girls will move into the apartment two miles from UAB Hospital and begin returning to the BMT unit's outpatient facility every day for the foreseeable future (30-100 more days.) There, [Anna's team] will continue to monitor her blood levels every day and treat as necessary any GVHD or other complication that may arise in this long but final stage of the transplant process.

Celebrate with us on Sunday; we have all earned the party!

Chris

*   *   *

5-9-10

Folks,

Today Tori and I moved the girls out of the BMT unit at UAB and into the apartment two miles across town that will be their home for the next several months. Pam had the room packed and ready to go as Tori and I and Pam loaded four carts of luggage, food, medicines, cards, magazines, pictures, games, computers, books, blankets, pillows, and every assorted thing that we brought and that you sent to us in the time we have been there. As we left, we stopped, and Anna ceremoniously rang the bell reserved for transplant patients who successfully leave the BMT Unit after recovering well enough to be on their own! And ring it she did, over and over to applause from nurses, attendants, physicians, and family watching and cheering a milestone accomplished.

The ride across town was quiet as was the unpacking of cars and cartage of all items into the apartment. There was no ceremony or loudness, just the quiet realization of being semi-free to move and breathe and stretch. Anna immediately took a long relaxing tub bath with bubbles, and she stayed in there as long as she wanted. Pam and I placed most everything where it belonged in the apartment and then Pam began cooking a simple, quiet taco and refried bean dinner, nothing fancy, just quiet. Over dinner, the first the entire family has had together around a table in over a month, we talked of survival, recanting stories of the last many weeks and those characters involved in them. Mostly we were glad it was over, and we were together for Mother's Day, one of the best we have had!

Peace,
Chris

Chapter 9

WHEN PAM AND I MARRIED IN NOVEMBER OF 1981, I was still an undergraduate student at the University of Alabama. Although Pam had completed her master's degree in 1979, after our marriage she still was deeply tied to the university, holding private piano lessons within the Community Music School. In fact, we were both connected to the university and its students. It was at this time that we, as a newly married couple, began the natural process of acquiring "couple friends" in addition to those friends we each had met on our own. We were not only connected to friends with music backgrounds, but backgrounds in the theater as well. We both had several years of theatrical experience, performing in the pit orchestras for various shows presented by the university's theater department and the Tuscaloosa Community Theater's productions. It was through our theater activity that we met Scott Tucker.

In 1982, Scott was cast into a Tuscaloosa Community Theater production of a children's show entitled *Androcles and the Lion* for which Pam was hired as musical director. While the production's cast was small, two of the actors became staples of our burgeoning group of couple friends. They included Scott and Ray Taylor, and they expanded our scope of theater friends, which already included Kathy Morgan, and Bill and Dianne Teague. Many more would enter our sphere within the next few years.

Scott was a gregarious personality, and he was an enthusiastic conversationalist. Whenever we had the opportunity to spend time together, a good time was had by all. As time went on, these people remained core members of our friends' group, those whom we rested, relaxed, and celebrated life with. Now, almost thirty years later, during the post-transplant phase of Anna's journey, Scott helped obtain the perfect apartment, satisfying our needs.

Scott lived in a historic two-story home in the "Southside" neighborhood of Birmingham, a highly desirable section, where many who worked in downtown Birmingham lived. The owner lived in the bottom story of the home; the upper story of the house had been converted into two large apartments. The other tenant in the house—that is, Scott's second-story neighbor—was leaving, and that tenant's apartment was becoming available. Scott informed us of the possibility that Pam and Anna could obtain that apartment, and we jumped on the opportunity. The notion of having Scott right next door in a location just two miles from the UAB complex where Anna had to receive almost daily outpatient procedures and checkups (and Pam had to accompany her) proved to be ideal. It was easy for Scott to talk to the homeowner and pave the way for us to acquire a short-term, month-to-month lease. No better situation was possible than to have Scott next door to help look after the girls and provide entertainment and conversation in an intimate setting where we were not concerned as to how we looked, how we felt, or what we thought or said, because Scott was family to us. He had been a core friend, part of family events and celebrations like birthdays, anniversaries, and most holidays, for almost three decades.

The apartment was bright with natural light. Each room possessed several tall windows allowing beams of sunlight to enter while offering spectacular views of the grounds of the estate, which contained mature trees and flowering foliage, generations old. The ceilings were high in the way that old homes were, and the rooms were large. The apartment contained two bedrooms, a gracious-sized den, perfect for lounging, conversation, and watching television. The only downside was the entrance to the apartment. Being on the upstairs floor, the only entrance to either of the second-story apartment was via a long, tall exterior staircase with twenty or more steps, not ideal for a cancer patient with limited energy and balance. The comical solution to using the staircase constantly when one wanted to visit with one's best friend neighbor and one had to descend their stairs, walk around the exterior of the house, and then climb the other staircase just to borrow some sugar, was to walk across the roof of the house, which was only slightly angled, and land on the stoop of the other apartment's staircase! This was an often-used shortcut.

Scott spent many hours in our den or kitchen. Laughter was frequent, conversation was comfortable and lively, and boredom or loneliness was never an issue for the girls. When a family is forced by circumstance to live apart from one another for a long period of time, I could not have asked for a better, safer situation for my wife and daughter.

* * *

5-10-10

Folks,

The girls arrived at the ICU for out-patient treatment and moni-toring at 8:30 am and Anna received blood tests and an antibiotic, and they were able to leave by 1:00 pm. Tomorrow they will do something similar. The doctors are monitoring her blood levels, liver functions, and several other processes that determine Anna's progress. Otherwise, they returned home and enjoyed napping and cooking dinner.

If you want to continue your letter and card connection to the girls, the address is 3308 Cliff Rd Apt. #4, Birmingham, AL 35205. I will cease to write every day now that the girls are in out-patient care. There is much repetition [during their days] and little change unless something out of the ordinary happens. In the event there is something to report, or there is a significant change, I will report on it to you so that you may continue in your support for us and Anna via your prayers and positive thoughts.

It is this support for which we cannot cease to thank you. Your journey with us on this walk has been vital to its success so far, I see no reason to change it now.

Chris

*   *   *

5-14-10

Folks,

This week at the apartment has been a mixed blessing for the girls. Anna has enjoyed, as best she can, more freedoms of movement (in that she can move around the house all she likes but when she leaves the house, she must wear a mask and carry an umbrella because she will forever be confined to staying out of the sun and UV rays) but she has very little energy to move around at all. Her red blood counts, the ones that carry oxygen to the body, are still below normal and Anna uses up what energy she has in no time.

She has issues with her stomach and digestive tract because of the effects of chemotherapy. She still gets sick every day or every other day, and nausea is an ever-present foe. She still is dealing with issues of liver damage. Those chemical counts are still high in her blood levels, somewhat due to returning to some oral prescriptions that she must take, but [they] have effects on the liver. Since leaving the hospital and its constant IV fluids to flush the kidneys, her kidneys are now trying to do the filtering load on their own and they are struggling to keep up with the necessary chores; there is much to filter. Finally, low-grade fevers sneak up periodically, too, during the week. These are what she endures and battles while being in a more comfortable environment. Sleep is still difficult for both Pam and Anna due to any of these four contributors and it is unpredictable also, becoming a factor in Anna's energy levels.

Going every day to the BMT unit outpatient area for meds, daily blood tests, blood products when needed, and fluids, their day is now full of transportation, parking, and home chores, adding a level of complication to the daily regime. The fight is for the stout and disciplined of mind and heart because it is such a long-term test of will.

We still request and require your prayers, good thoughts and positive energy focused on Anna and Pam. The process has merely transformed into a different playing arena with different challenges. I will keep you posted.

Chris

* * *

5-20-10

Folks,

This week saw improvements in Anna's liver and kidney situations, with both areas now showing test results in their normal ranges. The girls have gone to UAB several times but have also been given some days off this week as well, because Anna has been doing so well. The days they are there, however, can be very long, eight to twelve hours long, waiting in a single small room to receive meds, or fluids, or blood products when needed, all determined by blood test results done as soon as you arrive. The results often take a while to receive, then the orders must be given for blood or platelets or antibiotics. These orders, then, must be filled and delivered, often with pretreatments that can take hours to receive and infuse into her with a pump. So, while one day may be grueling, the next may be spent at home recovering from the energy [spent] going to the hospital. It is a cycle.

Yesterday, however, on her day off from the hospital, she decided that she wanted to venture out into the world. So, after resting until around four in the afternoon, we sneaked out for her first attempt at a movie, *Ironman 2*, and as luck would have it, we were the only people in the theater! We had an exclusive showing, just like Elvis back in the day! Laughter and fun were had by all with a healthy dose of popcorn! By the end of the day, though, nausea and puniness returned—alas, it still is cancer!

Little steps at a time…

Chris

* * *

5-25-10

Folks,

Pam and Anna were given two days off from the hospital, Sunday, and Monday, of this week. [Anna] is doing very well, and the blood tests are confirming normalization of counts. On Monday, the girls set out to purchase Anna some makeup, the first since late November 2009, when she left remission and began this long stretch. After the bone marrow transplant, she was told to throw away all makeup and start with new makeup that has not been opened and exposed to any possible organics that could bring her risk.

The girls went to the Summit and shopped at Belk's. and a new, refreshed Anna emerges from the adventure. I thought you would like to see, as well.

Chris

* * *

6-10-10

Folks,

It has been several days since I last wrote to you. So much time has passed, mainly because there is nothing earth-shattering to report. Life has been routine, meaning it has been remarkably better, not perfect, and not without some daily issues with which the girls have had to adapt, but Anna is feeling normalized. She can get out, go anywhere, do anything within reason and see people. There is a distinct lack of stress in comparison to the intensity levels that we all lived with for many months. This lack of stress has allowed all of us to relax, envision the future, and make plans for that eventual reclamation of our lives. We can see it, touch it, smell it, and be grateful for it.

The problem with these wonderful encouraging relaxing times is that we do not know if they are a mirage, a lull before another storm, or whether they are really an oasis of hope, allowing us to drink in the promise of a life returned. We will soon see in that there is another bone marrow biopsy scheduled for next week. These results will tell us if the engraftment is healthy and leukemia-free as it produces the next generation of blood cells. We were told that [Anna's] type of leukemia is stealthy, hiding in places, and it has the potential to wait and return after the transplant. This is the warning that one of the doctors expressed on the day Anna entered the BMT unit, almost derailing the transplant completely. This biopsy will determine if our less stressful month is a mirage or the beginning of a new life.

Anna had her twenty-third birthday early in the month and she is planning for life after transplant by applying for academic jobs in the area, at Samford University and the University of Alabama in Tuscaloosa, keeping her close to UAB doctors for the next year, before returning to school as a student. So, we will see what we will see next week. We pray for the best, know that you pray with us and continue to walk this walk by our sides.

More as it happens…

Chris

* * *

During her stay in the Southside apartment, Anna was discouraged by the Bone Marrow Transplant doctors who supervised her treatment, even during the post-transplant period, from seeking to return to Athens for graduate school. They argued that even after release from her daily visits to the outpatient care facility at UAB, she would require frequent checkups, scheduled for every two weeks. This, they said, would be overly difficult for her to maintain as a resident of another state and, according to their opinion, would adversely affect her condition, particularly if the appointments were not kept. Also, they argued, if there was any setback along the way, she would need to increase the frequency of her visits to the outpatient care facility. She might even require another hospital stay.

With this frustration in Anna's mind, she spent much time during May and June conceiving a way to continue increasing her exposure to higher education even if she could not return to pursuing the work she was engaged in for her graduate degree. She reasoned that if she could not work toward a degree in Athens, Georgia, then if she could obtain a job in higher education somewhere in the state of Alabama she would gain valuable experience. Fortunately, we lived in a central part of the state, close to many institutions of higher education of varying types. And summer was the season in which most of the open positions that universities and colleges sought to fill were advertised. Anna reasoned she could work at any of the institutions that existed within a sixty-mile radius of Birmingham, and still be regularly available to get to her medical appointments that would be required in the months ahead.

She set about updating her resume, gathering letters of recommendation from influential mentors in her life, searching through the *Chronicle of Higher Education*, a professional journal of higher education, for announcements of open positions, and then applying for those positions. The library within the institution where I worked maintained several subscriptions for this weekly publication, and it was easy for me to scour the want ads each week and bring her the most current position announcements within this geographic area.

She applied for positions within the student services areas of Samford University, Birmingham Southern College, and the University of Alabama in Birmingham, all within the city and suburbs of Birmingham. She also applied for positions at the University of Montevallo, only thirty-six miles away, and her alma mater, the University of Alabama, located in her hometown of Tuscaloosa, fifty-eight miles away, as well as other positions in various community colleges within that sixty-mile limit. After Anna had received all letters of reference, she wrote and emailed the following letter to Dr. Robert Witt, president of the University of Alabama.

July 2, 2010

President Witt:

Greetings from Birmingham! I am writing to report that my health is improving remarkably and that my last marrow tests indicated that I am completely free of leukemia! Consequently, I am beginning to make plans for the coming year as I continue to recover and monitor my health. Because I will not be able to return to graduate school for at least another year, I have already applied for a number of higher educa-tion positions at Alabama, as well as other institutions, so that I might gain some real work experience during this year of recovery. Positions at Alabama for which I have applied include Academic Program Advisor for Athletics, Scholarship Data Coordinator, Assistant Director for Advancement Services, and Admissions Counselor. I have no doubt that I would be able to perform well in these positions, despite my recent health difficulties. Outside of periodic visits to the hospi-tal, my energy and spirits are high, and I am of course eager to get back on track pursuing my education and career in higher education administration. However, I am concerned that I may not be the most attractive candidate for several of these positions due to my lack of a master's degree, although I was well on my way to attaining one before my efforts were thwarted by my relapse of leukemia. I was hoping that, considering my odd predicament, you might serve as a positive reference for me when it comes time for these offices to make their candidate selections. This is certainly not the way in which I had originally planned to gain my education and experiences in higher education, but I am doing my best to salvage a positive experience from this horrific one that I am overcoming. I appreciate any and all assistance that you could provide in this matter. I once promised that I would prove to be a worthwhile academic investment, and now I make that promise again, professionally.

Respectfully,

Anna E. Gordon

July 7, 2010

Anna,

I would be pleased to serve as a reference for all of these positions and I will speak to the directors I know and tell them they would be very fortunate to be able to add you to their staff.

Bob Witt

*   *   *

6-15-10

Folks,

Anna and Pam went to the hospital today, [underwent] blood work, the results of which caused the attending physician to do the anticipated bone marrow biopsy today. Anna's blood chemistry results were unusual with white cells and platelets descending but reds fine over the last ten days or so. Her kidneys are also bouncing around from normal to abnormal due to the doctor's balancing of cyclosporine levels, a drug necessary for anti-rejection [of the marrow transplant], every three days. Somehow the alternating of cyclosporine dosages affects the kidney's function and chemical readings. While there has yet been no indication from the doctors that Anna's health is taking a negative turn, blood levels jumping around at this stage is not something you wish to see. Therefore, the results of this biopsy will be significant in determining where things lie.

Suddenly, after a prolonged period of seemingly stress-free normalcy, we face the potential of a setback. We are anxious and we must endure the stress of waiting three days or so for the results.

It gets harder to stare into the darkness after you have seen the light.

Chris

*   *   *

6-19-10

Folks,

The girls had an appointment to return to UAB to see the doctor and receive the news regarding Anna's post-transplant bone marrow biopsy on Friday. The results were the best possible news they could hear, the marrow is 100% clear of any leukemia, and the system is 100% new, donor-related marrow, mission accomplished!!!

I was out of town performing with the Temptations and the Spinners, my first concert away since before New Year's Eve last year, and I was not able to write this note telling you about the results until today. We all are overjoyed with this news, and we expect a complete recovery and a restored life with all its potential for Anna Gordon's future.

While that restored life is not totally here today, there seems to be no major stumbling block in her way, and everything is beginning to look very bright!

Thanks be to God…

Chris

* * *

8-4-10

Folks,

I have not written in many weeks because I was waiting for all the necessary tests and procedures to be complete before I did. I did not want to declare victory while something might still be hanging out there. But now I can! The nurse just called Anna with the results of the spinal tap that was done on Tuesday this week. It has come back completely clean of leukemia in the spinal cord fluid. This accompanies the final bone marrow biopsy that was done three weeks ago which came back completely cancer free as well! With these good final reports, the end of the second phase of Anna's post-transplant recovery is over, and with the best of positive results.

Now, Anna will begin a schedule of [follow-up] checkups once every two weeks at UAB. She will begin the weaning off of cyclosporine, the main anti-rejection drug, opening the door for her system to become completely unaided and totally self-productive and self-sustaining. At this point, she can return to normal life and a normal life schedule of activity. The doctors will now watch her for any graft versus host disease that may become apparent at this time. While the schedule makes it too restrictive to go away to graduate school this year, Anna is applying for positions in higher education, her field of study, and she is getting interviews and call backs. We hope that she will obtain some position at an area university very soon, closing the loop completely, as she works toward re-entering a life at a level that she expects and is capable of living.

All of you have played a role in this complete recovery, through prayer, gifts, correspondences, and general good wishes. We have never experienced so much love and we are still laboring to process the meaning and significance of it. Please know that it has worked, currently we are well, and we expect to be well for many years to come. Rejoice with us! Sing, dance, smile, do whatever you do to express wonder and amazement at the accomplishment and the achievement of a thing that represents such a tremendous effort to acquire. Mostly, know that we did it together, and we thank you.

With gratitude and humility…

Chris, Pam, Anna & Tori

*   *   *

In early August, Anna interviewed by telephone and on-campus visits for several of the positions to which she had applied. However, in August, Rick Funk, director of admissions for the University of Alabama, interviewed and then hired her as an admissions counselor in the Office of Undergraduate Admissions and Scholarships. In this position, Anna corresponded with prospective freshman and their families, provided information, answered their questions, referred them to academic departments within the university where questions regarding academics were answered, scheduled on-campus visits, and led those campus tours when those students arrived in Tuscaloosa.

As soon as her hiring became official, it became necessary for her to find a place to live in Tuscaloosa. We immediately began to search for apartments that were both affordable on her salary and close enough to campus so as to ensure her commute would not be a burden. Anna obtained a two-bedroom apartment at The Links, just south of campus. We moved her into the spacious apartment, which had a balcony view of the golf course's sixth hole's green and fairway. Life was beginning to improve.

Chapter 10

9-26-10

Folks,

Just a note to keep everyone up to date on Anna's progress since the last time I wrote. Anna was applying for work at various universities, hoping to get interviews and ultimately to become employed in her field of study. She did have several interviews for various positions at the University of Alabama here in Tuscaloosa and she was offered the position of Admissions Counselor in the Office of Undergraduate Admissions and Scholarships. We moved her back down to Tuscaloosa and into her own apartment so that she would not have to commute each day to work. It was sad to say goodbye to the cute apartment in Birmingham with our friend Scott Tucker as a neighbor, but it has been the best thing for Anna's progress.

Her new address is: 1800 The Links Blvd, Apartment 1412, Tuscaloosa, AL 35405.

She has now been on the job for a month and enjoys working with prospective students and their parents from across the country who are interested in visiting the University of Alabama. She helps them plan visits here to campus, making them comfortable with all the areas that a new student must navigate when they make plans to attend a major university. Anna feels that she is truly helping young people and their families cope and make good decisions as they approach a major life milestone as an individual and as a family.

Medically, Anna has had a remarkable run of good reports over the time since I have last written. She is returning to UAB for checkups once every two weeks. She has blood labs drawn at that time and she gets checked visually by the doctors, but she has continued to have amazing reports. We have had to be creative with her physicians in maintaining a visit schedule that allows her to work during her regular work hours. So far it has been effective. She has endured a heavy case of shingles that emerged last week. Since her immune system is replaced, her antibodies from her previous body, which included chicken pox immunity, no longer exists in her system now. The virus that produces chicken pox in children hides in the nerve endings and it returns as shingles, causing great discomfort. The doctors have maintained an eye on it, and it is healing on schedule.

The physicians are continuing to reduce the cyclosporine levels in her medications, heading toward the closure of that medication soon. However, the danger is the possibility of graft versus host disease emerging as the anti-rejection medications decrease. Each person's reaction is different, and this is a critical time during the process. So far, Anna has done very well, and we hope she can continue to do well.

Pam has returned to work and except for a bout of diverticulitis that sidelined her, with many days of IV antibiotics and even one day in the hospital, she has been happy to return to her students and they are happy to receive her back to class.

Life has become normal or as normal as it can so far. We are grateful and we thank you all for your positive thoughts, prayers, and healing energy that have been offered on her behalf. Football and the Crimson Tide have been a positive healing force as we return to normalcy. We are grateful to indulge in the activities of life that preceded cancer. May we never return to those evil days.

Roll Tide!

Chris

*　*　*

In August, when it became clear to the UAB BMT physicians that Anna was planning to go to work and that she was applying for positions that would require her to begin working in a matter of weeks, their reaction was that of consternation and downright anger. In their view, Anna was to be available once every two weeks to come to the BMT outpatient facility for blood labs and other testing, Monday through Friday from 8:00 to 5:00; her employment, in their opinion, would make that impossible, therefore putting her recovery at risk.

Anna, on the other hand, had already researched every possibility affecting her decision to begin working in her field of interest in the state of Alabama and the Birmingham area. She discovered that the BMT Outpatient Facility's website, which the facility used to advertise its services to the public in order to attract new patients, stated that the facility was open and fully staffed seven days a week, and it was open from 6:00 am to 8:00 pm each day. This meant that there was adequate time to fulfill her regular two-week appointments in the morning or evening, Monday through Friday, and fourteen hours were available each weekend as well. It became obvious that her two-week appointments were not an impediment to her ability to begin a normal life schedule, in whatever way she chose.

Nevertheless, Dr. #3, the head of the BMT department, continued to resist, causing the atmosphere between the physicians who were supervising Anna's care—as well as the atmosphere surrounding the patient herself, not to mention all of us, as her family—to grow increasingly contentious. Just prior to Anna's release from the BMT unit, Dr. #3 came into Anna's hospital room and tersely demanded that Pam and I follow him into the unit's conference room. We looked at each other in confusion, as he spun on his heels and quickly began his trek, expecting us to follow him. We made our way to the room and sat next to each other in two chairs at the conference table. At first Dr. #3 was nowhere to be seen, but he made his entrance within a minute of our arrival, and he sat in a chair at the end of the conference table, three chairs removed from us. He placed a document on the table and began to speak in rapid, strong bursts. He stated that in his opinion, our decision to allow Anna to go to work placed her care in danger and that it was his recommendation that she stay at home and continue to come to her medical appointments as usual, indefinitely, during regular business hours (referring to Monday through Friday during the day). He then slid the document across the distance that separated us and declared that if we insisted that Anna do otherwise, we were to sign the document, releasing himself and the unit's staff from responsibility and legal recourse.

Pam and I stared at each other, immediately knowing what the other was thinking. I picked up the document and began to scan it. It was indeed a release from legal liability on the part of the physicians, and it was obviously a document that likely had been stored in the doctor's filing cabinet for use whenever the potential for litigation arose in a patient's case. We took a brief period to complete our review of the papers before we responded. The more I read the madder I became. Pam took far less time to achieve the same reaction.

We knew Anna was highly protective of her body and that she kept the best interest regarding continuing her progress toward achieving permanent good health at the forefront of her thinking. Afterall, it was she who bore the risks, she who endured the pain and misery of the procedures, and it was she whose very life and future were on the line. Her view was that the facility was open seven days a week, adequately staffed, and available for use by patients during nights and weekends on a regular basis. Additionally, because the facility was available with no decrease in the quality of patient care, and because it was advertised to the public in this manner, without further information being presented to her regarding how being employed would adversely alter her recovery's course, she should not only be allowed to begin a productive life, but that the physicians should praise her for the effort to return to a life interrupted.

I took a deep cleansing breath of air, looked up and made eye contact with Dr. #3 and said, "Can you present factual evidence to us demonstrating how Anna's decision will negatively impact her health as compared to her sitting at home doing nothing productive, only waiting from one two-week appointment to the next? Can you show us how idleness is statistically healthier?" He looked as if I had slapped him. He said, "Of course not, there is no such study. But I cannot be held responsible if she insists on coming to the outpatient clinic on the weekends."

The lightbulb went off in Pam's mind—and my own as well! Pam immediately responded, "So, your objection is not that she puts her health at risk, it is that you are saying the physicians would rather work only Monday through Friday, instead of as you advertise on the website. You are telling me that the care provided to patients on the weekends in the BMT Outpatient Clinic is the actual risk because it is below the level of care on weekdays? Is that what you're telling us?"

Dr. #3's face began to get red, and he stood up. "Of course not, the quality of care is the same!"

"Well then," I said, "if there is no difference in quality of care between the weekday and weekends in the clinic, and you cannot show us factual reasons why lifestyle choice leads to different patient outcomes, then no, we aren't signing this!"

Pam added, "In fact, we expect you to provide excellent care during her visits in the future during all times that you are open for business. We expect you to do your best, now and in the future."

We stood up. I slid the paper document across the table, returning it to him, and we walked out of the conference room.

* * *

10-30-10

Folks,

Anna and Pam went for a whole day at UAB last Wednesday. There were many blood tests, and she endured the eleventh bone marrow biopsy, so far. The day's visit was to prepare to release her from regular treatments. That is expected in one more visit or two. The results of everything came back, but the doctors failed to let us know; so, Pam finally called on Friday, after over a week of not hearing, and discovered that everything was good and showed no [adverse indications]. They just forgot to let us know about it. We are grateful to be winding down from contact with UAB.

Anna will have another meeting next Thursday; at which time [the doctors] should give Anna her exit schedule. Her shingles and her cellulitis are now gone, and she is finally feeling well and looking well at the same time. The future is promising, and we look forward to running toward it. We are especially looking forward to all the fall and winter holidays this year. Thank you for all your prayers and thoughts sent her way for her well-being.

Chris

* * *

Anna's return to campus was joyful! This is where she belonged. This was the environment in which she thrived. Being amid the energy of young people, full of hope for their futures, at a place where intellectual stimulation, creative work, research, and competition reigned, was thrilling. She felt useful. She felt plugged into the work of a university, deep inside the mechanics of how a campus functions, the decisions made, and the work of making the university experience the best experience for all students, energized her spirit. She was on the right path in the right place. Her work was exemplary, and parents often would write the university praising the helpfulness and enthusiasm that Anna displayed while interacting with students and their parents.

Adding to the enjoyment of her work was the sensory experience of fall's arrival. There is nothing like being on campus every day during the fall semester. Experiencing the changing of the weather, feeling cooler temperatures, observing the arrival of color in the autumn foliage as you walk the campus, and the thrill of Division 1 football on Saturdays, makes a university campus unique as a place to work and grow.

* * *

By this point, the relationship between Anna and Rob McDonald had begun to lose its steam. Not because there were problems relating to their personalities; rather, their relationship's end was due more to a situation similar to how her relationship with David ended. Strong women sometimes face this problem: they are unwilling to acquiesce to the upward trajectory of a man's career, and they choose not to follow a path that is best solely for the man. They do not wish to sacrifice what is best for their own dreams. Rob was heading quickly toward graduation from UAB Medical School. During the last year of study there, each student is expected to select the specialty in which they plan to practice medicine when licensed. Rob already knew what his specialty was going to be. He had known upon entering into medical school. He wanted to specialize in infectious diseases and run an AIDS clinic, this time as a physician, rather than as an administrator, as he had done for UAB in Africa.

Upon the selection of a specialty, the student begins the process of selecting at least five programs at other institutions (and their associated hospitals) that offer their field of specialization. The list of locations will lead to the student applying for a medical residency at one of those institutions. The individual medical schools will take the applications from the new doctors, evaluate each student's resume, credentials, recommendations, and associated examination scores. The institution will then accept the same number of new doctors as there are open positions within the specialty. This process takes many months and produces a lot of anxiety among the graduating class as they await the institutions' decisions. But when the time arrives and the announcements come in, indicating where each new doctor will go, to which city they will move, or whether they will receive an invitation at all, emotions are high.

Rob was in the fall semester of his senior year. He was consumed with the process associated with selecting the institutions he desired most and then applying for each of the five residency programs on his list. He was naturally focused on what was best for his career and he knew that all of his choices involved a move to another city. Obviously, his decision would take him away from Anna. He also knew she was actively engaged in doing what she was meant to do and that moving with him to another state, thereby leaving her medical team behind, would be difficult, and might well have an adverse effect on the quality of healthcare she received. . He and Anna spent many days discussing the dilemma as Rob made his residency selections. Anna knew straightaway what was best for her, and she knew full well the outcome. She had gone through this exact situation with David, only the year before. It was inevitable that Rob and Anna's relationship would end, and it did, early in September. But they parted company as the best of friends, each hoping for the very best for the other, with no regrets, only a short, but poignant, period of melancholy. Rob and Anna simply faded away.

* * *

11-17-10

Folks,

Pam, Anna, Tori, and I want to take this opportunity to inform you all that we are planning a HOLIDAY OPEN HOUSE and we want to invite ALL of you who want to come. This party will be our opportunity to celebrate, up close and personal, with all of you who have supported us so faithfully through Anna's illness, transplant, and recovery. We want to see, hug, and enjoy an afternoon with all those who wish to come celebrate with us during the holiday season. You may also receive an E-vite invitation, as I have created one and emailed it today. I figure the more ways to get the word out, the better!

ANNA'S HOLIDAY OPEN HOUSE CELEBRATION
When: Saturday, December 18, 4:00 pm until 7:00 pm
Where: The Gordon Home

We look forward to having fun and we hope to see you this season!

Chris, Pam, Anna & Tori

* * *

12-8-10

Folks,

I wish with all my might that I did not have to report that today we found out for sure that Anna's AML has returned for the third time. Everyone on the UAB staff is appalled and energized at the same time. Whereas they have not been known for their compassion in the past, there was true concern, disappointment, and human caring shared with Anna and us today. While now we are numb, moving around as if we know what we are doing, the doctors have already planned their attack, one that Dr. #3, the head of the bone marrow unit, heard presented at a conference just this last weekend.

The plan includes Anna returning to the 9th floor of UAB for yet another induction of chemotherapy, that process to kill the blast cells, and hopefully return her to remission, yet again. This will be done in conjunction with a new drug that Dr. #3 heard presented at the conference that is receiving good results in a research trial with post-transplant relapse patients. Then, after remission is reestablished, she will undergo another bone marrow transplant, hopefully from the same donor, with some differences tweaked in that process when it gets done. Right now, the plan is for her to return to UAB to begin treatment on Tuesday, as that is when the required medicine is expected to be received in shipment.

In response to the obvious question that we all asked today of the doctors, "How could this happen again and why?" their only reply was that [leukemia] is a very bad bug, the acute variety, and it is a devastating disease that can increase in no time and remain very deadly. It is not a good sign that she has relapsed, but they are determined, and we are cautious yet hopeful, for that is all we can be.

Again, I ask for your prayers and good wishes for Anna and for us all as we go down this path yet again. There has to be goodness in compassionate people who communicate with God on behalf of another, and that goodness can only be compounded when it is multiplied, as the people participating are multiplied. This, to me, is the last great hope of mankind, that the fervent prayers of compassionate and selfless people may bear fruit. Again, I ask for you to pass this on to whomever may want to know about Anna's situation and progress, as you have done in the past.

Lastly, I regret that we will have to cancel our open house celebration that was planned for December 18. We so wanted to see
you all and thank you for your contributions to Anna's recovery
last time. Yet, here I am asking for more of the same instead. We
will delay our party and plan for even a bigger one sometime in
the future.

Chris

* * *

12-9-10

Folks,

After a day to digest unexpected and devastating news, a shadow
of hope is emerging for us. The words of Dr. #3 and his plan have
given us direction and given us a plan to hold on to. We have been
here before; Anna knows what is coming and she knows that she
can endure for she has twice before. People have gathered, and the
ever-widening circle of caring people has expressed their renewed
support for Anna and for our family. We rest [assured] in your
support and concern. We could not do this without you all, and so
we thank you ahead of time for how little time it has taken for the
word to get out and for people to rally.

Today I returned to work to get things ready for my students'
final exams before the girls go to UAB. The girls spent the morning wrapping Christmas presents that they were able to shop for
this year since they were left out of all the details last year. The
sleigh knows how to get to the 9th floor of UAB, so we are getting
ready to spend Christmas there again this year. After lunch, Anna
returned to her office to say goodbye to coworkers and clean out
her cubicle of personal items. Her job must end so that she can get
well to get another one in the future.

Tomorrow she will go to DCH in Tuscaloosa to get blood work drawn and sent to UAB so [the team] can keep tabs on the chemistry and disease's progression in the days before she checks into the hospital. As I mentioned last night, the medicines that are to be used in this round must be manufactured and shipped to Birmingham, so she will receive her port on Monday at UAB, then return home until Tuesday or Wednesday when the meds arrive.

We know what is coming, we have been there before and we have the routine down pat; the stakes are just higher, but that does not affect the way that we approach what is ahead. Anna is optimistic. As she wrote regarding her Facebook status this morning…

"If … you can't believe, if you can't accept anything on faith, then you're doomed to a life dominated by doubt."
—Kris Kringle, Miracle on 34th Street

So, into the future we go, eyes wide open, with a host following right alongside us. There is no room for doubt!!

Chris

* * *

12-13-10

Folks,

Anna had the surgery to implant the port into her vein today. As is common at UAB (and in fairness this is true for many large hospitals) a procedure that should have taken an hour at most required almost seven hours. Anna was [instructed] not to eat the night before due to the surgery, and with the elongated time waiting for surgery and the recovery [from the procedure], tacked onto [which was an] X-ray [to ensure proper] placement [of the port] and speaking to Dr. #3, the girls were not able to eat anything all day until 6:00 pm. "Hurry up and wait" is the name of the game [taking place] in a room not designed for waiting.

We understand that the girls will move into the hospital on Wednesday, and [Anna] will begin the five-day chemotherapy treatment probably that day. We are packed, pretty much, and we have one last day at home to set things straight before moving day.

More as it happens …

Chris

*   *   *

12-15-10

Folks,

Today we moved into UAB for the long haul. We first went to the 9th floor and were given room W914, but we were told that a corner, more spacious room was being held for us but needed the heat fixed before we could move in. As Tori and I unloaded two cars into room W914 (5 cartloads full of necessities for a month or more stay) we arrived with the last cart in time to see Pam moving the first cartload into the bigger room, W934. I went to find lunch and bring it back and Tori helped Pam organize the room and even began to decorate for Christmas, complete with lights.

We ate lunch at 3:00 and Tori and I left Anna and Pam to make a home of [their room]. We brought the same small Christmas tree that all of you sent ornaments to fill last year, at Anna's insistence. We brought the usual Bear Bryant "I ain't nothing but a winner!" banner and a new addition that Tori gave Anna for Christmas, the Nick Saban quote on a red banner, "This is not the end, It's the

Beginning." So, Anna now has both banners in her room for this third run.

The girls have the 9th-floor sky view of Birmingham—well, the 20th-street view anyway—so they see the weather, the traffic, the sunlight, or lack thereof, and the medical helicopter landing pad. They have extended windows on two sides, so they will see Santa first! If you wish to send cards, letters or anything, the address is listed below.

Anna Gordon
UAB Hospital
619 19th Street South
Spain Wallace Building, Room W934
Birmingham, AL 35233

[The doctors] will start the chemo regime in the morning. This time, the chemo is supposed to be hard on the liver and kidneys. It has not been used at UAB in 6 years and it costs $30,000, so we are [venturing] into the experimental here, using an older medicine in a new way. We are anxious, but hopeful that the doctors know what they are doing.

Here we go………

Chris

*　*　*

12-16-10

Folks,

Not much to report today. The first of two chemo drugs was given to Anna today at 1:00 pm. The "new one" will be administered at 9:00 am. Anna visited with Tori and Pam most of the afternoon before succumbing to a three-hour nap. Tiredness is a large part of chemotherapy, even when there are no residual effects going on. [The girls] are working on getting their Christmas cards addressed and stuffed and I know they will be mailing them soon. Anna always likes to see cards, letters, and notes of encouragement come in her daily mail. As many of you know, all of the cards get taped up on the windows or walls and you can see from the pictures yesterday that there is a lot of window space to fill, so feel free to send what you want.

Some of you have mentioned a desire to visit. While it seems ungrateful [for me] to offer caution about visitations, I offer [my] experience that chemotherapy and its [effects] on the body can change daily. Often, plans get changed [due to] Anna's condition. Please ask Pam about all visitations because she is the best source of information regarding a very fluid situation.

More as it happens …

Chris

*　*　*

12-17-10

Folks,

Anna had a difficult day today (yesterday, actually, because I am writing this on Saturday morning the 18th) in that as [the team was] giving her the new chemo at 9:00 am, she began to feel "weird." She had heaviness in her chest and throat. She was getting anxious, and Pam called for the doctor, got none, then marched out to the hallway and insisted that someone come to check on her. Eventually the hall's nurse practitioner came and ordered an EKG and stayed to monitor Anna for a while. It seems that they are "tinkering" with the speed of the dosage, since it has not been used in 6 years at UAB, figuring stuff out as we go along.

After the treatment, later in the afternoon, Santa Claus showed up in the hall and in the room with his elves. Anna got her picture with them before having a special dinner with a friend who brought Indian food from a nearby restaurant, her favorite! This gave Pam and me the opportunity to get out, and I took her to The Fish Market just down the street for some snapper and wine. As we were walking back to the hospital in the cold, we looked up and were able to spot Pam and Anna's hospital room, all decorated and lit up in the icicle lights she has hung. It was a bright spot in the urban-landscape, one of hope and festivity in the middle of a drab dark wet concrete "mountain-scape."

Tonight, apparently because of the chemo, [Anna] had a fever of 102 that [the team] battled with antibiotics and Benadryl. This is a reaction that is arriving very early in the chemotherapy process as compared to the last experiences. This is new territory and we do not know what to expect. She is having two more chemotherapy treatments today and we will see what happens.

This journey will be different, I think. We know the road, but each mile of this trip seems like it will be new. I guess it will lead to a different place, which is the goal, I guess. Pray that [Anna's team] knows what they are doing. We roll the dice because there is no GPS [for this journey]…

Chris

* * *

12-18-10

Folks,

This has been a very hard day. More chemo this morning brought on nausea and sickness over and over again. Low blood counts originating from the pill-chemo Anna started a week ago while waiting to go to the hospital makes this period, the two weeks after chemo began, the worst period of sickness and tiredness, all while she is getting heavy dosages of two different IV chemotherapies. The new chemo drug causes concerns [in regard to] her kidneys and liver. It also is known to cause internal bleeding through the small capillaries of the blood system. When that happens, blood pressure drops, and heart rates go up. This is exactly what happened mid-day today. The physicians were very concerned. Everyone is very cautious with this procedure and with Anna since they have not done this at UAB in six years. The pharmacist who mixed the drug has even come to her room three times today. They are giving her two units of blood, in addition to all kinds of antibiotics to battle the fever which is caused by the chemo. They are giving her blood pretreatments of Benadryl, all while she is very ill. Anna sleeps when she is not sick in the bathroom, and she has not eaten much in two days. She says she is not hungry. This is intense, fast paced, and a very different road than we have gone down before, medically.

Anna's friends from the University of Georgia's graduate program made the trip to Birmingham just to see her. They are always wonderful, supportive, and encouraging people who love her unconditionally. They brought handmade paper snowflakes that are now hung up along the icicle lights in her room. Anna was not able to visit with them like she would like as she felt miserable during their stay, but she is very touched that they cared enough to come. They drove nine hours over and back to Athens just to brighten her day as much as possible on a very bad day. We love them for trying.

We are not playing; this is real and very hard. If we get through this, the good stuff better be on the way! Thank you for your prayers and the sending of positive energy and well wishes. They are all needed and appreciated, as usual, but more tonight than normal.

Chris

* * *

12-19-10

Folks,

Today was the fourth day of chemotherapy. It turned out to be fairly calm today. Some caution with blood pressure going too low and heart rate rising too high, but neither was a big issue today. Maybe they are figuring out the dosage or she is acclimating to it, or they are tweaking the pretreatment and getting it settled in; either way, today was better—not good, but better.

We will take that for now, let's see how the night goes.

Chris

* * *

12-20-10

Folks,

Today was a better day, the best day so far. Anna has acclimated to her medications and seems to be "tolerating them well" as they say. Her blood pressure has remained normal, and her heart rate is also [normal]. They have put so much fluid in her that she is uncomfortable but that is a small thing in comparison to fevers, etc., that have been going on lately. She ate parts of two meals today, a big improvement since she has eaten almost nothing for three days, and we have only one more day of chemo to go.

After this treatment, the effects will begin to manifest in her body and [all of] her blood count levels will go down to the bottom and she will have to climb back up out of that pit, which most of you know about. But we do know that when she was diagnosed, she had 28% blast cells in her bloodstream. A week later when she checked into the hospital it was 68% blast cells in her blood. That is how fast and virulent her type of leukemia is. As of today's blood

counts, she had 0% blast cells in her bloodstream! It comes fast…
and this time it is going faster. I hope that is why [the team] chose
this chemo treatment even though it is fierce on the body.

Thanks for the support and the prayers and the well wishes and
positive energy all sent our way. I am constantly amazed at the
diversity of experience and chosen paradigms of belief, all [of
which are] focused on Anna. I cannot help but share a brief
excerpt from a friend of 30 years who sent us this note. The reason I share it is because of the sincerity of the sender. It is so out
of character for him to write of his private spiritual life, but he is
invested to this degree, as are many of you, in doing what he can
for Anna's healing.

*"I went to the woods Saturday to pray for you all. I pray with a
sacred pipe, and it is in the Native American tradition that I receive
messages. As soon as I completed the prayers two woodpeckers flew
up to the tree above me. I take this as a wonderful sign. The wood-
pecker is the hardest working bird in the woods. They also mate
for life. They spend their time making homes and caring for their
young. I thought of you, Chris, and Anna and all the hard work you
have done. I also saw a hawk fly over. The hawk is considered to be
a direct messenger to The Creator. I will continue the prayers and I
have also asked my Native America friends to pray for y'all. Please
let me know if I can help in any way."*

I could share many more notes just like that from New York,
NY, from Washington DC, from Alaska to Florida, from Guin,
Fayette, Hamilton, or across the street…again it rolls downhill
into our mailboxes. I never cease to be amazed at the capacity of
the human heart to hold compassion for others. Isn't that what
we were instructed to do? Well, during this season of spiritual

reflection and quiet celebration of the gift of hope to the world, I can say wholeheartedly, and give names and addresses if required, that people are good, people are kind, people care and sacrifice for another, every day. It must have worked, all those years ago, I've got my own list to prove it; I don't bother to keep a naughty one…

Chris

* * *

12-22-10

Folks,

Anna has completed the chemo regimen that was outlined and now she is dealing with the things that come in its wake. Dropping blood counts that require blood and blood products is one of the expectations after chemo. She had platelets this morning. [She also had fever—then] blood cultures to determine if and what type of infections are occurring, and this ends in antibiotics until there are no more fevers. She has several antibiotics [that the team has given] her lately. She has gained 10 pounds of fluid weight in the last six days. The medical team is now curtailing her fluids and giving her meds to get the fluid out. The fluid and the chemo side effects affect her hands and feet. They are red and sore, and they make her uncomfortable. All in all, this part of the monthly cycle of chemo make her sleep a lot as the chemo continues to work inside the body for weeks as it searches out blast cells and hidden leukemia cells.

We hope that it does its job well this time, even though it makes her miserable. That is why they say you fight a battle with cancer. You endure and come out on the other side. We hope and we wait.

Chris

* * *

12-23-10

Folks,

Last night, there were low blood pressure [readings] and fevers that faded as the morning arrived. Anna got a unit of blood and began to feel much better by lunchtime. She felt well enough to get up and take a shower and change clothes. She actually wanted food for lunch as she had not eaten in a few days. She sat in a chair for a good bit of the afternoon, going through the large mound of mail that arrived today. Later in the afternoon, she walked with Pam and me through the hospital's ninth floor. She was hungry enough to want [food] and ordered her favorite Indian food, which I got her before the day concluded.

Energy is a great thing to have, even if only a little, that is an improvement from sleeping for days! Her blood counts are now down in all categories, having no white cells at all and thus no immune system. It will take two weeks or more for these counts to work their way back up to more normal levels, but again, no blast cells were seen in the slides the doctors looked at this morning.

We head into Christmas Eve and Christmas Day thankful to be well on the way to getting better. We certainly have the "room with a view" if there is snow to be seen in downtown Birmingham this weekend.

Let it snow, let it snow, let it snow…

Chris

* * *

12-26-10

Folks,

Merry Christmas from UAB Hospital! We were able to get through the holidays in pretty good shape thanks to the help of family and friends who called, came by the hospital, and brought gifts of time, thoughtfulness, food, presents, and well wishes. 'Tis the season of giving hope and we certainly are receivers of all of that and more, even though we are occupying the 9th floor of a hospital in Birmingham.

Anna awoke on Christmas morning to find that her name was in lights just outside her 9th-floor window on the largest marquee in Birmingham. She has had blood products, antibiotics, potassium, and other meds over the last three days. She has had some nausea and other not-feeling-great moments, but she is still getting good reports regarding no blast cells being seen in the daily blood tests. All in all, she was able to enjoy most of the holiday activities as they transpired. Snow was the main festive adventure that we did not count on. The view from the 9th floor was spectacular, but it was also mixed with urban steam that comes from the Birmingham underground.

Thank you for your support and we hope you and your families had a terrific Christmas this year!

Chris

* * *

12-27-10

Folks,

Today was uneventful for most of the day; however, Anna began to feel bad around 5:00 pm and now she is registering a fever. This is the first fever in a few days. I am sure [the medical team] will battle it with antibiotics, which cause her stomach to feel queasy, and in the morning's blood work, they will do blood cultures to determine which antibiotic to use to fight this specific type of infection. We will see what kind of night this leads to tonight.

Chris

* * *

12-28-10

Folks,

Today was quiet. Anna got a unit of platelets and is likely to have a transfusion of blood tomorrow. Her blood counts are still in the cellar and are likely to remain there for more days, before inching up. We are looking at another couple of weeks at least. One of her favorite doctors will take over her care starting tomorrow, Dr. #4. He is the academician of the bone marrow group of physicians and he spends a lot of his time in research. Dr. #3, the BMT head physician, told us a few days ago that Dr. #4 was "… on the verge of discovering a cure for cancer!" There is no one I would like to see do it more than he. He has been a consistent and positive source of encouragement and calm logic throughout Anna's entire ordeal since she first went to transplant physicians in March this year. We wish him well and we look forward to hearing about his research.

Pam is not sleeping very well. She is not finding the "chair" very sleep-inducing anymore. She has spent the better part of a whole year attempting to sleep in a chair bed—very uncool! She is my hero.

More as it happens…

Chris

*   *   *

12-30-10

Folks,

Today, the doctors performed a bone marrow biopsy to see if Anna is now in remission. Pam called me to say, "Stay home today." She knows that it bothers me both physically and emotionally (not that it does not bother her): I cannot stay in the room when [Anna] undergoes one of those [procedures]. It is too much for me to endure even though I wish to be supportive of Anna. Mostly, in addition to the sheer horror and brutality of taking what looks like a corkscrew and burrowing it deep into her hip to suck out four vials of marrow and knock off a piece of bone to extract and analyze, I cannot fathom how she is able to endure it for the four-teenth time, so far, without saying a word or uttering a sound. I cannot imagine what reservoir of inner fortitude she possesses to be able to accept so gracefully what must be done. I could not do it.

They will investigate the [extracted] marrow to see if there are, indeed, no more blast cells. If there are none, [Anna] will be declared to be in "remission." She has been in remission two other times before this third bout of leukemia. They cannot make fur-ther plans for her future treatments regarding another marrow/

stem cell transplant until she is officially in remission. With a positive result, we can at least move forward with what lies next.

I did stay home, and I began to dismantle the holiday decorations that the girls eagerly distributed throughout the house. Christmas did come, and it went. Unlike a typical year, where you anticipate the ritual of the introspection of self that accompanies the season of Advent, this Christmas came and left in numbness of heart and stoicism. In times like these, the heart is focused on the immediacy of getting through the day; on making the appropriate progress, to achieve the next rung on the ladder of wellness for Anna, for the whole family. We all have been like fish out of water. Like the television commercial advertising a medication for asthma; we, too, struggle to breathe the air of inner safety and peace of mind, those twin waters in which you swim within the sea of wellness. But, instead, for now, we float on.

In the meantime, Anna is in bed in a drugged slumber of Ativan, morphine, and Benadryl.

Bring on the New Year, please ...

Chris

*   *   *

12-31-10

Folks,

Anna has spent the day in pain control. Her bone marrow biopsy was extra aggressive—and extra painful the day after. She is bruised and has pain in her hip, back, and down her leg. She has been on morphine some of the day, but the doctors want to keep that to a minimum and use a mild opiate instead. I wish they would just get her out of pain.

We had a great family visit with Tori and Scott as well as Pam and me and Anna. Great discussions and love all around the room. It was a nice way to bring in the New Year as we throw this last one out!!

We wish all of you a great new year, too.

Chris

*   *   *

1-1-11

Folks,

Today is a new year, one we hope brings with it health and opportunity for us and for all of you. We enjoyed watching our boys execute possibly the finest game of domination and precision of execution we have seen all year. While it was a thing of beauty and pride, Anna kept falling asleep through most of the game.

She has no levels of blood counts; as a friend said today, "It's when your blood turns to water." This causes her to feel bad and have no energy and need blood products to reinforce her own blood counts. The unit of blood and the platelets she is to receive always come with Benadryl pretreatments that cause her to sleep as well. So, it has been hard for her to be an active fan today, but she was aware of the game's progress and cheered when she felt like it.

While the bone marrow will not be completely analyzed until mid-week next week, because of the weekend and the holiday break, the doctors did say that the initial [examination] indicates clean marrow, no blast cells. We are pleased and guardedly optimistic. In the meantime, she still has many days of recovery just to regain the strength needed to feel like she can function.

Happy New Year!

Chris

* * *

1-3-11

Folks,

Anna had a difficult couple of days. Fevers persisted. Low blood levels caused low energy and lethargy. She has had bone pain for the last two days and had little help from the doctor with pain management. On top of that, this morning her doctor had a particularly high degree of insensitivity, and then disrespect. Pam and Anna are ready to go home, emotionally, but physically, [Anna] is still two weeks or more away. The mind must battle on. It cannot just walk away...

Chris

* * *

Dr. #4 was Anna's favorite of the four BMT physicians who alternated being on call. Up to this point, he had shown the most empathy toward Anna, and he was the most supportive and responsive to her needs. He was her physician when she received the chemotherapy designed to put her leukemia into remission for the third time. One day, most unexpectedly, he entered Anna's room accompanied by a host of medical residents and medical students participating in oncology rotations. Altogether, it was a group of over twenty people, including one female social worker (all the others who came to the room were men). Such a large group is common, as UAB is a teaching hospital; medical students who are continuing their rotations as well as physicians in residency programs accompany staff physicians who not only practice medicine but hold faculty positions as well. The residents and medical students are exposed to each patient under the staff physicians' care and have the chance to learn about each patient's specific case. They learn the eccentricities of each patient's history, and the residents often participate in patient care.

Dr. #4 had come to Anna's room for a routine patient visit, and to examine her condition because she was receiving chemotherapy. He was also there to explain that day's treatment to Anna, describing what the procedure entailed and what to expect. All this took place as the mass of students and resident physicians observed the interaction between Anna and Dr. #4. After the doctor had completed his routine examination of Anna, he began to exit the room. Suddenly, however, he stopped. He turned back around to Anna. He told her to turn over on her stomach. Although this was an odd instruction (he had never made this request before), Anna immediately did as she had been told, believing the doctor was going to examine the two holes in her back—at the top of her pelvis bone—that were wounds from the previous day's bone marrow biopsy. Instead, without warning, without asking permission, without preparing Anna and informing her of what he planned to do, he reached over and removed Anna's pajama bottoms and then her panties, exposing her rectum and pubic area for more than twenty young males to see!

He then matter-of-factly began to discuss several rectal conditions patients who endure chemotherapy might develop. Anna had not developed any of these conditions. She had exhibited no gastric problems at all during the days leading up to this visit by Dr. #4; nor did she have any gastric problems on this particular day. Dr. #4 merely was using Anna's body as a teaching tool for the students and residents present. He was not even addressing Anna or Pam; he was lecturing to the people assembled.

Anna was immediately mortified! Pam was enraged. She stood up, threw her pointed finger in the air, and said, "*Get out!* All of you, get out, *now!*" Dr. #4 was shocked, as he was unaware that he was doing anything unusual. He could not immediately comprehend what his offense might be. Therefore, he looked at Pam as if she were a crazy lady, mentally unstable, someone who was behaving irrationally, in his view, but someone who was offensive to him—as if he were the victim!

They quickly filed out into the hallway, everyone embarrassed except Dr. #4, who was now angry that his moment of classroom instruction had been so rudely interrupted. Pam followed. She was not finished with him yet. As soon as she entered the hallway, Dr. #4 proclaimed his shock at Pam's dramatic action, and he had begun to dress her down when she cut him off mid-sentence. She began to tell him exactly how offensive and insensitive his behavior toward Anna—a cancer patient no less—was! She did not hold back, making certain he understood the degree to which his actions were unacceptable. All the students and residents were farther down the hall, but still within earshot of the heated conversation, as was the entire nursing staff working on that floor!

When Pam concluded her recitation of Dr. #4's inappropriate behavior, Dr. #4 responded haughtily: "There is no part of [your daughter's] body that is off-limits to me! This is a teaching hospital." He was immediately informed that with *this* patient, when examining her he was to limit himself to the parts of her body that concerned her primary condition, and that she was not a blackboard. If he wanted to use Anna as an example for medical students to learn from, he should ask permission of the patient first, or at least inform her of what he planned to do before it occurred, so that she could prepare herself emotionally. He yelled, "If Anna was offended, she could have refused treatment." Pam responded, "If she knew what was coming, she might have! She was not given the opportunity." Dr. #4, defeated by the facts, spun around and practically jogged away, humiliated in front of his students.

*　*　*

1-4-11

Folks,

This is day 22 of the journey so far. Anna has had three days of constant fever, often peaking at 102.5 but never [having the fever go] entirely away. [The medical team has taken] X-rays today to attempt to find an infection, but nothing has turned up. The

doctor will call for an entire body CT scan tomorrow if [the fever] does not break soon. She is on four medications now to combat this prolonged fever. Three are IV antibiotics and one is an anti-fungal. There is much drugged eye-shutting but not much sleep over the last three days and nights.

Some anxiety existed this morning as a nurse came in and reported that one of Anna's biopsy results showed a 10% blast-cell density, then left the girls to worry over that news for four hours before the doctor finally came in and reported, no, she is actually in remission and the 10% report was in an area that will clear itself up on or around day 30 and is not even something that is considered in determining remission status. So that is the good news of the last several bad days. Anna is now in remission, but she must recover from the very low blood counts that she is experiencing.

This is day 14 of having blood counts that are on or near the bottom. This is twice as long as it has been previously, before she begins to rebound in those categories. We do not know if this is because of the working of the new chemo that was used this time, or if it is as they have said in the past, "Each time she does this, it will be harder and harder for her to recover." We have not experienced that before, but his time it could be. This long, with prolonged high fevers and tremendous body-wracking and teeth-chattering chills, is all very new.

We wait and we pray, and we struggle to get through each day and still maintain a modicum of human dignity and optimism. Some days it is easier than other days.

Chris

*   *   *

1-5-11

Folks,

Things are still hard today. Anna had fevers all night and into this morning, reaching 103, and marking the fourth straight day of high fever. In the morning they did a full body CT scan to determine the cause and they saw nothing. Her liver numbers are up, not a good thing, and they have been up for two days. [The team is] doing an ultrasound on her liver and surrounding area to see what that shows. They have put her on ice today; little chemical ice packs (about ten) were used to cool her skin and body. They did this twice today, and around 2:00 the fever broke and fell dramatically to normal, the first time in four days.

She needed platelets and a unit of blood, but they were not able to give them to her until after the fever broke. Her blood pressure ran high today, go figure, and she has been faint. During the blood [infusion], she became nauseated and got violently sick, probably because of the fluid junk they made her drink to do the CT scan. Then violent body-wracking chills set in which upset Anna to the point of tears, fearful crying out of being out of control, and for the first time in two years not knowing what her body is doing and why it will not go back to normal.

The atmosphere within the hospital room is becoming more and more anxious and there is a sense of urgency in the nurses. This is all new; we have not been here before. Things are piling up and we could use a break of good news and good numbers.

Chris

* * *

1-6-11

Folks,

Today was slightly better than yesterday, which is a vast improve-ment! Anna still has fever. It came back last night, after it had broken for the first time, then leaped to 103 for a good part of the evening. This morning and today, she has been on a "cooling blanket" that they have installed in her room and on her bed. It is like lying in a pool of water with an adjustable temperature [that ranges] from very cool, to bring down fevers, to quite warm, to help her with violent body-wrenching chills that occur when she is about to have a fever climb back up. So, today has been up and down and up and down, body-temperature-wise.

She is now in pain, as well. This pain is muscle pain that comes from pulled and strained muscles, caused by the violent chills (yes, it is that bad, her muscles are sore) requiring Ativan and Demerol [for relief]. She got platelets today, as well, because yesterday's fever ruined the unit of platelets she received. With blood and blood products, of course, there are pretreatments of Benadryl. She is also getting the four meds, three antibiotics and one anti-fungal, plus regular fluids because the antibiotics are hard on her kidneys, and they want them to flush well.

The good news of the day is that her liver counts are down (they were elevated because of stresses from the meds) and the blood counts are beginning to go up (two straight days of miniscule improvement). This is what will make her feel better; the blood levels need to climb back up to normal levels, giving her strength and an immune system. The addition of the cooling blanket has helped in the fight against the fevers.

We hope that the chills go away and quit doing actual bodily damage. We also hope that the blood [levels] begin to dramatically rise, soon! Thanks for all the extra prayers and positive energy. We need all we can get this trip,

Chris

*   *   *

1-7-11

Folks,

I thought early on that it might be a little better day, but it was not. Chills still wrack her little body before fever begins. These have been so violent over the last three days that it has caused all the muscles in her body to ache with soreness and pain, making it difficult and uncomfortable to breathe at times. Mercifully, Demerol causes these chills to stop almost instantly, as if by magic. Unfortunately, it does not last long, so she has to have it on demand, roughly about every hour or two hours, depending on how much they give her. If the chills start and the nurse is busy in another room with another patient, or is delayed for any reason, even only five or ten minutes, [Anna] will violently twitch with every muscle in her body convulsing and contracting about 100 times a minute or more. Once yesterday at a shift change, the contractions went on for almost 40 minutes. Anna could barely breathe from the pain and began to feel anxious regarding her ability to breathe. Today relief has come much quicker, leaving more opportunity for rest, due to the nurses' watchful eye. But still, chills begin again every hour or two as Demerol wears off.

Today, she also endured her hair being taken off for the fourth time. The chemo has done its job and the hair is killed each time because it is fast-growing. So, another badge of the fight has been awarded. I think I will need a shadow box for the Purple Hearts she is accumulating.

The blood counts are continuing to inch upward. This should be a good sign and we hope it continues. I keep reminding myself that [Anna's progress] can be and is becoming very different than the patterns we have known in the past, so it is not with much confidence that I think this nightmare will end soon, but I can hope.

Chris

* * *

1-8-11

Folks,

There was more of the same today. I really have little to tell other than her blood counts are continuing to go up. She has no infections, all things look very good, and she still feels awful. The doctors cannot say why she feels awful, and she continues to have chills and medium-grade fever, hovering around 101. We still plod on.

Chris

* * *

1-9-11

Folks,

Another day like the day before; the battle continues, on the 9th floor. Here is Pam's Facebook status from tonight.

Another struggle of a day...fevers, chills, lots of Demerol, platelets, antibiotics, potassium, magnesium, lots of fluids...no appetite, no wonder. Fever is almost 103 again...She needs relief. When will prayers be answered? How many does it take? How sincere must we be? Do we need ten more people, one hundred? One thousand??????

Things are tense up there, especially with UAB being stressed with doctors and nurses being short due to the weather event today and tomorrow. When things get serious, you ask good questions!

The one bright spot has been a nurse, Danielle, who has stepped up and been proactive, calling the doctors to question their plans to decrease her Demerol and morphine ([she was] worrying that Anna will have had too much, leaving her to chill and shake for twenty-four hours if the doctors had their way). Then today, in preparation [before her shift ended] and wanting to make sure that Anna was being taken care of in the best way possible, she calls the doctors again and "encourages" them to make a more proactive plan. They responded with the idea [of giving] Anna a steroid that, in theory, will reset her hypothalamus, causing the fevers to subside. Now this is the first useful idea that has come forth in over two weeks, and it came because of a nurse who took her job seriously, taking care of her patients and not leaving until [what she wanted] was done. She is also not afraid to ask for it! Thank you, Danielle!

We will see if [resetting the hypothalamus] works. They say it might take twelve hours before they can tell anything. Now there is something to wait for.

Chris

* * *

1-11-11

Folks,

The last time I wrote, Anna had been given a steroid that was intended to "reset her hypothalamus." For that night it worked, giving Anna the most complete night of rest that she has had in the two weeks of high fevers and chills. All the next day, yesterday, she was calm and rested and playful, feeling almost well, reflecting with her actions and attitude the jump that has been seen in her blood counts in the last two days. She now has almost normal blood counts in all her blood levels. However, by early evening yesterday, the chills returned and with it, the high fevers. The respite of her perceived night and day without fever, promising the pattern of soon leaving UAB and returning home, was shattered by the reality of an even longer stay in her 9th floor prison and the return of the energy-draining sickness while [the team] figures out what is wrong with her.

Teeth-rattling chills that cause muscle pain, making it hard to breathe, recurring fevers causing low energy and restless interrupted sleep, coupled with emotional melancholy brought on by a loss of control and a loss of confidence, day after day over the last two weeks, finally overwhelmed her during a midnight walk around the hallways of UAB with Pam. For the first time, in her disappointed, exhausted, and angry state of mind, she let doubt fill her mind as to whether she has the physical, mental, and emotional strength to endure and survive the path ahead. The weight of knowing firsthand the physical realities of what still lies ahead of her, and what it takes to go through it, was almost too much for her last night. She put the burden down and let her humanity flow out in liquid form.

It is a tremendous load. She bears it with such grace and with such beauty that she rarely shows the weight she carries inside, making it look easy to the casual observer. It is not easy. It has never been easy. Unless you are around in the wee small hours when one of those rare times occurs where she succumbs to human fear and doubt and frailty and lets that hidden side of herself come out and be emotionally exorcised, you would never know. Last night Pam saw it. I have seen it before as well. There is not much you can say to help with her emotional recovery other than to be there and hold her up as she lets flow the river that has been dammed. Who could blame her? Who could carry her load?

She will restore herself; she always has. She will rebuild her determination, her confidence, and her swagger, to face what lies ahead. She always has. Fighting for your life is hard. It requires the will to do it. She will, again, in the coming days, rebuild and restore her will to fight and win. She must.

Chris

*   *   *

1-13-11

Folks,

Today was a better day; there was no fever all day and only a medium grade 100.5 for a while last night. Pam and Anna have relaxed today, even falling into deep sleep this afternoon after their first meeting with her new floor doctor, another attending [physician]. The doctors have found no infection, even after multiple scans and tests over several days. Therefore, they believe that her fever is being caused by the antibiotics themselves. Some have been known to cause fever. So, they were going to wean her off them one at a time and they have been doing that today. It may be working, [as indicated by] today's lack of fever. We will see if [her present state] continues over the next two or three days. If this continues, she can go home for a couple of weeks while she gets stronger, and [the medical team works] out the next step.

The picture included in this email is created by Anna's wonderful University of Georgia graduate cohort friends. They are terrific and we love them.

Chris

* * *

1-14-11

Folks,

Anna had a good day today, no fevers or chills for the second day in a row. The removal of antibiotics seems to have worked. I believe she had a reaction to one of the antibiotics, much like the "Red Man Syndrome" side effect she encountered with the antibiotic vancomycin a long while back (for those who remember that). Anyway, the good news is that [the doctors] will look at her numbers tomorrow and if her platelets are high enough, they may let her go home tomorrow. So, I will go [visit them] with the largest vehicle possible, ready to bring back the pack.

I'll let you know.

Chris

* * *

1-15-11

Folks,

The girls came home today. [Anna] has blood labs at DCH
early next week, then another bone marrow biopsy a week from
Wednesday at UAB. [The transplant team] will begin to set up the
donor schedule and we will hear in a week or so what the schedule is going to be. I think the earliest we could start would be two
weeks from now. We will see soon. For now, we rest and recover
and enjoy.

Chris

* * *

1-25-11

Folks,

Today Anna returned to UAB to receive her fifteenth bone marrow
biopsy. The results will show if she is still in remission, a state necessary for the marrow transplant—and its planning—to go forward. The results will come back over the remainder of this week.

The BMT unit is talking to the donor, the same one that donated
before, and they are setting up a schedule and process. As you
recall, everything starts with the donor's availability for harvesting, then [the transplant team] backs up and plans for all the
procedures that need to take place and be scheduled. If Anna
is in remission, still, as expected, it is looking as if Anna will go
through preparatory testing around the week of February 6, [then
go] into UAB for admittance around the next week, February 13,
ten days ahead of the donated marrow's arrival. Tentatively, the
transplant may occur on February 23.

So, we wait, and she recovers, and we try to enjoy the remainder of our time at home before the intensity begins again.

Chris

* * *

1-26-11

Folks,

I am pleased to say that the initial [examination] of the marrow results indicate that Anna continues to be in remission from her leukemia! This clears the way for the final stages of the transplant to begin to be planned. We will have a thorough schedule later in the week or next week. Right now, this is enough to celebrate.

Chris

* * *

During the weeks Anna was home from the hospital, waiting for the National Bone Marrow Registry to contact a donor and secure an agreement, she felt well enough to consider looking for another romantic attachment. It had been months since her relationship with Rob McDonald had come to an amicable end, and she missed that part of her life. Match, one of the earliest online dating companies, emerged as an interesting choice for Anna. It allowed her to investigate a pool of potential suitors from across a larger geographic area than did traditional dating, where she would have had to choose from among only those people with whom she had direct, day-to-day contact. Never being afraid of technology, Anna tried it. Soon she was "matched" with Kevin Rugani, an aerospace engineer in Huntsville, AL. Kevin was intelligent, handsome, sensitive, empathetic, and openminded. It isn't every day you come into contact with a young man who will take the time to seriously explore a relationship with a cancer patient.

They talked online for weeks, getting to know each other. There was enough interest between them both to continue communicating; eventually, their online conversations led to an in-person meeting. In mid-January Kevin came to Tuscaloosa, traveling down from Huntsville, so both he and Anna could further explore the possibility of dating. He was the real deal, the same in-person as he had been in his previous communications with Anna. He even had his own cat!

* * *

2-8-11

Folks,

We have been home for over two weeks waiting on information regarding the schedule for the upcoming transplant for Anna. Things have been very quiet and then, suddenly, many things occurred. First, we were told that the original donor has now backed out of a second donation. This seems to be the reason we went so long without hearing anything. After receiving the news, a couple of days ago, Pam called every day, pushing for a fast resolution to a new search, so that Anna would be able to get [the second bone marrow transplant] before she might have to go through another chemo consolidation. That would lengthen the process and Anna's suffering by at least a month.

The communication has been delayed because UAB cannot contact the donor directly; all communications with the donor must go through the National Bone Marrow Registry. If you remember, the first choice for a marrow donation was a man who had difficulty scheduling the donation; and, therefore, the [opportunity opened] for the second choice, the female, who could do it more readily, at the time, and so we went with her. Now, as we were told today, the man, the first choice, is available and willing! They are

working on expediting the donation and the scheduling. UAB is telling us that Anna may begin getting her organ tests and [evaluations] (which are done to get a realistic health picture of her organs, and to use this information as a benchmark, to compare back to, as she endures the serious chemical attacks [her organs] will receive when [Anna goes] through the transplant process) by this weekend. Things may pick up quickly.

Additionally, in the last three weeks, Anna has found a new boyfriend, Kevin Rugani, an aerospace engineer who lives in Huntsville and works as a subcontractor for NASA's space shuttle engines. They have been talking for months but they only met three weeks ago. He has played a large role in the improvement of her outlook and attitude. She now has something to look forward to and something that makes her happy. This is a good thing, especially now! We are grateful he makes her happy and we all enjoy his company.

More as it happens...

Chris

*   *   *

2-11-11

Folks,

Since my last update, things have changed daily for Anna and Pam. The latest, and I think final, version is that Anna and Pam went to Birmingham for blood work today. It turned out [to be] extensive blood work, beginning the intense buildup [before] her checking into the BMT unit for the transplant.

Replacing what we had been led to believe yesterday, there will be no additional chemo treatments before the transplant! This is a good thing. We were concerned that Anna would have to endure another month of chemo but the new donor, the man of the first search, can arrange to harvest on the earliest date of those that were given him. This allows us to plan the schedule.

Anna's schedule will involve a series of [tests to evaluate] her body and organs for [baseline] values to compare to as she undergoes the extensive medications and chemo to come. Today's blood tests marked the first of these tests. The remainder of the schedule is as follows:

Tuesday—Feb 15—Lumbar Puncture (Spinal Tap)

Thursday—Feb 17—a series of heart tests and other organ tests

Monday—Feb 21—review of the test results so far, and sign consent forms for transplant

Tuesday—Feb 22—Surgery to implant a second Hickman port

Monday—Mar 1—Anna receives the first chemo dose that will kill her native marrow. This will be done as an outpatient but will take all day

Tuesday—Mar 2—admittance to the BMT unit for daily chemotherapies to kill her marrow system

Tuesday—Mar 8—Donor will come to a collection site to donate marrow via blood machine

Wednesday—Mar 9—Anna receives her second bone marrow transplant.

This is what we know currently. [The moment of truth] is upon us, and we move forward with this schedule hoping that it will bring about the desired outcome for Anna.

Chris

*   *   *

2-15-11

Folks,

Anna had the lumbar puncture test today. It seems to have gone well with minimal reported discomfort, but with high residual anxiety. For those who remember, last time, Anna was found to have leukemia in her spinal fluid; thus, she underwent spinal chemo injections for several days under an excruciatingly painful process. This was the worst chemotherapy experience of any she had yet endured. Within the hour of my writing this, Anna received the phone call that the fluid is clear of leukemic cells! This is terrific news, clearing the way for transplant immediately following the remaining test processes and results.

As I mentioned in the last email, Thursday is the next battery of tests, including heart tests and other organ tests to establish a new benchmark regarding her organ's conditions prior to transplant. Next Monday, she will sign consent forms and receive the results of these tests. The Hickman surgery scheduled for next Tuesday has been delayed to next Friday.

Thank you for your concern and prayerful support during this week and this day's activity.

Chris

*   *   *

Chapter 11

Folks,

What a day! This is the kind of day you want to forget and bury in a hole in the yard. The day started early for the girls, getting up at 5:00 am to get to Birmingham for a 7:15 am brain scan, which was required today. Although early, this turned out to be the best part of the day.

The day [took a downward turn] when [Anna and Pam] made their way to the 6th floor of UAB (which is used for all sorts of testing, not just imaged lumbar punctures.) [They] were told by the 3rd floor BMT doctor, who made the test appointment, that Anna would have the same medications prior to the lumbar puncture that she gets when they do it on the 3rd floor BMT unit—if not more! They were told by the 6th floor physician in charge, however, that no, not only will Anna not be getting more than the BMT uses, she would not be getting any at all!! It is this doctor's policy to do the procedure without any medication. He announced that he is SO good, none will be required. (I might add that this is the only unit that does not use meds during this procedure.)

Needless to say, his announcement sucked the air out of the room and immediately caused anxiety for both Anna and Pam. The 6th floor physician was unmoved and had no compassion, encouraging Anna to "get over it" in essence and that her single option included not having the procedure done, it was her choice. Ugh, what?!?!?! Anna said, "No, that is really not an option"—and of course she had to go through with it. She was anxious during the procedure and was brought to tears due to the situation, the procedure itself, and for feeling like she had been misled by the physician downstairs and abused by the one upstairs.

Needless to say, the girls did, indeed, spend some time discussing the situation and circumstances with a patient representative on the 6th floor. For whatever good it will do, at least they had the opportunity to say their peace. Afterwards, on the 6th floor (after the 3rd floor was consulted), [the team] gave her some IV Demerol [to aid] her comfort. Imagine not having any med for a procedure that [the doctors] willingly give you meds for after enduring it!

On the way home, the 3rd floor BMT unit called, saying that the fluid sample looked good and seemed clean. [Anna's samples] had indications nothing [was] in her fluid! This was excellent news, but in my mind, the whole day was unnecessary. We still will wait on the final results [regarding] the fluid, which will come in a few more days. [The team], also, will have to schedule the remaining body MRI scans. So far, we got the same news last week from the other members of the team. I guess some physicians need to see for themselves so they can feel better, never mind how the patient feels about things. Go figure...

Chris

* * *

2-25-11

Folks,

Today the girls had to go into UAB to get the [remaining] results of yesterday's full body scan. The results are excellent and show no lingering leukemia. Therefore, there is no impediment to beginning the transplant. Also on the agenda was to get the first of a series of three shots and sign consent forms allowing UAB to do the transplant. However, in order to sign the forms, the patient always has to endure a horrible and merciless conversation with at least one member of the transplant team who, most likely due to previous litigation experiences, feels it a good thing to inform you of every negative and life-challenging aspect of what Anna will go through, even though she has been through it firsthand already. Needless to say, it was last year, and it was again today, heart-wrenching and sobering for the girls to hear. Psychologically, it has to be the worst possible way to start an already difficult and physically demanding procedure. Yet, they insist on putting Anna and Pam through it with all manner of flair and negativity.

They arrived at UAB at 11:30 and, at this writing at 5:30, they are still there due to having to wait on the doctor's availability to deliver the lovely news and because Anna had to have other tests and procedures done because she had a fever of 100.3 upon arrival today. They are trying to figure that out and test for various things before they will let her go home. The girls have not eaten, and they seem stunned, saying [their emotional state is] a 10 on the high anxiety scale, which is saying quite a lot since we have had much experience with high anxiety days.

While this is the last weekend the girls will be at home before they move into the hospital next Wednesday, they still have to go back to UAB every day for shots, including tomorrow and Sunday. There will be the Hickman surgery on Monday, outpatient chemo on Tuesday, and then move-in and chemo continuation on Wednesday—therefore, [this struggle] really has begun, they will just sleep at home until Wednesday. Today's verbal and emotional beat-down slams us all back into fighting mode, ready for war again against the known and the unknown. The tension and the mammoth hole in your chest return as an ever-constant companion until they walk back into the house for good.

We have all been through this before. It will be no easier this time, as a matter of fact it may be even harder. Like it or not, ready, or not, we are there, whether they have moved in or not.

Sigh,
Chris

* * *

2-26-11

Folks,

After a roundtrip to UAB for the second of Anna's pretransplant shots, UAB called her around 5:00 pm telling her to come back now to the hospital and check in. The blood work and blood cultures that had been done on Friday came back indicating a serious infection in her blood that required hospitalization immediately if her transplant schedule is to be kept in its current form. Apparently, her Hickman catheter has become infected, or so they think.

We arrived at the hospital around 6:30 pm, checked in to the BMT unit on the 3rd floor, room 356, and [the medical team] will take out her current Hickman tonight, start her on IV antibiotics via a regular arm IV and see how quickly they get her infection under control. There will be a tight window of time to work with before this postpones the transplant schedule. So we have entered the hospital a few days early.

Here we go…

Chris

*   *   *

2-27-11

Folks,

Anna has been pumped full of antibiotics today in an attempt to "sterilize her blood" of gram-negative infection in time to keep the transplant on schedule. They removed her Hickman port last night, inserted a regular arm IV, and are doing blood cultures each day. The results of the blood cultures, which the doctors are basing [Anna's] transplant timing on, are 24 hours old. They want to keep things on track but if it takes longer to "sterilize her blood" the transplant will be postponed until the next available date. No one wants that to happen, and we do not really expect her blood to take longer to "sterilize" than [the time] given us.

Tomorrow, Anna will have her seventeenth bone marrow biopsy. Today she had an ultrasound of her kidneys. She feels and looks good, despite her condition, and she is in good spirits. Kevin has been able to be here this weekend and he makes for good medicine.

Chris

* * *

2-28-11

Folks,

Anna's physician indicated that she has sepsis, a serious blood infection that has delayed her transplant until they can get rid of her infection. The chain of events seems to be a bladder infection that got outside the bladder itself and spread throughout the blood system before the antibiotics for the bladder infection could completely kill it. This spreading is what is now called the sepsis. It [has the potential] for rapid expansion, and it requires extensive IV antibiotics, guided by blood cultures that identify which exact strains of bacteria exists, (gram-negative and gram-positive in her case) so that the correct antibiotics can be chosen for specific kills rather than broadband antibiotics.

The bone marrow biopsy, which was scheduled for today, was delayed until she is better as well. [Her] condition can be a major complication if it is not caught early, but they think they have found it early, just as it was getting active. It is just bad timing, we hope…

Chris

* * *

3-1-11

Folks,

Since many have asked, here is the mailing address for Anna and Pam at UAB.

Anna Gordon
West Pavilion BMT 3rd Floor
Room P356

UAB Hospital
619 19th Street S
Birmingham, AL 35249-0018

Good news—Anna's blood cultures have again come back negative, meaning no infection for the previous gram-negative and gram-positive bacteria that she had a few days ago. At this point, the doctors say her blood is "sterile." This is what we were hoping for.

The bad news—she has a mysterious bacterium that has never been seen at UAB before. Therefore, a team of 10 infectious disease physicians, along with the ID attending physician, are all on top of the situation and they are working on her problem. They have also sent her "bug" to the "state laboratory" for further investigation.

In the meantime, Anna has had much [high] temperature, last night and into today, topping out at 104.6 before descending to 102 mid-afternoon. She is having another ultrasound of her back and kidneys, and a CT scan. She is on three antibiotics and an anti-fungal which they will play around with, swapping up, until something works or until they get further direction from test results or the ID team and state lab.

This is strange and frustrating. Thanks for the concern.

Chris

* * *

3-2-11

Folks,

Anna is better today!!! The temperature is down to normal and has been all day, but her blood pressure remains low. The doctors are giving her some medications to help with the low blood pressure. The mysterious "bug" still has not been identified, but it "may" have been eradicated with the broadband antibiotics that she has been getting. So, if her temperature remains normal and the cultures remain normal, it will not matter what it was. Anna received a unit of blood today and she is feeling very tired after the last several days of being "wrung out" with the fevers.

Today, March 2nd, marks the 2nd anniversary of her battle with leukemia. She was diagnosed on that horrible day by Dr. Bobo of Emergi-Care in Tuscaloosa because a cold continued for six weeks. What a journey—for all of us.

Chris

* * *

3-3-11

Folks,

Today was a good day for Anna. She had no fever all day and night. Her blood cultures are good. She was given blood again today (she got a unit yesterday, also) because her red blood cell count was down. She remains on the three antibiotics, and she will be on them for two weeks, the infectious disease team says, making sure that they kill the mystery bug which still has not been identified. Dr. #3, her main bone marrow doctor, joked that they may name it "AGordonism," or some such name. I wish they would!

She has felt very "shaky" the last couple of days because she has been on a high-powered drug to help bring up her blood pressure. The drug has worked and today we found out that it is virtually adrenaline. No wonder it works. But it makes her shaky—and I mean she shakes, all through her body from her eyes to her toes.

This is not chills like in fever, but tremors, lasting a long while. They treat the shakes with Demerol, the same as the chills, but she has to endure a good amount of [the tremors] because too much Demerol hurts her kidneys, which are already suspect due to the antibiotics. So it is a balancing act. The real bad part of [taking] this drug is that she has to be connected to a heart monitor and "vitals" machines, taking [measurements] every fifteen minutes, around the clock. She cannot get into a comfortable position for relaxation or sleep this way.

In addition, because her Hickman was taken out, she only has a regular IV, now in both arms, to handle all manner of fluids being pumped into her that she requires; saline, three different antibiotics, blood, Benadryl, blood pressure med, etc. The poor child is wrapped in wires, with bags on the pole, going through holes not designed for this much traffic, plus blood pressure cuff and heart monitor wires. She has not slept well for a week, either from illness or now because of the [treatment].

We were told that the donor is still flexible and excited and willing at whatever point Anna is ready. So things are not impaired from a scheduling point of view. That's a good thing!

Chris

*　*　*

3-6-11 (a)

Folks,

Anna has improved a great deal over the last two days. The nurses have removed both of the IVs from her arms, so she has regained her freedom of movement! She remains on some oral medications, and they are watching her as more blood cultures return, [conveying] past information. She will receive a bone marrow biopsy today, the results of which will determine if she is still in remission. If so, the doctors will let her go home on Monday, more than likely, while they request a new schedule from the national bone marrow association, which contacts the donor. Hopefully, Anna will begin her transplant process within the next week or so. More specifics of the schedule will immerge in the next few days.

Chris

* * *

3-6-11 (b)

Folks,

Plans change. We got word that Anna would be released today from the hospital. So, we gathered quickly and packed the cars and moved her back home. The bone marrow biopsy will be Monday instead of today. This way, she and Kevin will have one day at home before he returns to Huntsville.

Kevin comes every weekend and this weekend he stayed with Anna at the hospital and let Pam go to a friend's house, Scott Tucker, to sleep in a real bed! Thank you, Scott. When Kevin arrived on Friday, he brought with him a "promise" ring. He is promising to replace it with an official one when Anna gets through all of these procedures and can return home for good. Anna promised to get through this and receive the real one! We promise to be there for it all, and I promise to report on it when it happens!

Pam got home and built a fire, and we are getting on with what is left of a nice weekend!

Chris

* * *

3-7-11

Folks,

Anna had the bone marrow biopsy today at UAB then returned home this afternoon, late. The initial reading of the marrow slide indicated that she is still in remission and thus the transplant can be officially scheduled, again. They called the national marrow association and requested the earliest of the six options they were given. Their wish has been relayed to the association and now they get in touch with the donor and wait to hear back from him. When word comes back, we will have a schedule made that is official.

More as it happens.

Chris

* * *

3-11-11

Folks,

Anna had surgery today to implant two Hickman ports into her neck veins. She was to go into surgery at 7:00 am and be out of the hospital by 12:00 noon. They arrived at the BMT at 7:00 and the nursing staff could not get an IV line into her arm. Four different nurses tried for an hour and a half. At 8:30, they still had not gotten an IV into her and so they sent her on to surgery in hopes that they could get one implanted. Since Anna was held up from going to surgery, [the surgery team] took another [patient] ahead of her who ended up taking four hours. Anna did not get taken into the operating room until 11:30. The single nurse in surgery needed only one attempt to get things handled. Again, a simple task takes a multitude [of people], and she suffers more than necessary.

Of course the back story for all her day was that she could not eat until after the surgery. So, she and Pam ate breakfast at PF Chang's around 4:30 pm. The first chemo will begin on Tuesday, March 15, with the move into the BMT on Wednesday, March 16, for continued chemotherapies. Transplant is scheduled for Thursday, March 24.

That is the latest…

Chris

*   *   *

3-15-11

Folks,

Today the journey to recovery began again. Anna went to UAB to begin the chemo treatment that will kill her native marrow in the next eight or nine days and plow the ground for the transplanting of new marrow and stem cells to take hold and grow within her. Today, they give her the first treatment and they monitor and measure her body's response to it every hour for eight hours, in order to determine the exact dosage of the chemo that will again be delivered to her over the next several days. This will kill her native system and she must receive a transplant at the end of this time in order to survive. It is a calculated gamble that the donor will remain safe and healthy and then follow through on harvest day of March 22nd or 23rd. Anna will receive his gift of marrow and stem cells on March 24th and begin the climb back to health.

Tomorrow, Wednesday, March 16, we will move Pam and Anna back into the BMT unit on the 3rd floor of UAB, an intensive care facility, for the next month or more. Here the struggle will again be played out, a combination of scientific achievement and personal character. These will combine with fate and lead us to what the future will bring. We pray for a positive outcome, and we recognize that the journey, even though the end is not completely sure, has begun.

Onward we go, together, one day a time…

Chris

* * *

3-16-11

Folks,

Today was move in day at UAB's BMT unit. We were given instructions to arrive at 1:00. At 5:00 pm they finally gave her a room and we finally got settled in and completed moving in by 7:00 pm. Hurry up and wait is the rule in this place. As of this writing, at 8:45 pm, they still have not located a bed for Pam. So far, there is only a recliner for her to sleep in. Thankfully, [the team] did not have anything planned medically for Anna today. Chemo resumes tomorrow.

Her address is:

Anna Gordon
West Pavilion BMT 3rd Floor
Room P322
UAB Hospital
619 19th Street South
Birmingham, AL 35249-0018

More tomorrow.

Chris

* * *

3-17-11

Folks,

Today Anna received two different chemo treatments as the plan calls for the use of two, in various combinations, throughout the ten-day period, before transplant on the 24th. This is powerful stuff, designed to kill her native marrow. It works. While [we] have a memory of the same procedure last year at this time, reality still is surprising.

The procedure is quiet with not much to tell. The nurse hangs a bag of poison, processes it through a pump that uniformly pushes its contents into Anna's chest. The more poison enters the body, the more her body reacts. At first you can tell nothing, then, after fifteen minutes, her chest becomes heavy, and her heart rate increases to an abnormal rate. She feels anxious and asks the nurse to check her vital signs. She tells the nurse that she is beginning to be nauseated and asks for some anti-nausea meds. By thirty minutes into the drip, Anna cannot get into a comfortable posi-tion. She flops around in her bed trying to get comfortable, covers on, covers off, on her side, flip—on her other side, sitting up, lying back down, and curling into a semi-fetal position. Just as the nurse returns with the medications that have finally come from the phar-macy, Anna sits up, asks for a bucket-type pan, and proceeds to be sick for the next twenty minutes. The nurse and Pam hold her, wash her, clean her up, change her sheets, and administer meds for nausea and anxiety. Finally the poison is finished. She relaxes as best she can for the next hour or two.

Later in the day, some nurses from the 9th floor, who have cared for Anna during previous UAB visits and heard that she is back in the hospital, come down to pay a visit and try to lighten her mood and day. Anna smiles and laughs and is grateful for the thoughtfulness of girls near her age that have personally taken Anna's condition and care into their lives. After their ten-minute stay comes to an end, Anna returns to the bed, watches a little basketball, then manages to feel a hunger pain. She requests Chinese food from a specific Birmingham restaurant. Now I get to contribute to the day in a tangible way. I leave and find the restaurant, order, and get [the food] back hot, as quickly as possible, while [Anna] still might have an appetite before it flits away. We all eat dinner and I leave, needing to go home to walk the dog.

Early on in this process, it is quiet, then intense, and then quiet again. Poison is inside her; each day more and more will enter her body. All of it will continue to kill cells. The more that goes in, the more death inside her there will be and the weaker she will become, taxing all her organs in the process. She knows this, we know this. Her job is to get through it and live through the process. This all may be quiet, but it is not calm for anyone in the room. The nurses know—that is why they come to offer support. We know, Anna knows.

It's hard work to chase hope—Hope is not for sissies!

Chris

*   *   *

3-18-11

Folks,

Today was fairly quiet. Anna slept most of the morning since she could not go to sleep until around 3:00 am. By the afternoon, she received several pretreatments for the upcoming chemo (three pretreatments to be exact). These are administered before the chemo to lessen the effects of poison going into the body, so that the body will not notice so readily and react poorly. Then the chemo started around 3:00 pm, only one brand today, but the one that made her sick yesterday. She was able to sleep through most of the chemo delivery, but in the last half hour, nausea came and caused her to be uncomfortable for an hour or so. Then Kevin arrived!

The positive effect Kevin has on Anna's mind and body is immediate. The nurse and I joked that he needed to be bottled and put in a mister marked "Eau de Kevin" so that the positive effects [he has on Anna] may linger long after he's gone. The nausea settled into something manageable as the evening wore on. Tomorrow, she will have the two separate treatments again.

Chris

*   *   *

3-20-11

Folks,

Anna received two different chemos yesterday and today. This double-barreled shot of poison has made her nauseous and sick to a greater degree during this transplant regimen than last year's version. She has been sick both days. On Saturday, the premeds wore off before the day's regimen was completed, contributing to her extensive sickness. Today, the nurses and physicians tinkered with the order and timing of the pretreatment delivery. It seemed to help, indicating that in cancer treatment, there is a degree of "art" in the practice of medicine. There is only one more day of chemotherapy. It, too, will be a double-barrel day. There will be two full days of rest from any chemotherapy on Tuesday and Wednesday before Thursday's transplant.

She will need it…

Chris

*   *   *

3-21-11

Folks,

Today was the last day of chemotherapy given to Anna for the purpose of killing her native marrow and blood system. There will be two days of rest from chemical activity, Tuesday and Wednesday, with the marrow transplant delivered and given to Anna on Thursday. Again, Anna was nauseous and sick. The medical staff is trying to figure out combinations of medications that will take her nausea away and make her feel more human. This stuff is just toxic.

In addition to the chemotherapies that have been used, Anna also has received two of three doses of antibodies harvested from a rabbit, called "bunny gam." She has one more day of this and she will receive it on Tuesday. It, too, makes her sick and she has developed rashes and skin reactions from this treatment. They try to pretreat Anna with Benadryl, but it still has shown up [in the form of] reactions on her skin. All in all, these have been some rough days, physically. Emotionally, Anna is in pretty good shape. She is strong and motivated. Sleep has been hard to get over the last few days and last night was no different. I hope the girls get some isolated and consistent rest during this night, rather than one-hour naps that get interrupted continuously.

Transplant is soon!

Chris

* * *

3-22-11

A day of prayer, Folks,

Today was a day of rest from chemo for Anna, although they did give her the last of the "bunny gam" antibodies. Anna was still sick today, in the morning, but got better as far as suffering from nausea as the day progressed. The doctors have been very active in trying various combinations of medications, and their dosages and timings of delivery, in the attempt to battle the nausea. They genuinely wish to relieve [Anna's] nausea and make her more comfortable. Their efforts seemed to be somewhat successful, as she has been less sick in total today than any other day so far. It may be simply that there was no chemo today, but regardless, we are thankful for the reason. Tomorrow Anna will be given no chemo or "bunny gam" and fully enjoy another day of rest from sick-causing treatments. Thursday will be the transplant day.

Our hearts were warmed yesterday when we received an email notification that the church where I served as Minister of Music for almost six years, Fayette First United Methodist Church, is planning to have a day of prayer for Anna. They and other churches did this same thing last year on her transplant day. We are grateful for caring people who continue to support Anna and our whole family with their prayers, good wishes, positive energy, resources, and talents as they attempt to do whatever they can to bring comfort, relieve worry, raise money, or see that we are fed. I received word that my old Sunday School class at that same church, as well as my school's student ministry, are partnering to have a fund raiser on April 2nd, by sponsoring a concert of a local rock band, C+, for Anna's fund. C+ is a terrific band of local musicians in Fayette, all of whom are giving of themselves and their time and talent for her benefit.

The goodness of people abounds, and we are honored to be on the receiving end of their thoughts and actions.

Chris

*   *   *

3-23-11

Folks,

Tomorrow is the day, transplant day, Anna Gordon's 3rd birthday! It has come because a generous, thoughtful donor, decided to be helpful, marking the second person to which he has donated. It will mark the second time Anna has battled through the effects of an enormous amount of toxic liquid administered into her body over a two-year time period. She has endured the internal ravages of those liquids and fought the doubt and negativity it brings to her mind.

She has earned this birthday, and it has arrived with many party goers not attending; but they have sent their gifts of love and support for longer than she can count. All of us, everyone, will be blowing horns, throwing streamers, and eating our own symbolic piece of cake!

She is so weak, has felt so bad, and suffered so much just to get to this point over the last few days. It is no time to have a party, but it is essential to have it now. She will, in return, as her birthday present, only be given the opportunity to, in this desperate state, begin the fight to regain her health, one day at a time over the next several months, working each day in the hope of [again] building a future life [for herself]. We all will watch her walk toward hope.

In the end, though, we can only watch, and it will be she alone who will do the walking. While we all are walking with her, we [each] have our future [ahead of us], and we have [already] determined them. She is walking for hers and I am so glad she will have much company on her trip!

Thank you for your "presents" and your presence at this party; but do not forget to bring your walking shoes!!!

Chris

*   *   *

3-24-11

Folks,

Wow, what a day! Anxiety started the night before. Neither Anna nor Pam slept much. Anna had a headache that lasted about twenty hours, from last night through early evening today. The pain was so severe that, after trying many pain relievers, morphine did not even stop it. Her heart rate was high, and her blood pressure was almost double normal. I guess memories of last year's transplant process and some difficult moments kept going through her head. Also, when morning came, a favorite nurse, who had told them she was assigned to be Anna's nurse during the transplant, was nowhere to be seen and on this most important day Anna was assigned a nurse she had never met or seen.

Regardless of the [inauspicious] beginning, by 1:00 pm the pre-treatments for the transplant began and by 2:00 pm the nurse was hanging the bag of stem cells and marrow. Nerves combined with many hard drug combinations for nausea and pain mixed enough to make her sick briefly during the transplant. But, after 3:00 pm the bag was empty, and relief set into Anna's face and countenance.

She began to relax, the headache subsided, and her hunger returned, along with the desire to sleep. I hope the girls do sleep, deep and restful.

I thank all of our party guests, both those present (the nurses, Kevin, Pam, and I) as well as the hundreds of guests who wanted to be here. It was a horrible, terrific, wonderful, scary, GREAT day. There will be much bad yet to come, some of the bad will be quite soon, as it gets worse before it gets any better. But hope has been acquired, arrived, and now safely placed within her. Now we will see where we go.

Pass another piece of cake, please…

Chris

* * *

3-25-11

Folks,

Today has been difficult. Anna's massive headache returned, forcing the doctors to go digging and find out its cause. They did a CT scan, but results showed nothing. She has lost some motor skills in her hands and general muscle dexterity, causing her to feel unstable when she moves around and causing some mental and emotional anxiety as well. The doctors think so far that it is chemo-related but have not found relief for it as yet.

Anna has received loads of fluids, pain medications, and anti-nausea meds, and all of these have caused or created an environment where she has been sick all day. She has eaten nothing; she received vitamin K shots in her stomach, which will help her blood to clot as she is low in platelets. Tonight, she will have an IV feeding tube put in to help with her nutrition.

Last night was a much better night of sleep for both girls. I wish them another good night, but until the headache recedes, and its cause is identified and fixed, nothing will be good.

Chris

*   *   *

3-26-11

Folks,

Today Anna slept. She slept as long as possible, getting up only to take a shower, her first in three days. She is sleeping to avoid pain, pain from her headache which has lasted for four straight days at an intense level. The doctor thinks that her headache may be a side effect of cyclosporine, a drug used during anti-rejection efforts. So, she has switched Anna to another anti-rejection medication in the same class as cyclosporine. She is also sleeping to avoid pain from her mouth and throat. This pain is from the fastest growing cells in her digestive area being killed by the chemotherapies. This is one of the most dangerous effects of the treatment because patients cannot eat well, or at all. Open sores are created in the tissues, causing intense pain and hampering diet, but they may also hinder breathing. It is because of this that patients often have to go on a ventilator. [Anna] avoided the ventilator last transplant, but only barely. Last night, Anna was put on an IV feeding tube so that as she has more and more difficulty eating, she will still have nutrition. She will receive twenty-four-hour feeding from this tube, and she has a current regimen of 1400 calories. It will be moved to 2000 calories in the next few days.

The precise problem [that Anna is experiencing] was [addressed] by Friday's CNN announcement that NASA has developed a device that uses special light techniques to foster fast cell growth,

easing the pain and time required for [certain] cancer patients
to grow cells in the digestive area. The light source and process
was developed [to allow] rapid cell growth by food plants, and for
use on astronauts in the space station, by minimizing cell loss in
zero gravity. The first clinical trials of this device for use in cancer
patients was just recently done at UAB, with Anna's current physician spearheading the clinical trial.

With his NASA connections, Kevin knew of [the] advance [in this
technique] before it was announced on CNN. And it was he who
questioned if it could be of use in Anna's case. We have asked for it
to be used and asked if the physician can find a unit around UAB;
as some may have been returned we think it will be used. Kevin
may be able to locate one for us if UAB can no longer find one. We
will see. Now is the time when it could be helpful, and every effort
will be made to locate one of these devices.

Even though Kevin returned for the weekend, Anna remains
asleep. This tells all of us just how bad she feels. As I said a day
or two ago, things will get worse before they get better. We are
descending into this area. Many things can become problems—
eating, breathing—and these are known events, likely without
complications, causing the doctors to try to analyze what is wrong.
Her headache was an unexpected complication that has given her
great misery. We KNOW that these new mouth and throat sores
will be a problem she must endure.

We need to "hunker down" for the storms that are coming. We are
all now at the center of the battle!

Chris

*   *   *

3-27-11

Folks,

Some good news: last night, Anna's headache went away! The doctors think it was a side effect of the cyclosporine, which they [then] changed to another drug and the headaches eased and went away. She has been without the headache all day today. The bad news is that last night, too, they put her on a pain pump. She is on the pain medication Dilaudid, a synthetic morphine that is four times stronger than morphine. [The Dilaudid] is housed within a pump that Anna can push to inject herself when she feels she needs it. This is to counter the pain of the sores that develop in her mouth, throat, and esophagus because of the chemotherapy.

The Dilaudid works but it sends her into high orbit. Anna talks in her sleep, mixes consciousness and unconsciousness without knowing which she is experiencing, and sleeps a lot. She scratches at her skin, even when unconscious, as a side effect of one of her medications. Most frustratingly, she has muscle spasms that resemble large twitches, causing her legs to hop around on their own or her hands to shake, another side effect of her medications. She is on a LOT of heavy-duty drugs.

She is passing into the dark days this week, [the torment of] which will be determined by the severity of her throat and mouth pain. We hope for endurance, patience, and relief as we pass under the rod of time that is normal for this phase of the process.

Chris

*   *   *

3-28-11

Folks,

Today Anna was told the results of yesterday's MRI, [which was performed to diagnose] the cause of the headache pain she had last week. We were told that the cyclosporine, which [the medical team] suspected yesterday, indeed caused changes in the white matter within her brain. These changes are directly responsible for Anna's severe four-day headache, as well as her current muscle and leg spasms. She had already been taken off cyclosporine, but neurologists came in today to join her treatment team for the moment, until the cyclosporine gets out of her system and her brain's white matter fixes itself.

Also, Dr. #1, as seen in the link and subsequent video, found the light machine used in the study [I mentioned], and he brought it into Anna's room and gave her the first light treatment for the faster regrowth of cells in the affected area. She will get three eighty-second light treatments, each day, until she is better. We are grateful to NASA for developing it, to UAB for agreeing to use it on her, and to Kevin for telling us about it.

Anna is still in great pain and the dosage of Dilaudid injected with each pump was doubled today. She has to endure this week to get better. So do we. It is getting harder.

Chris

* * *

3-29-11

Folks,

Anna has been unconscious for most of the day today as well. She received medications from the neurologists to help reverse the effects of the cyclosporine, but as yet nothing has changed with her muscle spasms. We hope time will reverse the brain tissue changes. Anna's nose has started to bleed due to low blood counts, platelets count, and other chemo effects. She received another light treatment today! She is still in enormous pain, and she controls a vacuum wand, similar to ones used in dentist offices, that suctions off dead cells and skin patches that flake off in her throat. They want nothing to get in the way of her breathing properly. She sleeps; Pam has not spoken to her until tonight, when Anna woke half-way to look at the doctor when she visited. She made eye contact with the doctor and spoke a sentence or two to her, but it is difficult for her to make herself understood at this point. She cannot swallow.

Because she woke and spoke just a little this evening, we think she has improved a very small bit today. It's a beginning, we'll take it...

Chris

✳   ✳   ✳

3-30-11

Folks,

Anna was awake and talking most of the day today, even if what she was saying demonstrates a much-drugged body and brain. She is extremely weak, barely able to walk and needs help to shower, sitting on a built-in bench there. She is very weak with shaky muscles. We take today's activity as a good sign in that she has been unconscious for the last several days. Also, she has been talking; we take this to mean that her throat is somewhat better since it must not hurt her to talk as much as she has today. Maybe the light treatment is working, maybe she is on so many drugs she cannot feel her throat, who knows. At least [the condition of] her mouth and throat have not dropped down to lower levels of healthiness today. We want to stay off the ventilator.

She received blood platelets today, her third so far since transplant. Her doctors want to keep her on [the current] level of pain meds, because days still to come will need them. They insist that her mental and conversational difficulties are pain-medication caused and that she will return to normal when they are removed. Kevin is coming tonight for a visit. The third light treatment was delayed until he could get here to observe it.

This transplant has been more difficult, with new things to deal with that the other did not have, and levels of pain medications that are far stronger than before. I think one of Pam's Facebook quotes yesterday says it best: "I hope she can't remember this, and I hope I can forget."

Chris

*   *   *

3-31-11

Folks,

Today, Anna slipped back into a drugged haze where she can only mumble occasionally in an attempt to communicate. Her throat and tongue are swollen, and her mouth sores keep her in constant misery; so, her medication dosage has been increased, again. This is causing her to go back to the darkness. This is part of the process, but worse this year. The doctors actually feel she is doing pretty well; she is just a very sick young lady.

They gave Anna a unit of blood today. They will give her some steroids to help with the mouth swelling, and she remains on many fluids and medications with which I cannot keep up. I hope they sleep well tonight.

Chris

* * *

4-3-11

Folks,

Anna has taken a turn for the better over the weekend! Last week was miserable for Anna and hard to watch for all of us. Anna's pain medication has been the Dilaudid, [which she took] from day one this time through the transplant, while last year, [the doctors] used only morphine. The Dilaudid piled up on itself over the last nine days; while being a good pain reliever, it was a horrible hallucinogen. Anna fought [imaginary] battles, saw imaginary images, and by Thursday or Friday of last week talked to people, almost exclusively, about events that did not occur. By Friday, Pam was so uncomfortable with Anna's mental state that she asked the doctors to take Anna off of Dilaudid and go, instead, with morphine exclusively, like they had done last year.

By the end of one day on morphine, Anna [had] responded with a clearer mental condition and sharper body movements. By Saturday, she was standing up and walking on her own to the restroom and shower, talking coherently and engaged with real conversations and activities. Her biting humor and quick wit are beginning to return, as well. Anna says, and the doctor this morning concurs, that her mouth sores are looking better, and Anna's self-proclaimed pain index is now in the mid-range rather than the extreme, as it has been since even Friday. All of this is rapid and dramatic improvement.

Kevin came for his weekend visit on Saturday afternoon and brought an immediate boost into the room. Good medicine. We have made a turn from fearful and apprehensive to hopeful and encouraged. This [episode] looks like something we remember and from here, we know the way home…

Chris

* * *

4-4-11

Folks,

Today started very poorly. During the night, the back of Anna's throat sloughed off in a big chunk of flesh and blood, causing immediate concern for her safety, as gushes of blood followed, pouring from the hole that was left. Pam indicated that [Anna] suctioned and spit up "buckets" of blood all night, into the morning, and to some degree, throughout the day. The blood pooled in her throat so she could not sleep. In the two periods of time where she did fall asleep, she had terrible nightmares.

Anna's pain levels have been better today, and she is mentally much clearer. She is sitting up and watching television, looking forward to the basketball championship tonight. But her breathing depends on her suction wand which is vital in that she cannot swallow. Thus all saliva, all blood, or tissue release has to be suctioned out of her mouth, keeping the airway clear. She does this with a plastic wand, resembling a dentist's vacuum, which is connected via a plastic tube to a vacuum attached to the wall. The nurses change out the tubing and the wand as it is needed.

Today, in the afternoon, Anna was to go for a CT scan, which would take a considerable amount of time [as she would have] to go, wait, then be still, etc. When they came to get her in a wheelchair, she had to be disconnected from the vacuum (because it is in the wall), causing her to panic, knowing she would soon not be able to breathe since [her throat and mouth] would be filled with things that get in the way, especially with her blood and throat issue today. She refused to go until they figured out a way to provide her with a vacuum suction. They had not thought about that, now they are.

All in all, despite the two difficulties and scary moments, she is making very good progress, feeling much better than she has during last week and this past weekend. The light therapy seems to be working very well, promoting healing and rapid regrowth of cells. However, the light can only be held next to her cheeks and throat. Passages of throat and chest that cannot be reached with the light are faring much less well. I hope for sleep for them both tonight.

Chris

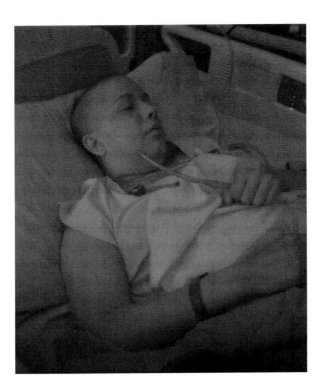

* * *

4-6-11

Folks,

On Tuesday, Anna bled so profusely from the hole created in her throat over the weekend, that it was necessary to give her two units of blood and two more units of platelets. She felt well enough to get up, walk around some, shower and go get the CT scan that she could not receive on Monday. The vacuum issue was worked out so that the only time she was without the vacuum pump used to suction her throat was on the way to and from the test.

Today, the CT scan revealed that Anna has pneumonia in her left lung. We were told that her liver and her kidneys were suffering under the current rates of filtration and their output levels were being closely watched and monitored. Her mouth bled all day today causing her to receive even more blood products today.

One step forward, two steps back. This is the way things are.

Chris

* * *

4-8-11

Folks,

I have not been able to come to UAB to see Anna and Pam since my trip on Tuesday afternoon because Tori has come down with an acute case of mononucleosis. She will be in bed for a week and possibly on a limited schedule for four to six weeks more. I am having to look after her health and needs while Pam and Anna have been self-sustaining these last two days. I did get to go up today and I saw a very sick girl.

She is losing her hair for the fifth time. Her eyes are jaundiced. Her mouth is too horrible and painful to describe. I do not see how anyone can bear the pain of it. Her liver and kidneys are distressed. They have called in a team of kidney doctors to oversee [the organs'] function and output. They are trying to avoid dialysis. Her hands and feet throb, burn, pulse, and need constant ointments to keep them from peeling, as they did last month, [from] the aftereffects of this new [round of] chemotherapy. She hurts everywhere, blurring in her mind what her body is telling her. The morphine does not stop her pain; it merely numbs her responses to it. Her poor hands shake as if she is chilled to the bone. She is under a warming blanket that is divine for her comfort, but she cannot sleep. She is on breathing treatments from a respiratory therapist for her pneumonia in her left lung and she received shots in her stomach of vitamin K. She has received six units of blood products in the last two days. She has had little or no sleep in the last thirty-six hours.

I have rarely seen someone in such agony, suffering so hard, trying to get better. She told me while Pam left to get something to eat and get out for a couple of hours, "Daddy, I am holding on from minute to minute." I believe her. I hold her and shake my head where she cannot see.

There is nothing I can do but be encouraging, recount how close she is to feeling better, and acknowledge her efforts to get out of bed, take a shower, change into new bed clothes, and start another day. It is one of the most poignant portraits of grace, courage, and inner strength I have ever seen. She has no alternative. She is willing herself to improve. It is painful to see, yet heroic to watch. I shake my head even now as I type this, recalling the look of her.

Sometimes I feel like Job, and I know how he felt when he asked God, "Why? When? How long?"

Sigh…

Chris

*   *   *

4-9-11

Folks,

Today was a horrendous day of tests and problems and bureaucracy. Anna received a CT scan of her lungs, an ultrasound of her liver, and had a chest X-ray. Her liver and kidney numbers are not improving, and her lungs seem to be worsening. She is sleep deprived and deeply confused, barely recognizing people. She has taken several steps backward in the last several days and no one seems to know why or has done enough things to cause her to turn back around to head in the right direction. Technical problems abounded today with many logistics having to be worked out satisfactorily just to get the three tests accomplished.

Again, a nurse stepped up, fought for her patient, and moved every possible stone to make sure her patient was cared for properly and in comfort. We cannot thank her enough for the fortitude and courage she has shown us over the last two days as our nurse. Nurses are God's hands and feet in the hospital, and we have been fortunate enough to have met several who have ministered to Anna and to us simply by caring and caring hard when it is necessary. I am proud to think that I teach future nurses and two of my former students have been Anna's nurse at different times throughout this two-year-plus journey. I must say they are among the best we have experienced, as well.

Kevin arrived this afternoon, allowing me time to take Pam out for an hour and a half to eat and talk and get away. He is a comfort and a positive help of selflessness. Things need to improve soon. Anna sees herself slipping back and she is beginning to be concerned for herself. We do not need fear to [rear] its head at this time.

Chris

*   *   *

4-10-11

Folks,

Today is a day of good and bad news for Anna. The good news is that her liver numbers are improved. The main good news is that her white blood cell counts have almost doubled overnight. This makes the fifth or sixth straight day of white cell growth. The more white cells she has, the better everything will be. In two or three days, she may feel much better and many of her conditions will improve.

The bad news is that her kidney numbers have continued to decline. She has kidney damage from the chemotherapy and her ability to filter her blood has been compromised for the moment and her blood stream is building up higher and higher levels of toxins. The team has been held off from doing anything for the last two days, hoping the numbers would level off and begin to improve. They have not yet done so. Therefore, tomorrow, Anna will go on dialysis in her room on a continuing basis, twenty-four hours a day. It is believed that it will only be needed for a few days, and [the doctors] think it will help her fluid retention, as she has gained twenty pounds of fluid over the last 27 days in the hospital, and it will clear her head as the toxins leave her body. She has returned to hallucinations and extreme confusions as her kidneys have declined. With the white counts coming up and the toxins being taken out, the next day or two should see dramatic improvement.

Additional bad news is that the CT scan of yesterday indicated that Anna has an inflammation of the colon, with a great deal of bacteria and blood from her internal bleeding over the last many days. The doctor has called for the most powerful antibiotic available on the planet to treat Anna's pneumonia and colon inflammation. She has to receive approval from the CDC, [the institution that] controls its usage nationally. These antibiotics will be critical to Anna's turn for the better.

The other bad news is that her physician [became] increasingly concerned about Anna's breathing as the day wore on today. The pneumonia is breaking up and affecting her breathing sounds. She may put Anna on the breathing ventilator tonight. I know this will not be a good thing for Anna to adapt to, especially since she is coughing so much right now. This could be a powder keg for Anna's psyche, which is not in good shape at the moment.

I feel that both the dialysis and the ventilator are temporary, and that Anna should show dramatic improvement within the next two or three days. She better [do so], there is not much lower she can fall.

Chris

* * *

4-11-11

Folks,

This morning Anna had surgery to implant another port into the upper neck area of her right side, so that dialysis could begin. She has gained almost forty pounds of fluid weight since she entered the hospital, seventeen pounds of which have been added in the last three days. By the time Anna arrived back in her room in the BMT ICU at 1:30 pm, the dialysis technician had brought in the machine, and they had it hooked up and running by 2:30. It will run continuously, twenty-four hours a day, and take off from her bloodstream a pound of fluid weight every two hours, so approximately twelve pounds of net fluid loss each day should occur.

Last night, mercifully, [the team] did not start a ventilator. It has been decided that as long as [Anna's] oxygen levels are good, we will push ahead. We all hope that the fluid will clear Anna's mind of confusion and toxic inspired hallucinations and that the white blood cell counts will continue to rise. Pam reports at 8:30 tonight that the kidney numbers are already trending downward [after] only six hours of dialysis! The white cells did double again during the day today, as well.

[The doctors] have [prescribed] another day of strong antibiotics for the colon inflammation and the pneumonia in her lung. We hope tomorrow will be upwards toward recovery in every way.

Chris

*　*　*

4-12-11

Folks,

Today saw some improvement in Anna's condition. There is an enormous amount of improvement to make, but she has begun to make it. The dialysis machine is taking off a net fluid amount of almost five liters during a twenty-four-hour day. She is in tremendous pain caused from the inflammation in her colon. The narcotics have contributed some to her colon problem, but they also have kept her pain at a level where she can sleep. She is getting good rest since the surgery of yesterday. She needs this concentrated sleep, and that is what is happening most today.

She is able to communicate better, even though the rate [of speech] is slow, and her voice is soft, and [her communication] is mostly motivated by pain, and the need for the adjustment of the situation or condition that inflicts it. We can tell that she [understands] the majority of what is going on, and she asks for clarification if she does not fully understand. We can recognize that it is Anna in there talking to us! Soft and slow as it may be, the fact that it is her personality that is speaking, this is a major improvement from the last several days. We look forward to her physical conditions improving to the degree that she can return to her former self in personality and in spirit. This will take several days, I think, but we have started down that path.

More as it happens...

Chris

*   *   *

4-14-11

Folks,

Today is another slow day of potential progress. The liver, kidneys, and bowel inflammation are still the three main problem areas. She is still half-delirious, still uncomfortable, and she still has pneumonia and its related cough, bacteria, and breathing issues. The good news is that her bowels are beginning to respond, slowly, the same is true with the kidneys, and the pneumonia. The liver is still bad, and its numbers may be increasing. Anna's movement is still a problem due to pain and delirium.

This week is a daily physical struggle for Anna and her caregivers. Pam, who tries to respond to almost constant physical demands, does not supervise as she should. She needs to allow the nurses to handle the load of physical procedures and care, while she can organize and instruct. She is going to hurt herself pulling and leaning over the bed rail hour after hour.

[Anna and Pam] do not sleep much. These are the hard days because Anna is suffering to a greater degree now, while also being somewhat improved. This stage needs to speed up, heading more to the next phase. But will it?

Chris

*   *   *

4-15-11

Folks,

This morning at 4:30 am, Anna was placed on a ventilator to aid in her breathing. She has been taking rapid breaths for four days, but her oxygen level remained good. Due to an increase in white blood cells, now over 5, these cavalry of infection fighters rushed to the area most infected, which was her lungs. The addition of those cells, and blood to the lungs, caused her oxygen rate to spiral downward, causing a breathing action similar to a mother who is nine months pregnant, panting with inefficient shallow breaths. In Anna's case, this condition occurred with the additional [impediment] of low oxygen transfer.

With the addition of the ventilator, [which] is considered life support, Anna's care has been transferred to a new team of doctors from the medical intensive care unit; she will remain under their primary care until she gets off the ventilator, which [is] as yet an unspecified length. This is for certain: Anna is in critical condition, fighting for her life right now. She still has liver damage, kidney damage, and continues on dialysis, and now has more lung and breathing issues.

[There is] further trouble: somewhere around 6:00 am, a round mass the size of a tennis ball arose in Anna's neck, near the line put in on Monday for use in the dialysis. Today's blood counts indicated a very low platelet level of 3, and the fear was that her vein was bleeding from the line used for the dialysis. They have been putting platelets into her all day trying to raise those rates, and they have packed her neck to hold pressure on the point of the bleeding. Only a few minutes ago, [the doctors] did an ultrasound of her neck to see if the hematoma was blood, or fluid, or what. They think it is not blood at all, nor fluid of any kind, but we have not heard from the radiologist yet to know what it is and what they will do about it. At least we do not expect her to bleed to death as we had feared earlier.

With today's ventilator, they have sedated Anna on a continual cycle, but not entirely, she can move her body but she is restrained in the bed from the waist up so she cannot move. Her hands are restrained to the bed, and her head [movement] is limited. Her body is a highway of tubes and wires, and the flailing around of the past few days is now over, due to the sedation. At least she is resting.

The good news in all of this is that as [the team] had her sedated, because of the placement of the breathing tube through her mouth and into her lungs, they went ahead and put a suction tube into her stomach, as well. It is now suctioning all of the mess that was in her belly up and out of her body, reducing the tight stomach area down to flat once again. This will make her feel much better when she recovers.

She must recover, but right now her body is failing her against her wishes. She has done her part and fought even through pain and suffering, but her organs are decreasing around her, and they need to rally, fast. This is what I know now.

Chris

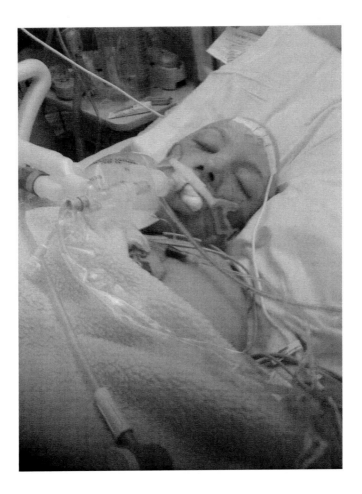

* * *

4-16-11

Folks,

Last night was bad. We all were devastated with a fast-paced bad day for Anna, and I must confess that I'm not feeling particularly positive about the day's events. By this morning's doctor's rounds, things changed for the positive. There are many things going on, each with side stories too numerous to get into here, but the gist of the doctors' discussion centered on why Anna got into this situation [where she needs a ventilator to breathe] and what the priorities were to get her out.

We came to understand this morning that in reality there is no pneumonia in her lungs as we had been told over the last several days. Instead, what she has are antibiotic-resistant E. coli bacteria that settled in her lung from some other area, either from her stomach, which was a problem for days as you recall, or from her throat. All the time in previous days she has been flailing around in the bed and panting, her body was trying to fight off the E. coli and its effects on her lungs, to no real success because she was on the wrong antibiotic.

They put her on the correct antibiotic when they got permission to use the very strongest antibiotic, which is safely guarded, but it had not had enough time to work on the lungs. For almost an entire week, Anna had been in distress and uncomfortable, as I reported here, with much physical movement, panting breaths, and coughing. This morning we were told her body simply wore out and got tired of fighting the E. coli bacteria. It was at that point that she and her tired body needed help in order to sustain itself and that is why they went to the ventilator, as her oxygen levels had dropped significantly by then.

Anna has slept peacefully and rested over the time she has been on the ventilator, giving her body some of the rest it needed to build up energy to fight again. Also, it provided two more days for the antibiotic to do its work. This morning they indicated that they were targeting Monday or Tuesday for her removal from the ventilator. By tonight's rounds, Anna's progress caused them to want to do a trial removal from the ventilator tonight! They will stop sedating her at 2:00 am tonight, gradually letting her come up on her own. They will then turn the ventilator off in the morning around 7:00 am, to see how well she can breathe on her own. It depends on how she responds as to what happens next. To me, it seems just like Anna Gordon to try and overachieve! Go Girl!! We will see…

Chris

* * *

4-17-11

Folks,

Today is the anniversary of Anna's first transplant. We are not sure it is a day we want to celebrate, but it is one we cannot forget.

This morning at 2:00 am the medical intensive care team gave the orders to lower Anna's sedation level so that she had the opportunity to come up to consciousness and focus on breathing completely on her own for two hours, as a trial of her ability to do so. At 7:00 am they turned the ventilator off, beginning the two-hour period. Anna rose up to a semi-conscious state, even opened her eyes and responded to questions with her head and hand motions. She did breathe on her own successfully throughout the trial period; however, she was more focused on her pains, discomforts, and limited freedoms, than on the breathing process itself. She indicated some irritation and distress during the process of the two hours, and everyone was relieved to see her more properly sedated when the trial period was completed. She rests when she is sedated properly, which is the point of why she was placed on the ventilator to start with.

The evaluation of the trial done by the intensive care team was excellent. They feel she did very well, and they will repeat the trial again tomorrow morning around the same time, and [define] additional parameters they wish to see. They say that they are very encouraged and at this point, they see her coming off the ventilator totally on Tuesday. Everyone is encouraged with this positive assessment. Anna likes getting "A's!"

Chris

*　*　*

4-18-11

Folks,

Today, Anna struggled more with the process of being on the machine. Unfortunately, to be calm on the machine requires considerable sedation to be able to allow yourself to tolerate a tube in your mouth going down to your lungs, as well as another tube going down to your stomach, and then having breathing treatments which force air and medicine down your throat four times a day, as well as other things to your stomach. She is still restrained at the hands and cannot move, except from the waist down.

Now to get off of the ventilator, she must be processing oxygen efficiently with her lungs, taking deep breaths, and most importantly taking slow breaths—less than twenty a minute is their goal. Now this is not difficult when you are sedated, but when you are conscious, with agitation, pain, irritation, anxiety, and downright fear—this is a large task.

Today, Anna was given no medication for pain for most of the day, since before 2:00 am. The doctors ran the two-hour test at 10:00 am, lasting until 12:00 pm. Without trivial details, there has been a continual parade of physical difficulties and emotional distractions throughout the morning and continuing through the test period, that caused Anna's breathing rate to be in the thirty- to forty- times-per -minute range, double the speed the doctors wanted to see.

This is the problem with trying to get off the ventilator—you must be willing to face anxiety and pain by controlling your breathing speed to twenty or less breaths per minute, to demonstrate you are healthy enough to handle breathing on your own. Yet, when they pull her off the machine for good, she will be able to have pain meds again, to make her comfortable while she continues on to address her other medical needs. The doctors designed for Anna to practice breathing in a real environment for almost twelve hours before they allowed her to have pain meds to a degree that brought some comfort. With this process in mind, you can see the frustration involved for her to do the practicing, experience the intensity of being calm while you are gagging and know it, and for all of us to watch. Practice makes perfect, we hope.

They will try again tomorrow morning. Tuesday was the predicted day all along, and we will see if Anna has built up enough endurance to pass the test!

Chris

*   *   *

4-19-11

Folks,

Today some realizations came to the Gordon household. One realization, at least for me, is that as a bone marrow transplant patient, Anna is going to have a more extended period of recovery from her current level of medical needs than we had hoped, including getting off the ventilator. I confess that I had no experience with a ventilator, and I knew nothing about how someone gets on or off of one. We hoped, as we were led to believe, that her breathing issues were recovering nicely and that she may only be on the ventilator for a few days, to let her body rest and regain strength so she could recover her ability to breathe and process oxygen. As a result, the doctors tried breathing trials each day, letting Anna breathe with little help from the ventilator, then no help at all. They did this again this morning. The results, as previously reported, show Anna improving in this area, but she is not ready yet to restore this skill now, although it may be soon. It will take longer, slower progress. This [experience] is much more common. Patients in her condition need time to heal and they get that time with the ventilator's help. Anna is making progress, real progress, but she needs more time on the ventilator just to restore her lung capacity. We need to slow down.

The next realization, again for me, is that Anna is very ill, critically ill, with complex and interrelated problems, caused by chemotherapy, associated with three [separate] regimens over two and a half years. This chemo is strong stuff, and it weakens organs such that they become susceptible to other medications that are used in healing, but these can tax the already fragile organ's ability to continue to work efficiently. These organs are interrelated, and they depend on each other. When one is overly encumbered, others are hurt. This is the nature of Anna's current conditions.

Today, the doctors called in a team of liver [specialists] because Anna's liver numbers continue to rise, and they need intervention. This team is looking at all the medications that Anna is currently using in all of her treatments, seeing which ones can have detrimental effects on her liver, again [an example of] medications used for healing having residual and unintended bad effects. Anna now has a bone marrow transplant team, a lung or pulmonary team, a kidney team, and now a liver team, overseen by a medical intensive care team. The bone marrow team, which is why she started this process, has to wait for the others to do their job, and restore Anna to them for transplant care again. The irony is that her transplant is going fine!

She is as ill as she can possibly be, and Pam, Tori, and I, as well as all of you, wait and watch. In writing these updates, often I have tried to edit, spin, or in any way make the story easier for all of you to read and digest. In doing that, I may be guilty of believing the brightest of scenarios. Anna is working hard. She is trying. She is also suffering, and she is weak. This does not mean she cannot recover; actually, in some ways, she is doing well. It means only that it will take more time than I imagined—or than any of us are emotionally prepared for. God help us, please!

Chris

*   *   *

4-21-11

Folks,

After much back and forth, at 1:30 this afternoon, Anna was taken off of the ventilator and is on her own completely. They removed her vent tube, her stomach tube, and they removed her hand and arm restrictions. She is calm and doing well. She even smiled briefly right after they did it.

We are all relieved and Pam said it was emotionally comparable to a birth, being in the room as things moved in the removal direction. She is now sleeping mid-afternoon and I hope she will continue [to sleep] throughout the evening. Her liver numbers have improved today as well, and she has lost twenty pounds of fluid weight as measured from her highest intake back a couple of weeks ago.

Things are trending in the right direction!!! THANKS BE TO GOD.

Chris

* * *

4-22-11

Folks,

Today was excellent and monumental in that Anna had a terrific night of rest and a very good day today as well. She was taken off of all oxygen, all masks, or facial obstructions. She continues to do very well in her pulmonary processes. The medical intensive care unit evaluated her this morning, and they were pleased. They turned her over to the bone marrow transplant physicians to continue her care from here. Anna received a swallow test this morning, which she passed, and she is now able to take liquid medications by mouth, as well as a liquid diet by mouth. She has not eaten anything in nearly a month, so this alone is an excellent improvement.

Dr. #3, the primary BMT doctor, indicates that the emphasis will now shift to getting her liver and kidneys back into shape. The liver has already begun to recover, having dropped ten points in the numbers that are considered. These have trended down for the last two days. Her bowels are doing well, and they have begun to eliminate antibiotics from her regimen of IVs. Anna is still confused but we are reassured that this is from toxins in the body and blood from the liver, and kidney damage. As these organs clear, so should her head and mind.

We celebrate this turnaround and we give thanks for the physicians for their skills, in spite of their shortcomings in consumer services. We are thankful for great nurses, who have shared and cared, well above the call of duty. They have worked with [all] their heart, and we are grateful. Further, we are grateful for all the prayer, the positive energy, the well wishes, and all of the concern that has been sent in our direction over the last many days. We walked close to the "valley of the shadow…" and we have made a turn toward the light!

Thank you for your support and your role in [getting us to] where we are right now!

Chris

*   *   *

4-23-11

Folks,

Anna has been taken off of all continuous pain medications at this point. She is able to have them on demand, but they are not [administered constantly] anymore. Her lung sounds are good, and they continue to improve. Her liver numbers look better, and they are slowly improving. We are still waiting for her kidneys to begin working again.

The doctors have slowed the dialysis machine's rate of fluid removal because Anna has lost thirty pounds of fluid, and fluid is now not a breathing problem for Anna. They want her kidneys to begin to work on their own. If the dialysis rate is high, the kidneys will feel no need to kick in again.

As [Anna] regains consciousness, she is more active, flipping and flopping again, requiring more supervision. We are waiting for her to want to eat again. All of this is new to us since this transplant is different. We do not know exactly what to expect but [the recovery] is likely to be slower.

Happy Easter!

Chris

*   *   *

4-25-11

Folks,

Anna was taken off of all monitors today. The only thing remaining attached to her is the dialysis machine leads and the lines to the ports. They are stopping another antibiotic today, so, that too means less fluids going in. We are still waiting for her kidneys to restart working.

Anna began a regimen of physical therapy today, mostly stretches and the like on the first day. The goal is to get her more active and up and walking since she has been in the bed for weeks on end. Her poor little body is frail and thin, having not eaten in a month or more, and not moved. Becoming more physical should help jump-start the kidneys. There has also been some discussion of cutting dialysis back to three days a week, so that her body will have to take up more of the load. The liver numbers are down to 13 from the 26 posted last week at this time.

All things are looking up and heading in the right direction!

Chris

*   *   *

5-1-11

Folks,

I have not written because I have not had internet since
Wednesday at 5:15, the moment the largest tornado outbreak
in US history came through the state and into my house. Yes, we
took a direct hit in the tornado that hit Tuscaloosa, and two trees
have entered my house. I am in the process of cleaning it out and
up. I have talked to my insurance adjuster, found a contractor to
rebuild, who is already been to the house and begun to measure
and estimate. I have had a mountain of volunteers, people I know
and people I have not known, many bringing chain saws, others
bringing ideas, supplies, and food. These people have helped
move, pack, clean, saw, tote, push, pull, lift, and give of themselves,
at a level that I could have only imagined. Because of all of their
caring and efforts, we are in as good a shape as we can be at the
moment. Life will be forever changed, and we will go day by day
from here.

Anna has had a difficult week of extreme diarrhea due to medications, and from her conditions. She has been given a liquid diet,
but she has not wanted to eat much all week. If she does not eat
soon, she will be placed on a stomach feeding tube which will go
through her nose to her stomach. The doctors have reduced [the
dosage of] a lot of steroids, backed off of some antibiotics, and
reduced much of what she was getting before. This has been done
in an attempt to make her liver better. The liver is somewhat better,
but she is now feeling well enough to feel absolutely miserable. Her
body aches, she is bruised, and she has been in the bed for forty-five days. Her kidneys have improved, some, but she is still on
dialysis, but at a reduced rate in hopes she will make her own urine
in greater amounts. Pam is tired and needs a break. Both girls are

finding it harder to be "up" in their attitudes. They need [to see] improvement now.

Still, there are others who are in difficult conditions as well and many who have been killed. Others have not had the help and love that we have been given and we are grateful to all of you for your support and love. These are hard times, but people are being terrific all over. In their efforts, there is hope.

Chris

* * *

On Wednesday, April 27, 2011, the state of Alabama experienced the largest tornado outbreak ever recorded. Sixty-two tornados dropped from the sky, causing a combined six hundred and ninety-one miles of track damage. Central Alabama, where Pam and I live, saw twenty-nine of those tornados race across the ground, in two waves. One of the most dangerous and dramatic of the tornados made a direct path to Tuscaloosa from the southwest, initiating in Greene County. It traveled the length of Tuscaloosa County then continued northeast into Jefferson County. Ultimately, the tornado arrived in Birmingham, Alabama's largest city, before it lifted back into the evening sky. The National Weather Service categorized it as an EF4 tornado, and its path stretched continuously for eighty and one-half miles. As a result of that one tornado, sixty-five fatalities and fifteen hundred injuries were recorded.

James Spann, the most trusted weatherman on Alabama television, always breaks into regular programming when the National Weather Service issues a tornado warning for locations within his station's broadcast area. On April 27, a warning occurred for Greene County at 4:43 p.m. Spann displayed video from a network of cameras mounted in various towns and cities; the cameras were pointed at the horizon. Most of the north-central Alabama viewing audience was riveted to their television screens as the weather event dominated local broadcasts that day. We watched a mammoth tornado track toward our location in Tuscaloosa, taking direct aim.

Our family was spread out in various locations. Pam and Anna were in the BMT ICU on the third floor of UAB Hospital. Tori was at work at The Woodlands, a large apartment complex located just behind Target. I was at home, alone with our dog and three cats. We all were watching James Spann, keeping abreast of the current weather situation playing out in the state. We could all see a half-mile-wide nightmare approaching. Spann was talking excitedly but using a tone of impending doom.

As the storm reached the I-359 corridor, making its entry into the city, we watched as power lines erupted into showers of electrical sparks, one after another. Suddenly, my television went black as most of the city lost power. We all knew the direction of the track. The tornado had been on the ground for thirty minutes already. If it remained on the ground and on its current path, the storm would pass through the southeastern heart of Tuscaloosa and continue on a course toward downtown Birmingham, with its many suburbs.

Our whole family was texting each other, making sure that we were in a safe location. I gathered our pets and moved to the only storm shelter in our house, a small centrally located bathroom on the bottom floor, farthest away from windows and doors. UAB was already moving patients to shelters in anticipation of the tornado's arrival. Pam texted that Anna's team was moving Anna into the hallway, away from the windows in her room. This meant that a host of nurses had to roll her bed through the doorway while simultaneously rolling all machines, pumps, IV poles, electrical cords, and tubes attached to Anna. Tori was also in the safest place at her work. She and I had to now wait out the emergency in the silence imposed by no electricity and no information, while Pam, Anna, and the staff at UAB continued to watch on television.

With the door closed, in the confined space of the "powder room," I sat on the lid of the toilet seat and waited with my nervous and confused animals. My family was scattered, my daughter was in a hospital in another city in desperate condition with her mother fearing for her, and for us. Now nature was wreaking havoc. Seconds felt like hours in that anxious silence. Then I heard it, initially faint, but slowly increasing in volume over the eternity of the next five minutes. Now a roar, my stomach knotted while I continued to wait, not knowing if I would be sucked through the roof or spared as the tornado passed me by. With the sound now deafening, and my anxiety at its highest level, I heard—I *felt*—a tremendous bang. The house shook from a huge weight. Glass broke, air whirled, spinning just on the other side of that bathroom door. I reached over to grab hold of the doorknob, pushing with all my might to keep it closed. At the same time, my other hand, on its own, rose into the air above my head, forming a defiant fist. I heard my own voice yelling into the terrible cacophony—""Why!" I was forced to listen as the roar took as much time to diminish as it had taken to crescendo. When I could no longer hear the roar, I stood up and opened the door.

I was overcome with the smell of broken trees, and I could feel the warm wet air still moving inside the house. I made my way in the direction of the blowing air, toward the living room. As I reached the foyer, to my left I saw the destroyed picture window containing mangled plates of glass, chards strewn over the entire floor. I could see two enormous trees uprooted, leaning on my roof and outer wall. I also saw limbs sticking through the picture window, perched inches above Pam's grand piano where she practiced and taught. Mixed with the smell of damp lumber was something more unusual, more immediately dangerous—the unmistakable smell of natural gas!

I managed to get the front door open, and I precariously walked onto the front porch, bowing underneath—and between—low-hanging tree limbs. I soon emerged on to the sidewalk leading to the street. I inched forward as far as I could before I could go no farther. I turned and looked back toward the front of the house and stared in disbelief. The scene I observed looked like something in a war zone. Two trees joined together by a combined trunk were *inside* my house. The ten-foot-diameter trunk of the two trees had blown over. The base—a hundred years of root growth, spreading downward and outward beneath the topsoil—was no match for the swirling 190-miles-per-hour winds of the EF4 tornado. The fallen trees had cut a huge gash through my roofline and sunk down six feet into my attic. The middle portion of the trees leaned their weight on the drooping roofline; the lowest branches rested, mid-air, inside my living room. The trees' enormous root ball flared up into the air, the trunk protruding from a flat layer of topsoil, angled forty-five degrees to the ground. Underneath the layer of topsoil, ripped roots dangled in a huge mass of mud. A hole, seven-feet deep and eight-feet across, was exposed where the tree had formerly stood as the centerpiece of my one-acre lot. I looked and counted eleven hundred-year-old oak trees covering my front and side yards, each with a hole and root ball configuration similar to that of the trees in my house. My house had survived intact—except for the damage created by the weight of two fused oak trees. And all I could smell outside was natural gas! I needed to investigate where the smell was coming from.

I walked to the side yard adjacent to the living room and heard a loud hissing sound. As I inched forward, toward the hissing, navigating the holes and strewn limbs of fallen trees, I discovered that the root ball of the tree that fell onto my house had pulled the gas line away from the gas meter. The line was askew, pointing skyward, venting pressurized natural gas into the air. As each minute passed, more gas was pouring into my neighborhood!

I backed away and continued to explore the back of my house. I saw that two trees were blocking my driveway, keeping me from moving my car, which remained untouched. I was trapped from leaving my house, and I knew that I could not stay in it: the sun would soon be setting. I pulled my phone out of my pocket and texted Pam: "We're Hit!" I could not make a call—I tried, but the call did not go through. I texted again, but this time the text did not go through either. Later, I learned that Pam received the first text, and she knew our house had been hit, but she could not call or text me, as all cell towers had been destroyed; there was no communication into or out of the area of Tuscaloosa where Pam and I lived. I was without communication. I could not leave my house, and I could not communicate with Tori, either. If Tori and I stayed in the house overnight, we would be sleeping in a house exposed to the elements, with no electricity, the food spoiling in the refrigerator and no way to cook it!

I walked back to the street and looked at my neighbors' properties. Trees were twisted and ripped from the ground as far as I could see. Those left standing were mangled and disfigured. But my house was the only one that had sustained major damage My immediate neighbor to the north did have a large tree limb fall onto his roof, but there was only one small hole.

Neighbors began to exit their houses and gather in the street. We gravitated to each other, making sure each was okay. All the while, we could smell the natural gas pouring from my meter's hose line. As we were talking, a police car slowly cruised through our neighborhood, inspecting the damage. I stopped the officer in the car, telling him of the gas leak and the danger it posed to the neighborhood. I also told him that I wanted to call the gas company and report the danger, but that no one had cell service. The officer radioed the gas company and notified the company's personnel to send a truck to cut the gas off from the street. Soon an Alabama Gas Company truck arrived and did just that, preventing a second disaster.

Then, within fifteen minutes of the gas company's arrival, I heard Tori's voice, screaming hysterically, "Daddy, Daddy!!" She was running down the long street our house was on. Police had already installed a barricade at the entrance to our neighborhood, preventing traffic from entering our Claymont subdivision from Veteran's Memorial Parkway. Tori could not get to our house by car, so she had parked on the street near the barricade then climbed out of her car and run the half-mile distance. I was standing in the front yard when I saw her turn the corner, heading toward our property. When she reached me we held each other, experiencing a surge of emotional relief. She saw the house and yard, and she burst into tears again. We were both shaken.

She had seen it, this mammoth tornado, pass directly in front of her. She was only two blocks from McFarland Boulevard, a main thoroughfare:

the tornado had tracked near the middle of the boulevard before turning. When the tornado tracked northeastward, it came within a block of the DCH Hospital and Cancer Center. As soon as it was safe to leave The Woodlands, Tori had gotten in her car and driven the mile and a half from her job to our neighborhood. But because the tornado's path had left a trail of strewn debris, the drive took almost twenty minutes. Tori was forced to take several detours because roads were impassable due to downed trees, downed power lines, and other structural debris.

In Birmingham, Pam and Anna were panicking because they could not get a call or text through to us in Tuscaloosa. Instead Pam called Holli Moss, our dear friend who lives in Gordo, twenty-eight miles to the west. Holli answered the phone, and Pam told her that our house had been hit and that there was no communication in or out of Tuscaloosa. Holli assured Pam that she would ask her husband, Harold, to drive over and check on us. You can imagine my shock when about forty-five minutes after Tori and I embraced each other in front of our house, up drives Harold Moss and his son Clint.

Somehow, Harold was able to navigate a route into Tuscaloosa from the west, approach my neighborhood, and bypass barricades. He parked his pick-up truck directly next to my house. To this day, I do not know how he got through. He and Clint got out of the truck, shook my hand, and assessed the situation. Without another word, Harold and Clint reached into the truck's bed and lifted out two chain saws. They cranked the engines then walked directly to the trees blocking my driveway, impeding my car's exit. Neither Moss stopped until the tree they were working on lay in small pieces. We cleared those pieces from the driveway, and I was free!

Harold and Clint loaded their truck and promised to give Pam a report telling her that Tori and I were fine. Just as quickly as they had arrived, they drove away.

The Mosses had heard a call for help. They immediately stopped what they were doing, got into their truck not knowing what they would encounter, and drove straight to me. They wasted no time relieving me of my problem, and they informed my wife of our safety, easing her anxiety. They chose to help without hesitation. Not only did they provide me freedom of movement while at the same time informing Pam of our situation when we ourselves could not, but also, because of their efforts, Tori and I were now able to travel to Anna's apartment, where we could safely spend the night in air-conditioned comfort. God was helping me, through the Mosses, in my time of need, allowing Harold and Clint to arrive at my house within ninety minutes of the worst disaster of my life.

Tori and I got into our cars and drove to her apartment, which was located on Helen Keller Boulevard. We wanted to see if she still had a place to live. Her apartment was within a few blocks of Alberta City, one of the most damaged areas in Tuscaloosa. We had to take a circuitous route to avoid all of the other damaged areas, but we managed to get through. After confirming that her complex had not been damaged, and that the apartment she shared with three other roommates was intact, we continued south on Helen Keller until we came to a barricade at the entrance to University Boulevard East. We parked on the side of the road and walked into Alberta City to view the damage. It was like nothing I had ever witnessed.

Alberta City was completely destroyed. The half-mile-wide tornado crossed McFarland Boulevard, leaving behind the destruction it had caused to the Forrest Lake neighborhood. It then plowed through the Highlands, destroying some of the most beautiful homes in the city. Then it continued east-northeast, along University Boulevard East, leveling everything in its path. It then took aim at Holt.

We walked in the middle of the street, observing damage to churches, businesses, a fire station. Then we noticed hundreds of people emerging from crushed houses, or from under rubble, walking out into the street. They were coming toward us. We saw people helping injured neighbors, holding, carrying, or pushing them toward the hospital a mile away. Most were dusty and dirty, others bloody, some not able to walk at all, but being carried. They were all heading toward the DCH's Emergency Room. It looked like a scene out of a war movie. Three days later, the president of the United States, Barack Obama, walked the very same path as Tori and I did that evening.

We had seen what we needed to see. It was time to go.

Tori and I returned to our cars and drove south to Anna's apartment at The Links. We were together, we had a roof over our heads, we were comfortable, and we had power!

The next morning, Thursday, I discovered that we had cell service. I called Pam to hear about the experience she and Anna had endured. She reported the scary, hurried actions of the nurses, who had been charged with moving the patients, even those in critical condition, into internal hallways, in preparation for the tornado's arrival. She told me that the tornado had shifted course slightly and missed their area of town. She talked of a night of high anxiety and little sleep. Anna was in bad shape.

After our conversation, I returned to our house to keep watch. It was damaged, and I wanted to be a hinderance to looters. Then it dawned on me that one-third of the city of Tuscaloosa was destroyed, including hundreds of damaged homes. It also occurred to me that local contractors would be swamped with work repairing homes for insurance claims…they would be backed up for months before any of them would be able to get to my house. Then I remembered Sammy Renfroe, a contractor who had been in my Sunday School class at Fayette First United Methodist Church. I knew his company was primarily engaged in commercial contracting, building hotels. But I took a risk and called him. He answered right away. I asked him if he would consider acting as the contractor to rebuild my house, even though I was sixty miles away. He readily agreed. Not only did he accept my proposal, but Sammy also showed up that afternoon with a crew. They immediately set to work tarping the holes and gouges in my roof. He wanted to keep the house dry, as more rain was predicted for that night.

When I got off of the phone with Sammy Renfroe, I called my insurance agent. My insurance agency is unknown to most people. Decades ago, my father, working as a principal in the Jefferson County School System, selected an Alabama Educators Association endorsed insurance company, American National Property and Casualty, as his insurer for our home and automobiles. When I became of age to drive and pay for my own auto policy, it was easy for me to continue with the same company. Now, decades later, I was still insured by ANPAC. When I called the claims number, I was given the name of my adjuster. I called him directly. He told me he had only three homes insured in Tuscaloosa, so he could be at my house the very next morning.

When Sammy and his crew arrived that afternoon to tarp the house, I told him of my conversation with the adjustor and his availability for the next morning. Sammy said he would be here at the same time, which would allow them to speak directly with each other. The next morning, Friday, both men appeared at my house at nine o'clock. Sammy had prepared a budget, which he gave to the adjustor. The adjustor walked into the house, looked through every room, surveying all the damage. Then we all walked back outside, and the adjuster said to both Sammy and me, "I see your estimate. It's a good one. But I am adding thirty thousand dollars to this total. We don't fix things. We're not going to patch anything. Since there is a crack in the ceiling of your master bedroom, I'm not going to patch it, I'm going to replace it completely. I don't want you calling me back in two years saying damage from this claim is recurring on its own. We are going to replace everything that is affected." Sammy and I looked at each other, and we both thought, "You don't hear *that* every day." I thanked Sammy for meeting with us, and he left.

The adjustor then took me over to the tree still wedged into my house and roof. He said, "We can't do anything until that tree is gone. Call whomever you have to call to get it removed so Sammy can begin. We'll cover the cost of tree removal." We shook hands, and then he left.

I realized that within thirty-six hours the universe had supplied me with a place to sleep, a contractor who was available and willing to help, an insurance adjustor who had already shown up, talked to my contractor, and increased the contractor's budget by thirty-thousand dollars, all of which had occurred despite the disaster my family and I were in. Standing in my ruined front yard I looked up to the sky and thanked God for providing what and who was needed to come to my aid.

My neighbor, who also had a small hole in his roof, had a father-in-law who was a commercial contractor living in North Alabama. That same morning he arrived with a trailer attached to his pick-up, which was hauling a small crane. He had come to remove the limb from the top of his son-in-law's house and to clean up the other fallen trees and debris in his yard. I watched as he removed the large branch from the roof. He was easily able to get the limb into the metal jaws at the end of the crane's arm. He lifted the limb and set it on the ground nearby. The idea occurred to me that I should ask him if he would like to make some unexpected money while he was here.

I told him my predicament and of the conversation with my insurance adjustor. I then asked him if he would come over and remove the tree from my house, so my contractor could begin his work. At first, he was hesitant, but then he seemed interested. I called my adjustor on the phone, told him I had a person who was interested, and I handed my phone to the man with the crane. I let them talk and negotiate a figure. When he finished talking, he handed me back my phone, cranked up his crane again, and drove over to my front yard. Within an hour, the tree was removed from my house. Sammy's crew was due to start work the next morning!

That same morning, I told my neighbors, who had gathered in the street to watch the tree be removed from my house, that my construction crew was scheduled to arrive at 10:00 a.m. the next day. I told them of the damaged areas, including the living room picture window and floor, and the master bedroom's ceiling, bathroom, and closet. Hearing that I was going home to begin to remove items from those rooms and relocate them out of the way of construction, my neighbors decided to follow me home. They entered after me and followed me to the master bedroom upstairs, where we formed a bucket brigade. I selected an item from my closet and passed it to the person next to me, who then went to a location on the other side of the house unaffected by damage, laid it down, and returned to the back of the line, waiting there to carry another load. Everything had to go: clothes, shoes, jewelry, drawers, bedding, furniture—everything. We did not stop until the affected area was empty and ready for repair. Sammy and Debbie Watson, Tom and Sharon Hale, and Marilee Brown-Wells had stopped what they were doing and worked for almost three hours in the heat of midday! I had not asked them for help. They just helped! When they left to go back to their homes, I shook my head in wonder and disbelief.

The next day was Saturday. I arrived at my house to work inside, cleaning up as best I could. Unexpectedly, I heard voices and noises coming from the side yard below me. I looked out and saw several young people gathering, talking excitedly as others continued to arrive. I had no idea who these people were or what they wanted from me. I descended the stairs and went outside through the front door. I approached the closest person to me and inquired what was going on. The young man introduced himself, told me they were athletes from the University of Alabama, and that they had been sent out from the Athletic Department to go into the community and help whomever they could find.

Twenty young people were now gathered in my front yard. They walked from the university, two miles away, into the heart of Alberta City and its surrounding neighborhoods. My house was the first one the group saw with damage, so they stopped. They did not ask my permission. They just informed me as to who they were and why they were there, and they began to organize themselves. Before my conversation had even concluded, they had already begun cutting the remaining trees with the chain saws they brought with them. They were members of various sporting teams: ten young men and ten young women, including one woman who walked with artificial limbs below each knee joint. She was a member of the wheelchair basketball team. All of them began lifting and carrying armloads of tree branches, cut logs, and debris to the street where the city of Tuscaloosa would pick them up and haul them away. I told them they did not have to do that. They informed me that they wanted to, and that Coach Saban had spearheaded the effort to inspire the student-athletes of the University of Alabama to give back to the community. Again, I watched in awe and utter appreciation for these students, whose homes were in other places, far away; yet they were out walking the streets of Tuscaloosa, looking for ways to help those they did not even know! The Universe strikes again!

* * *

Chapter 12

5-2-11

Folks,

Anna is more "responsive" today. That means she is more aware, awake, and willing to talk. She still did not eat. She received platelets and tomorrow they will do a colon biopsy to pinpoint what her problem is. [The doctors] will look for the beginning of graft versus host disease, GVHD. When they determine the results, they will make a final decision regarding [Anna's] diet and nutrition.

On the home front, the trees are now off of the house, although more damage was caused in extracting them. This was not unforeseen. Sammy Renfroe, my contractor, brought a crew to tarp and close all exposed holes in the event it rains tonight, and he will begin working in earnest in a few days [once] he has worked out the final plan.

This is all we can do at this point.

Chris

*   *   *

5-3-11

Folks,

Anna was more alert today and she was diagnosed with "C diff," a virus that attacks the colon. This is the cause of her diarrhea problems over the last week rather than GVHD. This also means that she can be treated with medications that are common for this problem and there is no need to do a colon biopsy as had been discussed yesterday. She managed to try and eat today, drinking some amount of juices, Ensure, water, and some spoonfuls of spaghetti for dinner this evening. We hope that this eating [pattern] continues, especially when the medications to calm the colon may allow her appetite and desire for food to return. Decisions [regarding] her feeding tubes have been delayed.

Sammy Renfroe, our rebuilding contractor, henceforth referred to as Sammy, and his crew managed to finish tarping the last of our house early today. Because of their efforts and hustle, water was kept out of the house on this rainy day.

We roll along and along…

Chris

*   *   *

5-5-11

Folks,

Finally, after waiting all day, we had a discussion with the doctor about the feeding tube. [The doctors] attempted [to insert the feeding tube] last night but it was unsuccessful. At 5:30 pm the tube was successfully placed into her stomach. They will begin to feed her when they can take an X-ray to make sure it is past her stomach and placed into her colon. This is done to avoid any regurgitation that may be attempted; nothing would be in the stomach to come up.

She is still battling the blood infection, C. diff in her colon, and a virus that may be holding down her white cell counts, which are now below one. We hope that nutrition will begin to make her feel better. Today is three weeks without any nutrition.

We need for things to turn around, she is miserable.

Chris

*   *   *

5-6-11

Folks,

Last night Anna had some distress and she awakened Pam, who discovered that Anna's respiration rate was high with oxygen saturation low, her blood pressure was dangerously low, and her heart rate was high. Pam called the nurses, who all came in the room, and the doctor was called as well. While there was much confusion, Pam suggested that Anna was dehydrated, and that the dialysis machine had siphoned off too much fluid. As it turned out, that is exactly what happened.

The doctor agreed [with Pam] and called for a bolus of fluids to be put in Anna's line. Like magic, her body retreated back into calm and normality over the next half hour. She slept for another two or three hours then had an additional spell, and more fluids were given to her. Her body returned to normal again. In the meantime, Anna pulled the feeding tube, placed last night, halfway out. It was repositioned again this morning by a GI doctor. Anna resumed being fed this afternoon on a continuous flow.

[The doctors] are changing her antibiotics to readdress her lungs, blood infection and virus. Her kidneys are the same, and we have not seen her liver numbers today. She is back on pain medications as needed.

We will celebrate Mother's Day this weekend as best we can, but for tonight, Pam will settle for a decent night's sleep.

Chris

* * *

5-9-11

Folks,

Pam called me at 8:15 on Mother's Day to say, "You need to get here, now." Of course I got in the car and drove to Birmingham immediately to find Anna surrounded by a throng of physicians. After a good night of rest on Saturday night, Anna's blood pressure [began to drop], and with it went her oxygen levels, heart rate, and breathing speed, all [tumbling in] different directions. It was decided that she needed to be placed back on the ventilator, and thus [I found] the "Gold Team" of the Medical Intensive Care Unit in full throttle when I arrived.

After many procedures, tests, X-rays, etc. it was determined that Anna was suffering from three different problems, each deadly serious in their own right. She has a bacterial blood infection that is very bad and getting worse even though it is being treated aggressively with antibiotics. She also has a virus, and she has the pneumonia. Because of all three conditions multiplying simultaneously, her blood is septic, and she has a dangerous degree of acidosis, or her blood is out of pH balance with far too much [acidicity] than is good for her.

The doctors are fighting with everything in their power. After he finished a procedure and while making his exit, one young doctor looked at her door, on which hangs a poster of Anna's photographs from happier times, and he broke down emotionally as he left. Everyone here loves Anna. She creates a positive bond with each person who comes in contact with her. She always has, from the day she was born. Every doctor and every nurse is moving heaven and earth to keep Anna going, but we have been told that despite all their efforts, her condition is too grave, and she is too sick, in their estimation, for her to recover. They told us that it is only a matter of time before her body will give out, possibly in the next 48 hours. Twenty-four of those precious hours have almost gone already. We begin the second day this morning.

Anna has fought all of Mother's Day and failed to fade away. She rallied after midnight and remained relatively stable most of the evening. At this writing, 5:00 am, her oxygen levels are beginning to fall and the balance of fluids, blood pressure, oxygen, heart rate, etc., will do a dance again today. We are here, holding her hand, talking to her. She responds in her eyes, her hands, she knows we are there. She may recover, her awareness is a good sign, but the adversary is imposing.

We have been waiting and praying, watching for whatever comes next. She deserves to rest and not suffer anymore…

Chris

*   *   *

5-10-11

Folks,

Anna Gordon passed away at 10:02 pm, Monday evening, May 9th. It was a difficult passage, but she was surrounded by loving family and friends until the end. She is at peace, and she is released from the struggle that was put upon her. She bore a ravaging disease with grace and with elegance, battling for dignity until the very end.

Her arrangements are:

Funeral will be held at Tuscaloosa Memorial Chapel on Thursday, May 12, at 11:00 am with graveside service following at Tuscaloosa Memorial Park. Visitation will also be at Tuscaloosa Memorial Chapel on Wednesday evening May 11, from 6:00 until 8:00 pm.

Anna specifically requested a few weeks ago that we create a scholarship in her name and memory. Dr. Witt has helped to set this up, and anyone wishing to contribute to the scholarship in lieu of flowers will be honoring Anna's life and love of learning in perpetuity and at the same time assisting a young person pursuing their college degree. Memorial gifts should be made to the Anna E. Gordon Memorial Endowed Scholarship, P. O. Box 870122, Tuscaloosa, AL 35487-0122.

We are humbled and honored that you have chosen to invest your time, emotions, resources, and spirit in following our journey with Anna. While it came to a negative end, we trust that the journey was valuable for us all. We are thankful for her life and legacy, and we will forever be made better for having known her.

"Well done ..."

Chris

* * *

The Tuscaloosa News

GORDON, ANNA ELIZABETH

Anna Elizabeth Gordon, age 23, of Tuscaloosa, passed away May 9, 2011. She was born in Fayette, AL in 1987. After living for a period in Columbus, MS, she relocated to Tuscaloosa with her family in 1994. She attended Tuscaloosa City Schools, and eventually graduated a Valedictorian at Northridge High School in 2005. She entered the University of Alabama and earned her Bachelor of Science degree with a double major in Psychology and Spanish, with a minor in Blount Studies, graduating summa cum laude in 2009. She was awarded entry into the honors organizations of Phi Beta Kappa, Golden Key, and a host of other scholastic honoraries. She received the inaugural Norman R. Ellis Endowed Scholarship from the Department of Psychology in 2008. She was awarded the Recognition for Academic Excellence by a Major in Psychology award in 2009. She also earned the Outstanding Senior Award from The Blount Undergraduate Initiative of the College of Arts and Sciences at the University of Alabama. While working toward her BS degree, Anna worked for three years as Resident Assistant at the Lakeside Community in its first year of existence, where she earned the Most Valuable Veteran as well as the Most Valuable Player awards. In the spring semester of her senior year, Anna was diagnosed with Acute Myeloid Leukemia. She battled through chemotherapy treatments to be able to enroll at the University of Georgia in Athens in the fall semester of 2009, studying higher education when she relapsed with her disease. She received a bone marrow transplant at UAB in April of 2010. She went into remission for a second time and was hired at The University of Alabama in August of 2010 as an Admissions

Counselor for Alumni and Volunteer Recruitment within the Office of Undergraduate Admissions at the University of Alabama. In December of 2010, she relapsed yet again and began her journey toward a second transplant at UAB in March 2011. Her journey ended in peace on May 9, 2011.

Survivors are her sister, Victoria K. Gordon; parents, Christopher P., and Pamela G. Gordon; uncles and aunts, John and Kay Daughtry and Stephen Gordon; and grandparents, Dr. Horace G. and Nadine Y. Gordon and Jean Guthrie. Funeral service will be held on Thursday, May 12, 2011, at 11:00 am at Tuscaloosa Memorial Chapel Funeral Home, with burial immediately following in Tuscaloosa Memorial Park, with the Rev. Kathy Griffith presiding. Pallbearers are Dr. Marcus Ashford, Thomas Furlough, Josh Kavanaugh, Dr. Robert McDonald, Dr. Chris O'Rear, Shane Porter, Nathan Smock, and Sammy Watson. Honorary Pallbearers are Dr. Phillip Bobo, Dr. John Dubay, DCH Cancer Center Nursing Staff, DCH Second Floor Nursing Staff, UAB Ninth Floor Nursing Staff, UAB Third Floor Bone Marrow Transplant Unit Nursing Staff, Scott Tucker, the Harold Moss Family, and the University of Georgia's CSAA 2011 Cohort. The Gordon Family would like to express appreciation for the help and support provided them by the following during this time—University of Alabama and Dr. Robert Witt, Bevill State Community College, Fayette First United Methodist Church, and the "Sunday Morning Live" Class of FFUMC. In lieu of flowers, memorial gifts should be made to the Anna E. Gordon Memorial Endowed Scholarship, P. O. Box 870122, Tuscaloosa, AL 35487-0122. Tuscaloosa Memorial Chapel directing.

* * *

5-9-2012

> *I find it hard to reflect on May 9th, 2011, without thinking about November 15th, 2009.*
>
> *We were working on our presentation at the last minute, which was typical for Mark and me, yet atypical for Anna. Sitting in that apartment, I remember feeling the weight of our project and the nerves stirring in my stomach. Anna wasn't feeling well, either. I kept telling her it was probably stress-related, or maybe the crushed red pepper flakes. She knew, though. It wasn't her stomach. It wasn't her nerves. It was something bigger.*
>
> *I remember the fear in her eyes and feeling the fever in her forehead. She excused herself to go to the bathroom, but I followed her a few seconds later. I found Anna on the floor, next to the toilet...and she was crying. At that moment, life became very real. My head was previously focused on CAS standards and PowerPoint slides. Yet, my heart led me to sit on the bathtub ledge next to her. And there we were: an innocent, beautiful, young girl facing leukemia...and a clueless friend, scared out of his mind, who didn't know what to do.*
>
> *There was nothing I could do to change what was happening. The only thing I could do was help her realize she wasn't alone. I placed my arm around her shoulder and sat there until she was done crying. That night changed everything. I may not have realized it then, but I certainly do now.*
>
> *Last year, when I got the news of Anna's passing, I fled. I drove straight to Athens to be with those who would help me remember that I was not the only one going through that moment. There was nothing anyone could do that night—nothing except take time to remember that, even in death, we are not alone.*

Life is not about pride, or homework, or making yourself look good, or deadlines, or hiding from the world, or even knowing the way. Life is about those moments when you are afraid and you don't know what to say, when you're unsure how to act and you can't predict what is about to happen. Life is about those moments that remind you that you're not alone, those moments when all you know to do is love. Life is about moments like November 15th and May 9th.

Sure, those nights brought horrible pain, tears, suffering, distress, loss, and feelings I wouldn't wish on another human being. But I would be lying if I said those nights didn't save me. Those nights reminded me that I am not alone...that Anna was not alone...that none of us are alone.

So, tomorrow, I encourage you to do whatever you need to do to remind yourself of that. Even though I will be in South Carolina, my heart will be with Anna and with my cohort tomorrow. I will wear my button for each of us in CSAAlidarity.

Never alone...Always 20.

—Alex Miller, CSAA 2011, UGA

(Text of email sent to me on the one-year anniversary of Anna Gordon's death. The words "Never alone...Always 20" refer to the number of students in Anna's cohort at the University of Georgia.)

* * *

Chapter 13

WHEN WE LEFT THE HOSPITAL ON THE NIGHT OF May 9, 2011, Pam, Tori, and I drove to Tuscaloosa to spend what was left of the night at Anna's apartment at The Links. This would be our home for the next six months or more. We were fortunate to have a place to go, given that our home was under reconstruction to repair the damage caused by the EF4 tornado on April 27, 2011. We arrived after midnight and spent a while just being together, mostly in silence, but not wanting to leave each other. Silence is what we often used as a default means of communication, as speaking felt as if it would confirm the reality of what had just happened. Nevertheless, our Anna, our firstborn, was gone. In silence, we spoke volumes. Eventually, we allowed ourselves to go to bed and sleep, suspended in our reality.

Sometime in the late morning, something closer to noon, I awoke and quietly exited the bedroom. I went into the kitchen and made a pot of coffee. When it had brewed, I took my cup and went outside to sit on the balcony at the patio table, overlooking a putting green, already filled with golf enthusiasts. The golfers were focused on their game and made little conversation. The quiet of the morning and the beauty of the scene afforded me the time and opportunity to stare into the distance. I was emotionally numb.

Eventually, Pam and then Tori woke and filled their cups. They joined me on the patio. So did our animals. Silence, still, was our form of conversation. The patio balcony became the place to think, to feel, to plan, and to grieve—all of which are perhaps best done in the inner cathedral of silence.

There was, however, the necessity of planning Anna's funeral, writing and submitting her obituary, and purchasing a gravesite, casket, vault, headstone, and footstone. We had none of these things. Death was not something we had planned on, yet. We knew it would come in time, but we had no idea that it would come so soon. We were unprepared.

Just before noon, there was a loud knock on the door. Pam and I looked at each other and confirmed simply by eye contact that we knew of no plans for visitors. Then the knock came again. We were dressed in our bed clothing and wore robes, but I answered the door expecting to see some close friend or family member, coming to grieve with us collectively. When I opened the door, however, I saw two men in their mid-thirties whom I did not recognize. They came into the apartment, and the older one began to speak.

"I am the manager of The Links," he said, "and it has come to my attention that the one whose name is on the lease has passed away. It is the policy of the company to lock the apartment at this time. I am here to inform you that you will have twenty-four hours to vacate this apartment. Also, you may take nothing with you except one change of clothing. I will return tomorrow at this time. I will lock the apartment and you may not reenter."

I was stunned. Not only was the man's demeanor rude and inconsiderate to our bereaved family, still mourning the deceased, but also, where would we go? I told the man, with increasing hysteria, that we were Anna's immediate family. We were grieving and we had no other place to go, as our home had been rendered uninhabitable by the tornado only eleven days earlier. I told him that Anna had a lease that extended until next August, and that we intended to honor her part of that lease. He said, "I'm sorry, but it is the policy of the company that [the vacating of the apartment] happens at the death of a lessee. I will return in twenty-four-hours." With that, he quickly exited.

My only instinct was to call my lawyer, Gar Blume, of the Blume & Blume law firm. Gar was my friend as well as my lawyer. I knew that if something could be done to stop the horrible injustice The Links' manager was about to inflict on us, it was Gar who could do it and do it fast!

I picked up my phone and dialed Gar's office. The secretary put me through. Gar picked up on one ring.

"Hi, Chris, what's wrong?

"Gar, Anna's apartment manager just came to kick us out of her apartment! He said that it is the company's policy to lock the apartment within twenty-four hours of a lessee's death. Gar, we have no place else to go! He's coming back at this time tomorrow to kick us out, and he says we can only take one change of clothes with us. I've already moved a lot of clothes from the house into [the apartment] because this is where we plan to stay until the house is repaired. All our stuff is here! Can you do something?"

"Give me his name and number!" Gar said.

I did.

"I'll look into it. I can't come there, I've got court most of the day today, but I'll call and talk to him."

I know Gar. He is passionate and persuasive. His main line of work is juvenile defense. He and I served on the board for the Parent Booster Club supporting Central High School's softball team. He and his family were as passionate about competitive softball as we were. His daughter, Rachel, was the same age as Anna, and she was Anna's catcher on the team. Gar's older son, Zach, was Anna's first boyfriend. We were very connected in each other's lives. If anyone could do anything about this problem, it was Gar Blume. We trusted he would take care of the problem, but we went on with our day. We had to make plans, quickly.

We dressed and made our way to the Tuscaloosa Memorial Funeral Home. The hours spent there were some of the most surreal I can remember. We had to purchase a plot. While we were doing it, we chose to go ahead and buy a plot for the entire family. They would be needed eventually. We also paid for embalming, paid for the opening and closing of the gravesite, bought a vault, a casket, and arranged to have Anna's funeral at the funeral home's chapel. Selecting a casket for your child is not something you are prepared for or expect to ever do. It was another emotional benchmark, making us very aware of the reality that we were now living.

We left the funeral home after completing the arrangements. We shopped for the clothes she would wear, another emotional hurdle. Mercifully, we quickly found something appropriate and returned to the apartment. When we arrived, we began working on the service itself. Pam planned the music and asked the faculty woodwind quartet at the University of Alabama to perform prelude music during the upcoming service. She selected two pieces of recorded music for use within the service: "Smile," a song composed by Charlie Chaplin, and "Over the Rainbow."

I wrote the obituary and sent it to the *Tuscaloosa News* and the *Birmingham News*. After discussing who Anna would have wanted to speak about her at her service, I set about writing emails to Dr. Joan Barth, Dr. Jennifer Jones, Dr. Robert McDonald, and Sammy Watson. All immediately agreed to deliver a eulogy. I then called Kathy Griffith, Associate Pastor, Fayette First United Methodist Church, and my friend, to inquire if she could officiate Anna's service. She, too, readily agreed. Anna would have been very pleased to have a woman officiate. Then, Pam and I selected pallbearers and honorary pallbearers. I sent emails to the pallbearers, asking if they would serve on May 12, 2011, for the funeral.

Then, I went to visit my parents, who lived at Capstone Village on the campus of the university. I ran into Ray Taylor, who was decorating for a function to be held there. Ray works for the President's Office, overseeing all necessary social events, hosted by the president of the University of Alabama. Longtime friends, I asked Ray if he would do the flowers for Anna's funeral. He accepted, and I purchased a blanket of flowers for the casket and requested Anna's favorite flowers, snap dragons, roses, and lilies.

The next day, Wednesday, just before eleven o'clock, the loud knock on the door returned. I opened the door, and the same manager walked in the apartment, but took only a few steps inside.

"I don't know who your lawyer is, but he's a bulldog! There was no need for you to call your lawyer" he said.

"You spoke to him then?" I asked.

"No, I was out of the office, but he left a message!" He smirked. "Anyway, you can stay."

He immediately turned and exited, never to be seen again.

* * *

The "visitation" was scheduled for Wednesday evening, May 11, from 6:00 to 8:00, for all those who wanted to express their support and condolences. We were not in great shape emotionally or physically, but we knew it was something we must do. We had to allow others to grieve with us. We dressed and drove to the funeral home early so we could spend some time alone with Anna's body. This was the first opportunity for us to view her body since we had left the hospital on May 9th. We wanted to see how she looked in the clothes we provided. We wanted to know if her visage would prove too shocking to allow the public to view her. The decision as to whether we wanted an open casket at the visitation and funeral had to be made.

The funeral home had done the best job they could. Still, there was no denying that our beautiful Anna had suffered, hard, during her struggle. There were visual reminders of just how much the cancer, the chemotherapy, and the treatments had altered her appearance. We decided that the opportunity to view her face, neck, and arms would not be too shocking. Rather, Anna's altered appearance was only moderately noticeable: her face no longer looked vibrant when compared to the large portrait we placed on display next to the casket.

The first person to enter the funeral home's chapel was Dr. Robert Witt. He arrived fifteen minutes before the top of the hour, when visitors were scheduled to begin arriving. He was on his way to a board of trustees meeting, but he wanted to visit with us before leaving town. Two days earlier, I had asked him to speak at Anna's funeral. He informed me that his presence was required at the meeting scheduled for the same day. Otherwise, he would be honored to speak. He suggested, instead, that we allow him to schedule a memorial for Anna, to be held on the university quadrangle, at Denny Chimes, when school returned for the fall semester. He wanted the opportunity to speak about Anna, then. Also, he told me that upon his return from the weekend, he would check his calendar and call me with a suggested date.

Dr. Witt spoke with each of us individually, Pam, Tori, and me. Then he made his way to the casket, touched Anna's hand, closed his eyes, and stood over her in silence. Then, he opened his eyes, backed away, and took his leave.

People began to arrive. They came from Tuscaloosa, Northport, Gordo, Fayette, Aliceville, Birmingham, Cullman, Huntsville, Muscle Shoals, Prattville, Columbus, MS, Nashville, TN, Athens, GA, Atlanta, GA, Pittsburgh, PA, Charlotte, NC, and Daytona Beach, FL. Our little family lined up across the front of the chapel, first me, then Tori, and finally Pam, closest to the casket. The idea was for people to greet each of us, one at a time, before viewing Anna. They could then find a seat in one of the chapel chairs or make their way down the center aisle. Before long, people were standing in line along the left-hand wall, then snaking back toward the chapel entrance. The line soon backed up into the lobby of the funeral home before backing up through the doors into the funeral home and down the sidewalk outside.

Tori, Pam, and I spoke to each person who came. But when the line was empty, it was almost 10:00 pm. It was wonderfully heartwarming and heart-wrenching at the same time. We were exhausted, physically and emotionally.

* * *

Celebration of the Life and Legacy of Anna Elizabeth Gordon
Rev. Kathy Griffith
Associate Pastor, Fayette First United Methodist Church
May 12, 2011

Words of Grace

The eternal God is our dwelling place, and underneath are the everlasting arms.

The Lord is near to the brokenhearted and saves the crushed in spirit.

The Lord heals the brokenhearted and binds up their wounds.

Great is our Lord, and abundant in power, whose understanding is beyond measure. [United Methodist Book of Worship]

Greeting

We have gathered this day to celebrate the life and legacy of Anna Elizabeth Gordon. We come together in grief acknowledging our human loss even as we celebrate and give thanks for her courageous and beautiful life. A life that was lived well! Twenty-three years of life lived to the fullest—full speed ahead, embracing the world, confronting the world, impacting the world and the lives of all those she encountered. Such beauty, such elegance, love, stamina, and grace! We seek to honor her wishes this day as we refrain from having a "funeral" for her but instead, we seek to celebrate her life.

At this time we recognize her strong and courageous family, no doubt a source of strength for Anna as they walked this beautiful and difficult journey of life alongside her. We pray God's comfort and blessing upon you during this hour and in the days ahead:

Anna Elizabeth Gordon,—born June 5, 1987, was preceded in death by her grandfather, Mr. Harry L. Guthrie. Survived by her Sister, Victoria K. Gordon; Parents, Christopher P. Gordon and Pamela G. Gordon; Grandparents, Dr. Horace G. and Mrs. Nadine Y. Gordon…and Grandmother Mrs. Jean

Guthrie. Uncles and Aunt—John and Kay Daughtry and Stephen Gordon. *May God grant us grace that in pain we may find comfort; in sorrow, hope; in death, resurrection!*

Let us pray—

O God, who gave us birth, you are ever more ready to hear than we are to pray.

You know our needs before we ask, and our ignorance in asking.

Give to us now your grace, that as we shrink before the mystery of death, we may see the light of eternity.

Speak to us once more your solemn message of life and of death.

Help us to live as those who are prepared to die. And when our days here are accomplished, enable us to die as those who go forth to live, so that living or dying, our life may be in you, and that nothing in life or in death will be able to separate us from your great love in Christ Jesus our Lord. Amen. [United Methodist Book of Worship]

As I reflect on Anna's life and the words of this historic prayer, I fully believe that Anna indeed embraced and lived this life as one who was prepared to die—not by making plans for this day, but by making plans to live. She was always looking forward, making plans for her future, continuing her education, making plans for marriage, and career, and how she might continue to impact our world. Living life completely and fully, she was not one to look back, but one who pressed on. In so doing, I believe that Anna was indeed given the grace to die as one who went forth to live. And her living and in her dying, God's grace was and is sufficient for her. God's grace remains sufficient for her because NOTHING in life or in death can separate her from God's love.

As we celebrate Anna's life today you will hear words of remembrance from different individuals who knew her from different perspectives—we'll hear from those who knew her growing up, those who knew her as a student, a colleague, friend, and neighbor. I did not know her from any of these perspectives. I did not know Anna personally; I only knew her through others. I had the privilege of serving on staff with Anna's daddy, Chris, at Fayette First Methodist, where he was our music director and where I continue to serve as associate pastor. Chris joined the Sunday Morning Live Sunday School class that I am privileged to teach. We could always count on a good discussion when you were present, Chris. I became acquainted with Anna through Chris and his daily briefings so wonderfully penned about Anna's life, her journey, her struggles, and the struggles of her family. And I am here to give witness to what an impact their life and journey has had on all those like me throughout our church and community—indeed throughout our world—who have been moved, who have been changed by having known Anna in this manner. Time and time again, I have witnessed the faith, the hope, the prayers, the outpouring of love in response to Anna's beautiful life!

Thanks to Anna, we have dealt with real life issues, we have struggled with and had deep conversations about the problem with pain in our world and the impact that has on our faith and our belief in a loving and merciful God. We have grown closer in our relationships with each other and with God. We have broken through the barriers and the facades of pretending all is well (because all was NOT well) and we have acknowledged our hurt, our pain, and our doubts...and through it all God's grace, His abiding love has been experienced on a deeper more intimate and more real level than many of us have ever experienced before. And through it all, the faith we profess became more than a profession—it was embodied in loving action. It became real!

Time will not permit me to explain the many ways Anna's grace-filled life has impacted so many of us, but I did want to share with you one of the times when our congregation's response was particularly inspiring. We have a prayer-shawl ministry, where members from our church and St. Michael's Episcopal Church prayerfully knit or crochet beautiful shawls for individuals. Prayers for the one in need are woven into every stitch, and then the shawl is brought before the congregation and dedicated to the person it was made for. The shawl is then presented to the individual as a gift—representing the enfolding love of God and the love and prayers of God's people. A prayer shawl was lovingly made for Anna. It was dedicated to Anna during one of our Sunday morning worship services, and at the end of the service the prayer shawl was left at the altar. The senior pastor and I dismissed the congregation with a blessing, and we proceeded to the narthex (the front doors) to greet the people who would be leaving the sanctuary. Standing at the outer doors ready to greet them, the choir finished singing, and we waited...and waited...and no one exited. We both looked at each other a bit puzzled—wondering why no one was leaving the sanctuary, and as we looked back inside, we witnessed our entire congregation at the altar, on their knees with hands outstretched, touching the shawl or touching each other and praying for Anna. It was a beautiful and moving sight to behold. I believe our congregation was changed that day by the grace of God experienced in the outpouring [of] love and prayers for Anna and her wonderful family.

As we continue our celebration of Anna's life and legacy, I do want to share with you a few words of scripture that came to mind for me and for her parents particularly over these most recent days. They come from the Old Testament book of Ecclesiastes:

While trying to be faithful to Anna's request to keep this [ceremony] light and not have a "funeral," I do believe that it's important up front that we all acknowledge our loss...that we acknowledge our pain. It seems so unfair that her difficult and courageous journey ended her life here on earth. The pain, the suffering and anguish that she so gracefully endured...have been at times more than we thought we could bear.

After all that she has been through, we had hoped, we had prayed that the outcome would have been different. And in the midst of it all, there was always hope. Chris shared with our Sunday School class one day these words: "We have two choices—Hope or Despair, and to be honest, despair at times seems to be the easier choice, but still I choose hope." We acknowledge that it has been a difficult time and a difficult season. And over the last few days the seasons began to change...the hope that was embraced was redirected to the hope of resurrection and complete healing and wholeness in life eternal.

Listen to these words from Ecclesiastes 3:1

> *To everything there is a season…*
> *There is a time for everything,*
> *and a season for every activity under the heavens:*
> *a time to be born and a time to die,*
> *a time to plant and a time to uproot,*
> *a time to kill and a time to heal,*
> *a time to tear down and a time to build,*
> *a time to weep and a time to laugh,*
> *a time to mourn and a time to dance,*
> *a time to scatter stones and a time to gather them,*
> *a time to embrace and a time to refrain from embracing,*
> *a time to search and a time to give up,*
> *a time to keep and a time to throw away,*
> *a time to tear and a time to mend,*
> *a time to be silent and a time to speak,*
> *a time to love and a time to hate,*
> *a time for war and a time for peace.*

What do workers gain from their toil? I have seen the burden God has laid on the human race. He has made everything beautiful in its time. He has also set eternity in the human heart; yet no one can fathom what God has done from beginning to end. (NIV)

This is the word of God for the people of God. Thanks be to God.

Amen.

Let us continue to celebrate this beautiful life.

* * *

Anna Gordon: A Remembrance
By Joan Barth
May 12, 2011

"*I believe that every action is a self-portrait of the person who did it. Consequently, I have always sought to autograph my work with excellence.*"

This is what Anna wrote in her statement of purpose for her graduate school applications. Indeed, she did sign her work at UA with "excellence." Her list of accomplishments is long:

- *GPA was 4.0*
- *Norman R. Ellis Endowed Research Scholarship*
- *2008 Outstanding Junior, Department of Psychology*
- *Crimson Achievement Scholarship—awarded by UA President Robert Witt*
- *Future Leaders Scholarship—awarded by UA President Robert Witt*
- *Outstanding Leadership Award—Lakeside Residential Community*
- *Most Valuable Player—Lakeside Residential Community*
- *Phi Beta Kappa*
- *Phi Kappa Phi*
- *Golden Key Honor Society*
- *Phi Eta Sigma*
- *National Society for Collegiate Scholars*
- *Sigma Alpha Lambda*

On her one-page resume, Anna reduced the font to 9-point to get it all in! The reason I mention these accomplishments is not because they somehow summarize Anna's experience at UA, but because they reflect her energy, her love of learning, and how she just shined wherever she went and in whatever she did. Let me share with you a little about the Anna I knew.

When I work with students, one of the conversations I try to have [with them] early on is a discussion of their career goals, where they see themselves after they finish schooling. Anna told me her goal was to work in higher education administration. When I heard this, I thought, "Really? That's what you want to do? Unbelievable!" Most psychology students I had worked with before aspired to maybe "help children" or "research how families affect emotion processing." Not to put the other student's goals down, but here in front of me was a young woman who wanted to run a university!

As we talked more, she wove together her experiences as an RA, her internship with student affairs, and her research interests, and I thought to myself, "Joan, you better be careful here—Anna could be running UA one day!"

Anna worked with me on her project titled "Self-Efficacy and Performance: Explanatory Factors for the Attrition of Females in Math and Science-Related Fields." Her honors thesis piggybacked on a larger research project I was conducting at the time. Anna became part of my "A team"—three women whose names all began with the letter A: Anneliese, Arngenel, and Anna. The A-team's job was to try to recruit freshmen engineering students to complete a 15-minute survey. The engineering students got paid $20 to complete the questionnaire, so you wouldn't think we would have too much trouble getting students to participate, but we did. We had been going to the engineering study hall to try to recruit students but were not having much luck. When it was Anna's turn to go, we weren't too optimistic, but thought we would give it one more try. In two hours' time she had something like 20 students signed up! We were shocked! She became our good luck charm—none of the rest of us could get students the way she did. How did she do that? It was her gift, her glow...well, it was just Anna.

Last night I reread part of Anna's thesis proposal—it is really good. Her intellect, her clarity of purpose all shine through. Her project made a real contribution to my research and helped me understand my questions a little differently. I am so grateful for this.

When I was writing a note to let my colleagues know of Anna' passing, I said that in describing Anna, words like brilliant, smart, insightful, warm, and caring seem accurate, but just fall short of describing a truly delightful young woman. There are certain students who come into our lives who are special, *not just because of their capacity to learn, but because of their character and how they make us shine as teachers.*

In closing, I want to offer one more excerpt from Anna's graduate school applications. She included this quote from William Butler Yeats:

"Education is not the filling of a pail, but the lighting of a fire."

Sometimes when you are really lucky as a teacher, it is the student who lights your fire. Anna was just such a student. We will all miss her terribly.

* * *

Dr. Jennifer Jones

Hello. My name is Jennifer Jones. I am an Assistant Professor in the Higher Education Program at the University of Alabama. I had the distinct honor of having Anna as a student in my class during the fall of her senior year. Our class was called "The American University." In our course, we have explored the history, organization, governance, and policies of higher education institutions. We [held] our class in Altson Hall, in a classroom that had stadium seating. Anna always sat in the 3rd row on the end, to my left. She never missed class, and she always showed up on time and was prepared. Most days, she was more prepared than I was.

To be honest, that fall was my first semester as a full-time faculty member. I had taught freshmen but not upper-class students. And the course I was teaching, I had never taught. In that kind of situation, my goal was to stay one chapter ahead of the class. It became very clear to me early in the semester that Anna was always two chapters ahead of me.

With each topic we explored, Anna's interest in higher education as a field of study grew. Her intelligence allowed her to grasp the complexities of higher education, and she would continually ask really good questions. She was asking better questions than my graduate students. I learned a very important professorial skill during that semester. "You ask a really good question, Anna, what do YOU think about that?" It allowed me more time to come up with a semi-intelligent response. But most times, I didn't need the response as Anna typically had it all worked out for me. It was always a bit awkward for me to be taking notes so I wouldn't forget what she had said.

Anna made me a better teacher. It is one thing to know about a topic, it is entirely a different skill to know how to teach that information. Anna continually challenged me to explain it better, to ask harder questions, and to expect more from my students. The greatest gift Anna gave me as a professor was her genuine interest in my field. She became so interested that she decided to make it her own course of study. There is no prouder moment in teaching than when a student likes your class so much they want to do what you do.

As the fall wrapped up and we moved into the spring semester, Anna asked me to serve as a reference and write letters of recommendation for her for graduate school. Dr. Witt was also on her list, so I felt like I was in good company. Last night, I read through the reference letters I wrote for Anna as she was pursuing a graduate degree. It was really hard to write letters for Anna because I didn't want my gushing to come across as fake—you know how rec-ommendation letters can be—but with Anna, I meant every word.

Here are a few excerpts from letters I wrote:

- Anna is the type of young leader we need to cultivate as a future leader in the Student Affairs profession.
- As a professional in higher education, I believe Anna is the type of person we need as a future leader.
- Anna is bright, thoughtful, and insightful.
- Anna is an independent and self-motivated learner. She will thrive in graduate school.
- Anna has confidence in her convictions and is conscientious and respectful in sharing those with others. She will be an asset to your learning community.

And those accolades didn't begin to scratch the surface of the type of learner she was. Anna was the type of student that every teacher wants in his/her classroom. She loved learning. I loved watching her think and process information. She would stare at me intently—which always made me a little uncomfortable because I thought maybe she finally saw through my charade and [had] figured out she was smarter than me—but I could just see her tossing around the thoughts in her head. She was confident in what she knew and how she felt. However, she also allowed me to challenge her, and she was willing to consider things differently. A mark of a true scholar.

As I was preparing my remarks for today, I read through old email exchanges and assignments Anna submitted. I would like to share feedback I sent to her on a photo-journal assignment: "You far exceeded my expectations for this assignment. You are such a tremendous asset to our campus community, and I really feel fortunate that you decided to take my class."

Anna set a standard for all the students that followed her in my classes—as well as ensured that I never show up to teach class without being at least THREE chapters ahead.

Throughout her journey with cancer, I always admired the way Anna remained committed to learning. She never stopped thinking, analyzing, asking good questions, deconstructing ideas, and trying to make sense of her world. This was challenging in a situation that made no sense at all.

I am sad that I lost a friend. I am also sad that my profession lost a brilliant future leader. To Pam, Chris, and Tori, I am honored and humbled that you allowed me to share in your journey over the last 2 ½ years, and that you would include me in the celebration of Anna's life.

To Anna, your grace through your valiant fight has forever changed me. I am better for having known you. You will always be my hero.

*   *   *

Anna Elizabeth Gordon
5 June 1987—9 May 2011—Forever
Dr. Robert McDonald
[Complete Text of Eulogy]

Anna Elizabeth Gordon, what a beautiful, remarkable, vibrant woman...who comes from one of the best families I have ever met. I've known Anna and her family since I was a medical student, when Anna was first diagnosed by Dr. Phillip Bobo. There wasn't much to those first encounters at UAB. Anna was a bright, athletic young woman who had developed a blood cancer. She received treatment, sailing through chemotherapy in a relatively easy manner, if losing her hair and staying in hospital for weeks on end can be called "easy," for what was to be the first of several times. Her room had Christmas lights in it, and there were always snacks there, readily shared with those of us working there.

And there was the sign:

"I ain't never been nothin' but a winner."

—Paul Bear Bryant

And there were the cards that covered the walls, tended [to] by Pam and Anna: gestures of love, humor, compassion, sympathy, and camaraderie.

Anna was a proud graduate of the University of Alabama, here in Tuscaloosa. Have you ever met a graduate of Alabama who wasn't proud?

She went on, matriculating at the University of Georgia for graduate work in higher education. After she left, I contacted her via Facebook, as is done these days, to tell her that I was glad she had done so well, and that if I could ever do anything to help, to let me know.

Time passed and chapter two began with a message from Anna, "My cancer is back." I went to the room where Anna was going to be at UAB, and found Pam in a rare moment...standing, alone in the room, holding back tears and fear...signs that evaporated when I walked in after knocking. I could see her, in that moment, steeling herself.

I can't say enough about the Gordons. I promise, you have never met more extraordinary parents in your life. Pam has spent more time in the hospital than I have, and that's saying something. She never left her daughter's side. She never, ever left her daughter's side. She protected Anna, spoke up for her, questioned, permitted, failed to sleep, failed to eat, breathed her breaths with her. She was always, always, always gracious, polite, and straightforward. It's easy to see where Anna got it from. Chris kept the outside world appraised and continued to work, continued to maintain the health insurance that gave Anna the chances she had, and kept his family together. Tori was also there, with grace and caring.

I visited Anna to talk to her, to hear her story...and I began to see what an extraordinary woman she is. She was a recruited, college-level softball pitcher, but she elected to go to Tuscaloosa for [the school's] academics. She told of approaching Dr. Witt, President of the University, to describe a gap in some of the scholarship programs available, and that she thought the university should invest in her. She was right, and President Witt did. I won't reiterate all the accolades she received...She graduated in the top 10% of graduating seniors at Tuscaloosa, proving what she knew, that she was capable and valuable.

She continually demonstrated herself as winning, and NOT in the Charlie Sheen sense.

Anna was serious, matter-of-fact, pleasant, quick-witted, and very much alive. There was never a question of cancer beating her. Never. It was more like this: "What unpleasant things do I need to do to get through this so I can get on with my life. Because I have plans, and this is really inconvenient."

Anna was protective of herself. She was a package deal, with her family always a part of her. Chris, Pam, and Tori are as interwoven into the fabric of Anna's being as she is in them. It has been a grand privilege to be permitted to add some threads to the fabric of the Gordon family.

Anna received a bone marrow transplant at the end of chapter two, suffering the unspeakable difficulties of this ordeal with grace, elegance, fortitude, persistence, and steadfastness. She would follow any direction she got from her nurses and doctors, as long as they made sense and were consistent. She made her caregivers appreciate the fact that she wasn't just a pretty face—she's got a brain, is able to use it, and "you all better get your story straight and treat me with respect while I'm here, entrusting my care to you." She fired those who deserved firing. She spoke up when she was treated as anything less than a beautiful human being. She forced people to listen, and she got people to listen. And...as very rarely happens...she rang the bell in the Bone Marrow Transplant unit, signifying a victorious departure from the Bone Marrow Transplant unit.

Anna took incredible care of herself. She never abused her body. She was so careful to protect herself. She was good to people. Her family was good to people. She had plans...good plans...helpful plans...plans that would improve her corner of the world. She therefore was faced with unanswerable questions—why would God permit this to happen? Why on Earth...for what reason...why do bad things happen to good people?

I will interject a story here. Anna has a phenomenal winning spirit. She is good at whatever she does. Academics? Certainly. Athletics? Certainly. She had to receive chemotherapy in her spine prior to the first bone marrow transplant. She was imprisoned within hospital walls, with Pam, trying to make the most of it, as always. Wine was occasionally involved. Jesus understood.

We went for a walk, breaking unreasoned rules, and by virtue of indoor corridors, made our way to the Children's Hospital. They have a place called Safe Harbor, with games and...a basketball court! We played H-O-R-S-E. Now I love basketball. And I don't like to lose. I don't like to lose no matter how pretty my opponent is. You hear me?

Anna, however, also does not like to lose. And a little cancer and spinal chemotherapy...a large, new Catheter under the collar bone on her shooting arm...these inconveniences were not going to get in the way of this. And I mean I tried. This was not even a little letting up to show sympathy for "the cancer girl." She wouldn't have any of that, and neither would I. And God bless it if she didn't beat me.

OK...three times.

Pissed me off...not in a bad way...in a way that you couldn't help but be completely, utterly admiring of her. And all the time with that smile that lights up a room. With those looks that turn heads everywhere she goes. With that quick, sharp wit that was characteristically hers.

After the bone marrow transplant, Anna returned to the UA and worked, reapplying for graduate programs in her field, determined to discount the inconvenience of cancer. I think Bear Bryant would have her on his team, any day of the week.

There has been suffering, tears, loss, grief, heartbreak, hope, faltering, wavering Faith. There has also been incredible outpouring of love and support, from the University, from church communities, from family and friends and loved ones. Jess Lee, Nathan Smock, Kevin Rugani...there is everlasting love there. The cohort of people at the University of Georgia showed great support, as did many others.

Young Kate Moss took it upon herself to make Anna-bags, and to sell them to raise hundreds of dollars to help with whatever Anna needed. Dr. Witt personally became involved with the Gordons and has supported Anna at every step of the way. Hundreds if not thousands of you have prayed and given of yourselves to help. This is a tribute to the Gordon family, who have been the most gracious, accepting, long-suffering people I have ever met in my life. It is because of them, and you, and Anna, that I will always hold a special place in my heart for the people of Tuscaloosa.

I left off many chapters, but I will leave snapshots as my closing remarks:

Anna told of how, when she was growing up, her parents would play with her and Tori, doing whatever the girls wanted, because Pam and Chris just wanted to...because there was nothing they would rather do than be with their girls. I remember thinking, with wonder, because this was so remarkable to me, isn't that how it ought to be? What wonderful parents they are. What wonderful people.

Anna told of how the differential between her fastball and her change-up was her greatest weapon in softball. And of how there were rituals on the diamond when she was pitching, of her spinning around, and her teammates patting her backside as she turned. Her face would light up, happy to recall accomplishment, and happy to recall a team working well together.

She told of how she appreciated thoughtful songwriters, like John Mayer. Her life followed the rhythm of her own drum, and she appreciated other musicians who did the same.

Where do we go from here? That's a question I'm not qualified to answer. What would Anna say? Well, she has said it in one way, by establishing the Anna E. Gordon Memorial Endowed Scholarship at the University of Alabama.

What would she tell me? She'd tell me to treat patients well. To treat them like they're human beings—like loved individuals, deserving of respect. She would tell me to listen. She'd be reasonable. She'd tell me not to be stupid, and she'd do so in a way that would make me feel smart. I look forward to seeing those bright eyes and that winning smile again, on the other side.

✶   ✶   ✶

Anna Elizabeth Gordon
Sammy Watson

The Gordons moved in two houses from Debbie and me in the spring of 1996. Anna was eight years old and Tori, five. The girls loved to come to our house and play with my cocker spaniel. Our pool was a place they enjoyed, too, on hot Saturdays in the summer. I had the habit of washing my cars in the driveway of our house on Saturday mornings. The girls would come talk to me as I did my work, entertaining me, and sometimes helping me wash. Many good times and good meals were enjoyed with The Gordons.

I remember the first time I shared the joys of a "potato-gun" with them. Now, if you have never seen and experienced a potato-gun, then you've missed out! I had a piece of PVC pipe, long and large in diameter. One end of the pipe was threaded, and I had a stopper that had a tiny hole in the back. When the girls came over, I would gather together the potato-gun, a can of Aqua Net hairspray, and a regular dinner-spud, and take it out back in my yard. I would take the can of hairspray and spray a whole bunch in the back of the gun. Then I'd screw the stopper on, lean the pipe on a rock or cinderblock, and take a match and light the little hole at the end. It would go off with a bang, hurling that spud over the fence and above the trees, in the woods behind my house! I mean it would GO!! The girls were AMAZED, and Anna always said, "Again, again, again..." We had such fun.

I remember once when Pam, Chris, and the girls were going on a vacation to the beach. Both girls had gotten American Girl dolls for Christmas the year before, and they played with those dolls for the next six months, Anna especially. The morning the Gordons were packing the car to leave on their trip, Anna comes over to our house carrying her doll and a bunch of gear. She asked Debbie and me to babysit her doll, Kirsten, while she was away. She said she didn't want her to be lonely! She showed us all the pieces that accompanied the doll, its bed, its clothes, all laid out and planned for each day of the week, its pajamas, etc., and she went over the schedule that she had planned for Kirsten's maintenance routine: You need to feed her these foods. You need to hold her, and dress her, and take her to school, and pick her up from school, and play with her, and talk to her, and put her pajamas on, and put her to bed at 9:00 each night! Will you please do this for me while I'm gone. "Oh yes," we said, "We can do that. Don't worry, she'll be fine!" Of course we did none of that while Anna was gone—but she was happy to know that her well-loved doll was taken care of in her absence.

Chris asked me to share with you just a few of the comments made by people on Facebook when she passed away. I'm happy to share them with you.

Alex wrote: "I ain't never been nothin but a winner." Anna had a life filled with fierce love, hope, courage, and strength. I think she's one of the biggest winners I've ever known...and we're all winners for being part of her life

Skip writes: "It is with tremendous sadness in my heart that I bring you the news that Anna Gordon lost her long struggle with cancer last evening at approximately 10:00 PM. I know that all of us have followed Anna's brave fight for a long time, offering our thoughts, prayers, well wishes, and support. There is no question that we have all developed unparalleled admiration, respect, and feeling for what Anna and her family have gone through. I simply hope that Pam, Chris, and Tori will find a way to come to peace with this situation, as we know that Anna now has. I know that at this point our collective hearts are broken as we care so deeply for this family and what they have endured. But I know that I personally will never forget what I have learned from Anna Gordon.

Sally writes: "In high school I considered killing myself. Anna was the one person willing to talk to me. She saved my life, and she will forever be in my thoughts. My heart is with your entire family. She was an amazing person."

Susan wrote: "*Thinking back on the last 24 hours, I must say that although I'm saddened by the loss of this very young woman, I'm also awestruck of the outpouring of emotions about this journey that we all have experienced in following the Gordons' plight. It comforts me to know that the spirit of kindness, goodness, selflessness for a fellow human in need is still alive and well in our less than perfect hearts. If this hasn't been a great example of what The Master meant by love (one) another and blessed are those who believe yet have never known me, then I don't know what is. '... and a little child shall lead them'.... Thank you, Anna, and your family. The spirit of human kindness lives on in your memory & burns brightly through us.*"

Denise wrote: "*I have only met Anna briefly, but she seems to be a very courageous and strong young woman. I did stop her one day as she was leaving for lunch and told her I admired her strength and her spirit. Wearing her hair natural when it started growing back really touched my heart. On the Wednesday before Christmas this year I noticed slurred speech in my Dad, and I was shocked to learn that day that it was in fact a brain tumor. Things happened quickly and we landed in UAB, Dad had surgery. I'm writing this mainly to say that while I was staying with my Dad at UAB, from his room I could see the large marquee (in downtown Birmingham) that I recognized from your pictures....as well as a corner room across the street with large windows and twinkle lights. Every time I looked out that window and saw the lights it touched my heart and I thought and prayed for Anna. We were in the North Pavilion—could this have been her room? I just wanted you to know that your emails and pictures touch me each day and I keep your precious family in my prayers. Seeing the lights in that room just made it more than a "room across the way," it personalized it and made me stop and think about Anna each day. She has a beautiful smile and when I see her smile in your pictures it is contagious.*"

Suzanne wrote: "*I am so sad to hear about my friend Anna. When describing her, I would say that she was a pro at everything she tried. Graham and Ben coached us on the church softball team, and she was a constant starter.*

And when we danced together, she knew how to conquer a class with confidence. Then when we were in AP Spanish, I always knew who to ask the last question before a big test. She was a rock star. When we both went to Spain in 2008 with UA, I felt a sense of comfort knowing she'd be there too. Knowing that she would be there gave me the same kind of confidence that she had in ballet so many years ago. It was a good feeling. I've always admired her amazing intelligence and grace. I just wanted you to know that she was a shining light in my life, full of comfort and strength. I can only wish to be more like Anna. I feel much love for your family. What a loss for this world."

Carol writes: "I am too many miles away right now to embrace you two in love and support. Words fail. She taught us lessons in how to live."

Shelia writes: "She was too bright a star for this ugly old place."

Melissa wrote: "Thank you for letting those of us who never met her, love her all the same."

* * *

Dismissal

Two choices—Hope or Despair. Let's continue to choose hope. (To Chris, Pam, and Tori): Thank you so much for allowing me to be a part of your lives, your struggles, and to bear witness to Anna's beautiful life, it has been an honor and a privilege.

Such a beautiful life. Well done, Anna. Well done!

(Stand for the blessing.)

And now may the Lord bless you and keep you. The Lord make his face to shine upon you and be gracious to you. The Lord lift up his countenance upon you and give you peace. Amen.

Commendation
(Graveside)

Let us pray:
God of us all, your love never ends.
When all else fails, you still are God.
We pray to you for one another in our need, and for all, anywhere,
who mourn with us this day.
To those who doubt, give light;
to those who are weak, strength;
to those who have sinned, mercy;
to all who sorrow, your peace.
Keep true in us
the love with which we hold one another.
In all our ways we trust you.
And to you,
with your Church on earth and in heaven,
we offer honor and glory, now and forever. Amen.

[United Methodist Book of Worship]

Listen to the words from 1 Corinthians 13...

If I speak in the tongues of men or of angels, but do not have love, I am only a resounding gong or a clanging cymbal. If I have the gift of prophecy and can fathom all mysteries and all knowledge, and if I have a faith that can move mountains, but do not have love, I am nothing. If I give all I possess to the poor and give over my body to hardship that I may boast, but do not have love, I gain nothing.

Love is patient, love is kind. It does not envy, it does not boast, it is not proud. It does not dishonor others, it is not self-seeking, it is not easily angered, it keeps no record of wrongs. Love does not delight in evil but rejoices with the truth. It always protects, always trusts, always hopes, always perseveres.

Love never fails. But where there are prophecies, they will cease; where there are tongues, they will be stilled; where there is knowledge, it will pass away. For we know in part, and we prophesy in part, but when completeness comes, what is in part disappears. When I was a child, I talked like a child, I thought like a child, I reasoned like a child. When I became a man, I put the ways of childhood behind me. For now we see only a reflection as in a mirror; then we shall see face to face. Now I know in part; then I shall know fully, even as I am fully known. And now these three remain: faith, hope and love. But the greatest of these is love. [NIV]

Into your hands, O merciful Savior,
we commend your child Anna Elizabeth Gordon.
Acknowledge, we humbly beseech you,
a sheep of your own fold,
a lamb of your own flock,
a sinner of your own redeeming.
Receive Anna into the arms of your mercy,
into the blessed rest of everlasting peace,
and into the glorious company of the saints of light. Amen

[Adapted from the United Methodist Book of Worship]

Well done, Anna. Well done!

Blessing

And now may...
The peace of God which passes all understanding
keep your hearts and minds in the knowledge and love of
God,
and of his Son Jesus Christ our Lord.
And the blessing of God Almighty,
the Father, Son, and Holy Spirit,
be among you and remain with you always. Amen

[United Methodist Book of Worship]

* * *

Chapter 14

IN APRIL OF 2011, AFTER ANNA HAD SUCH A DIFFI-
cult time and had to go on the ventilator, she verbalized her first doubts as
to whether or not she had the strength to survive the recovery process from
the second bone marrow transplant. For the first time, she spoke of dying,
as if she felt it could be a reality at some point. Anna talked. Her mother
and I listened as she spoke of it, matter-of-factly. She talked of her being OK
with it. She told us she was satisfied with her life, that she could have done
no better with it, and that she had no regrets. She was not emotional about
death as a possibility; rather, she thought of it as a natural process, one each
of us would have to experience. Hers was just closer, she said. When Pam
and I recognized that Anna's discussion of death had been initiated not out
of fear, but more out of fact, we began to speak.

We knew that Anna might find it comforting at that point for Pam and I
to accept her premise and treat the discussion as an opportunity to allow her
to make some choices known to us, to plan for the possibility of her death in
a way that she preferred. To me, it felt like she not only wanted to make her
preferences regarding her funeral clear to us, but also like she was trying to
comfort us and guide us, her parents. It was as if she was helping us to prepare
for the event and for us to have knowledge of what she wanted.

I asked her if she wanted anything specific. She said she wanted to be
buried and not cremated. She suggested names for her pallbearers. Then
she said, "I want a scholarship in my name at The University of Alabama. I

want it to benefit a student in the Psychology Department." I then asked her what type of student would she like it to help? She said, "I think it should be a rising senior, somebody that's proven themselves as an achiever, and somebody who's interested in research." I told her that I would call Dr. Witt and find out what had to be done.

Pam and I did not feel unusually awkward in the face of Anna initiating this discussion. It did not feel macabre. Instead, we were calm but reflective. And buried within that reflection was a sense of gratitude that Anna was wise enough to prepare all of us. I do not know if she had a premonition or if she was just being logical and recognized the best moment to bring up the topic. Maybe she needed to talk about it, to make the possibility of her death real, so that she, herself, could process it. Regardless of the motivation, it is a moment with Anna Gordon that I continue, all these years later, to remember.

* * *

On May 10th, 2011, the morning after Anna passed away, I called Dr. Witt's office at the university. I told him of Anna's death, and I mentioned the story of her request for a scholarship in her name. I asked him what it would take to create such a thing. He immediately said that he would take care of it and that he would call me back later in the day. I thanked him and hung up. I went about helping Pam and Tori with the tasks we had planned to work on that day. Before too long, my phone rang. I answered it, and Dr. Witt told me, "It's all set up." I told him what the name of it should be and that I was going to publish an announcement noting the option for people to donate to her scholarship instead of buying flowers that would quickly fade away. He told me how people could donate so that I could get the word out. I thanked him for his constancy to Anna and our family. I told him that Anna will be pleased, now.

* * *

As the weeks passed after the hurry of the funeral, Tori returned to her apartment. Pam and I were left alone in Anna's apartment, surrounded by all of her possessions. Not a minute went by without our thoughts centered on what we had endured for two years and two months. We went through the normal progression of grief, including anger and, eventually, depression.

One day, about six weeks after the funeral, Pam said to me, "We've got to do something! Anna was treated so inhumanly by those doctors. She endured so much that was unnecessary, we've got to do something to ensure no one else is treated that way!"

I knew Pam was angry. I knew Pam was depressed. But she was deliberate, and insistent, even manic about the notion that we had to do something to ensure no other patient was treated as insensitively as Anna had been treated. Initially, I tried to be supportive of what I viewed as Pam's progression of grief. We had both read Elizabeth Kübler-Ross's book, *On Death and Dying*. We were familiar with the author's assertions regarding the grieving process. As days passed, I tried to give Pam time to grieve in her own way. But every day, she would come to me and bring up the topic again: "We've got to do something!"

I knew Pam had witnessed every procedure, every test, every chemotherapy, and every office visit Anna had undergone. I knew that she had slept in a chair throughout each of Anna's hospital confinements. She had witnessed unspeakable pain and suffering inflicted on her first-born child. Every bout of sickness, every kindness, and every disrespect—nothing escaped her seeing and knowing. I knew that in addition to moving through the various stages of grief, Pam must have had at least some degree of post-traumatic stress disorder. She could not avoid it. She had seen and experienced too much! I kept trying to be graceful with her insistence on "doing something."

I nuanced my conversations with her as best I could, until one day, about a week after the topic had first been brought up, Pam said it again: "We've got to do something! Anna would want us to do something!" This time, Pam brought with her Anna's journal, the one Anna wrote in while she was in the hospital.

I suppose Anna journaled as a coping tool. Maybe it was a way to document her treatments, I wasn't sure. Nevertheless, Pam turned to specific pages in the journal and handed it to me to read. She said, "This is how she felt about it. She describes each encounter, the negative and the positive, until she felt too bad to focus and write anymore. Here, read it. It's in her own hand!"

I did read it. On page after page, Anna described her encounters and her reactions to negative events that occurred with her BMT physicians. No other doctors were so described, throughout the whole process, from the beginning of her diagnosis until she could not write anymore. It was only the four BMT doctors. She even described alternative ways a sensitive physician should interact with a cancer patient, offering a way to teach them how to have empathy and engage with them humanely.

I was stunned by what I read. I now realized the source of Pam's anger and insistence. Her passion regarding treating cancer patients humanely was not Pam's, it was Anna's! It wasn't Pam's grieving progression, it was Anna's. Anna was writing in her own script, knowing that nobody would read it, knowing nothing would change, but expressing her feelings and insights regarding how to ensure future cancer patients had a more humane experience than she had had. Her words amounted to a private prayer sent into the ether, expressed within the pages of an unfinished and closed book, just like her life—a book that would find its way to a bookshelf, collecting dust somewhere, stored in our house, unused, but somehow not able to be thrown away.

When I finished reading those pages, Pam said, "See what I mean? We've got to do something." I said, "But what? What can we do that will make any difference?"

We sat in some silence for a while, and then Pam said, "We've got to identify the CEO of UAB, whoever runs the joint, and you'll have to write a letter to him telling everything they did to her."

"I can do that," I said, "but he gets that type of thing every day. I'm sure he will just throw it away, like all the others. I'm not sure it will do any good, but if it will make you feel better, I'll write it."

It took me a week to investigate to whom I needed to write the letter, and then to write it. Writing the letter was hard. As I wrote I grew more and more angry. I couldn't help myself. I tried to edit out any insensitivities on my part. Over and over, I edited. In the end, when I was satisfied that the facts had been told, not personal exaggerations or emotions regarding events, just the facts, then I was satisfied. I had described only one encounter with each of the four doctors, although there were many left untold. I felt it was unnecessary to harp on and on. I didn't want it to be perceived as a whiny, emotional tome from the parents of another dead cancer patient, writing to ease their grief. No, I wanted it to reflect the no-nonsense style in which Anna had written herself. She wanted to teach the physicians, not about medicine, but about being human, being empathetic with their patients, being sensitive, and being kind.

I gave the seven-page manuscript to Pam to read. She read it over and over. When she had finished, she handed it back to me and said, "Mail it!"

*   *   *

Dr. Michael R. Waldrum
Division of Pulmonary, Allergy & Critical Care Medicine
1530 3rd Avenue So, THT-422
University of Alabama at Birmingham
Birmingham, AL 35294

June 30, 2011

Dear Dr. Waldrum,

We are the parents of Anna E. Gordon, who passed away May 9th in the third floor Bone Marrow Transplant Unit. Having had some time of repose, away from your hospital, where we spent the majority of two and a half years, we have come to the opinion that we have many things of which to tell you, in hopes that through the telling, it will inform, empower, and embarrass you to the degree that you will be motivated to make policy changes necessary in that unit, to ensure that no other patient receives the same disrespect, lack of empathy, and mental and emotional abuse that our daughter endured at the hands of your physicians charged with dispensing "care" in that facility.

While we are considering litigation, our initial aim is to make you aware of the deplorable lack of humanity dispensed to patients by your physicians. We intend to point out extensive breaches of concern for the feelings, the emotional well-being, and the appropriate level of human respect that ought to be a part of a patient's experience with your hospital. The expected level of satisfactory "customer service" should be in accordance with the prices charged for your services. We are here to say that in our case and in our opinion, they certainly were not and are not in such an accord. We are also here to say that the lack thereof created lasting and far-reaching emotional scars on our daughter and ourselves which cannot be undone.

In writing this letter, we appeal to your sense of humanity with which we hope you will desire to maintain the highest standards of professional behavior for your units and staff, not only medically, but interpersonally with patients, as well. In addition, we appeal to your sense of professionalism with regard to the hope that you will desire to maintain your institution's reputation and positive public image. If you do not have a desire to make right these breaches, we intend to let every cancer patient that we come across know of our experiences with your institution and its physicians, telling the reality of our daughter's experiences there, and giving them fair warning as to what to expect if they entrust themselves to your "care."

Before we list a litany of negative stories regarding your physicians and nurse practitioners, let us first say that your nursing staff met or exceeded our expectations with regard to medical professionalism and, more importantly, personal empathy for our daughter and her medical and emotional needs. They were and remain on the front lines of human interaction, and were often a comfort, often a resource of procedural information, often working tirelessly and selflessly to bring about healing, comfort, and reassurance, not only to our daughter, but to ourselves, in the middle of an atmosphere of fear and anxiety. They are to be cherished and nurtured as they labor for the maintenance of professional medical nursing practices, and they should be thanked and appreciated for their efforts in maintaining the only level of compassion and interpersonal dignity that we experienced from the hands of your medical staff. We are grateful for them, and we have done our best to make them aware of our thanks. We think you should, too.

Let me say that as we experienced issues regarding our daughter's care, we attempted to use the resources available to us already in place within your hospital. On two occasions we sat down with patient representatives to express our concerns when specific instances arose. The patient representatives took copious notes and listened. In both cases, however, we never heard back from them regarding any progress, outcome, or resolution of the issue in question. In fact, we never heard a response at all. We can only conclude that the available resource in our case was ineffective and of no use to us.

In another instance, we discovered, through a UAB PR website, that the message [being enunciated by UAB] touted the innovation and effectiveness of a program for patients called "Nurse Navigators." This service described a thorough and calming orientation to procedures, facilities, and services offered to new patients as they enter treatment units with which there would be extended stays. While the website publicized that the BMT unit offered this orientation service, we never received it, nor did we ever see anyone else receive the services described in our entire time of treatment in the BMT unit, both as outpatient and inpatient. Again, we conclude that if such a service exists, it is ineffective and not uniformly available. It is because of these breaches that we report to you now and hope for a follow-up personal meeting with you, so that every attempt can be made to not duplicate our negative experiences with future patients. No one should have to endure such treatment on top of having to battle the disease itself.

In order for you to grasp the context of our complaints, a brief history of Anna's disease is required. She was diagnosed with acute myeloid leukemia in Tuscaloosa in March of 2009, when she was a senior at the University of Alabama, where she graduated summa cum laude, with memberships in Phi Beta Kappa, Golden Key, and numerous other academic honoraries. She completed a double major in Psychology and Spanish, and held a minor in The Blount Undergraduate Initiative, a rigorous program of humanities and western thought literature. She was a multiple scholarship recipient and gained recognition in the Psychology department for her undergraduate thesis research, and she was given the award for Academic Excellence for a Student of Psychology. In addition, she garnered the Outstanding Senior award for The Blount Undergraduate initiative. She was brilliant, hardworking, ambitious, and highly effective. She was also kind, engaging, and she was a campus standout in her unselfish interaction with faculty and fellow students. This was evidenced by her receipt of the Most Valuable Player and Most Outstanding Veteran awards presented by the Lakeside Community, with which she served as a three-year Resident Assistant. She maintained the highest degree of professionalism and interpersonal grace in all her dealings with a wide range of people from distinguished faculty to apathetic students alike. She expected the same from an academic teaching hospital with a national reputation for excellence. In the end, she was highly disappointed, as were we.

From March until August of 2009, Anna endured chemotherapy treatments at UAB's ninth floor Hematology unit. She often returned either to UAB or to DCH Regional Medical Center in Tuscaloosa, to treat subsequent infections. In every instance of admittance, the physicians associated with DCH were kind, effective, and comforting, while UAB's were emotionally cold, uncooperative, and insensitive to Anna's desire to maintain a focus on "living" and returning to a productive lifestyle. Often, as a response to her wish to go forward to graduate school, she was delayed, thwarted, and discouraged from even contemplating a return to normal activity. This she found intolerable, thinking that the goal should be to support the patient in their desire to defeat the disease and continue with life's journey. Instead, she felt they desired her to acquiesce to the disease and gracefully accept it as a death sentence, drawn out over many months. She would not!

She applied and was accepted to study at several prestigious institutions in an attempt to pursue her goal of a master's degree in higher education administration, including: William & Mary, the University of Indiana, the University of South Carolina, the University of Maryland, and the University of Alabama. She chose the University of Georgia's top-five program in Student Affairs, where she received a full tuition grant with an assignment to work in the Vice President's Office for Institutional Effectiveness. We moved her to Athens to begin study and work in August of 2009, only a week after her last hospital stay at UAB, where she was declared to be in remission. The week before Thanksgiving her cancer returned and she was forced to return to UAB, this time to receive chemotherapy to reestablish remission status and then receive a bone marrow transplant.

Again, Anna endured chemotherapy at both UAB and DCH, for treatment of infections in order to achieve remission. It is at this point that we came in contact with the BMT physicians on a regular basis. The first introduction to the physicians at the BMT unit was when Anna and my wife, Pam, the designated live-in caregiver, met with Dr. #1, to receive the overview of the bone marrow transplant process and to sign consent forms. This notorious exercise is where the physicians feel it necessary to enthusiastically inform the patient of every negative aspect of the upcoming procedure, listing facts on survival rates and telling of complications that other patients have faced. This was a mean-spirited conversation, seemingly designed and delivered with the intent of scaring the patient off from undergoing the procedure, rejecting their only hope of cure and return to normal life, and protecting the staff from litigation in the aftermath by ensuring the defense of "you were fully told of the possibilities, yet you chose to move forward anyway." After long periods of aggressive conversation from Dr. #1 to which Anna responded with no negativity, Dr. #1 retorted, "My, you surely are a very mature young lady," indicting by inference that most patients succumb to despair and tears as their response. Right from the outset, the impression was given that it was "us (the physicians) against them (the patients)." This is no way to comfort and set the patient's mind at ease regarding the path that lies ahead. It had the opposite effect, the impressions of a hard and unforgiving road filled with stress and physical discomfort [lying] ahead.

Pam took a leave of absence from her faculty position at the University of Alabama, and she and Anna moved into the BMT unit ready to begin the chemotherapy treatments that would kill Anna's native marrow system, opening the door for transplant. The second disturbing encounter with BMT physicians occurred after the chemotherapy treatments, when Anna underwent tests to determine remission status. This time, Dr. #2, the physician on call for that time period, entered the room and announced that while the tests were clear, she suspected that cancer cells remained in Anna's body. She announced that the transplant would be worthless, in her opinion, and that we should consider calling in hospice! Anna and we were left with despair, feeling all must be lost, and that Anna's battle would be over before it had even begun. We appealed to Dr. #3 for clarification of Dr. #2's comments, looking for hope. He declared that we should dismiss her suggestion and pronounced that we would "of course go ahead with the transplant." Anna received the transplant in April of 2010 and progressed toward health in record speed, surprising even Dr. #3 with how quickly and thoroughly she seemed to recover compared with other patients.

When Anna was released from the BMT unit on Mother's Day in May 2010, she and Pam moved into an apartment on the Southside in Birmingham, where they could return daily to the outpatient facility of the BMT for regular blood tests and other treatment. This they did for almost four months. In the outpatient facility, Anna experienced regular delays, where patients are left to wait for long hours before test results or treatments [can] be administered. Long, tedious, daily routines were experienced, with physicians paying little heed to the time needs or daily activities of the patients. The attitude was that the patient was to be available at all times to receive information or treatment at the convenience of the physicians. All else was of no importance to them. Any request or deviances made from the normal [routine] was treated with disdain and rebuke, as if the patient were not taking seriously their healthcare obligations and would thus bring upon themselves negative health consequences that the physicians were desperately trying to have the patient avoid. This was their explanation for delays and inattention [displayed] by the physicians to the outpatients, who were kept there for long hours with no choice [regarding] the remainder of their daily tasks.

When Anna was released from daily visits to the outpatient facility and allowed to return home to Tuscaloosa in August of 2010, she was told that she would have to continue to return to UAB for regular evaluations, forcing her to remain in Tuscaloosa where she could more easily return to Birmingham. Rather than return to her graduate study in Athens, where the frequency of these visits and the length of travel to receive checkups would be cumbersome, Anna chose instead to apply for employment within her chosen field of study at area universities. In August 2010, she was hired as an Admissions Counselor for Alumni and Volunteer Recruitment within the Office of Undergraduate Admissions at the University of Alabama. She was determined to not waste a year of activity leading towards advancement in higher education. If she could not study, she would work. Anna announced to the UAB physicians that she was beginning to work, and that she would need more flexibility in the scheduling of her visits to UAB for checkups. We referred to the UAB BMT website and pointed out the pronouncement of services offered seven days a week to outpatients, and she requested a similar schedule to other patients who were being served on the weekend. She was met with disdain and discouragement. She was told that she should not go to work and must be available to them during workdays from 8:00 o'clock until 5:00, Monday through Friday, and that if she insisted on coming on the weekends for treatment, as was advertised, she would receive inferior care and endanger her health. When we pressed the doctors to live up to the messages that were advertised to the public in an attempt to recruit patients for the BMT services, we were ushered into a conference room with

Dr. #3, who informed us that in doing this, we would be risking the care of our daughter, and that they could not be held responsible. He then produced a document, saying that we released him and the UAB staff from any responsibility incurred from our choice of action. We told him that we would not sign any paper relieving him of his responsibilities, and that, further, we fully expected him to work with Anna to restore her not only to health but to a useful and productive life. He and his staff would have to adjust in whatever small ways were necessary so that Anna could live a life full of promise and happiness, rather than be bound by the inactivity and slothfulness associated with the year ahead that they expected. We said that this was not a singular request, but that it was already being done for other patients. Again, we left with the impression of "us versus them." We did not bend to intimidation.

Both Anna and Pam returned to their work at the University of Alabama for the fall semester of 2010. Anna moved into a new apartment of her own, throwing herself into her work with vigor and enthusiasm. She was met with acclaim and gratitude, from the family clients which she served and her colleagues in the Office of Undergraduate Admissions alike. She consistently maintained her appointments at UAB, scheduling them after work hours during the week, and the physicians begrudgingly accommodated her schedule. For a time, all was well, until crushingly her cancer returned for the third time, in the first week of December.

Yet again, she endured chemotherapy treatments that killed her native marrow system with plans to proceed through a second bone marrow transplant. While receiving the treatment on the ninth-floor Hematology unit, our fourth insensitivity issue with UAB physicians occurred. Dr. #4 was on call, and on this particular day he was making rounds with a team of student physicians, with a social worker in attendance. He was talking to Anna and making a regular physical examination. He asked her questions and talked for a bit, when without provocation and without leaving Anna time to think, he exposed her intimate area for the room to view and proceeded to do a rectal examination. When this first began, Anna only thought that he was going to inspect the wounds in her back, created from the bone marrow biopsy performed the day before. Never had a rectal examination been done before, and there were no symptoms of issues in this area at this time. He viewed the procedure as a "teaching moment" for those assembled. He acted as if this was standard procedure. Embarrassed and humiliated by this exposure in front of a team of male physicians and a lay person, Anna later expressed mortification that he would do such a thing to her without due diligence and emotional preparation. When they left the room, Anna cried all day, feeling violated. Later, Pam took Dr. #4 to task for his insensitivity to Anna's feelings and modesty. He insisted that this procedure had been done in the past as a matter of regularity. It had not! It had never been done. He then declared to Anna, when he begrudgingly apologized, saying, "No part of your body is off limits to me! This is a teaching hospital and if you didn't desire this to occur, you could have denied treatment!" His lack of [preparing Anna] for what he wished to do, combined with the emotional humiliation the patient endured while he went about his business, seemingly unaware of any impropriety, serves as an example [of] the deplorable lack of feeling and respect your physicians [convey].

Later, as Anna was entering the BMT for transplant, this time the "orientation" lecture was given by Dr. #4, who seemed to relish the delivery of every agonizing detail, as if in retribution for the embarrassment he suffered when being challenged for his lack of empathy earlier. When Anna complained of the insensitivity of the presentation, Dr. #4's response regarding his verbal onslaught of the "orientation" lecture was, "I told you this would be a difficult conversation!" Anna knew full well what the lecture entailed and besides, she had lived the experience. Why must she endure another emotional assault, as a matter of "policy," especially with the seeming personal satisfaction on the part of Dr. #4 for having delivered it? In addition, during the lecture Pam asked Dr. #4 what counseling services were provided by the hospital with regard to emotional and psychological support for patients and their families so they could less stressfully endure the process. He responded that he could be of no help because he knew nothing along those lines, and that we should ask Dr. #3. The nurse practitioner added that, "No one has ever asked that question in here before!" We were informed that there was no such service at the BMT unit.

In order to again determine that Anna was free of leukemia cells, Dr. #4 scheduled a Radiology department spinal tap examination. Anna had already endured many days of repeated spinal taps due to treatments of chemotherapy in her spine, and she knew full well what was involved with the procedure with regards to pain and discomfort. Anna was told by the bone marrow transplant coordinator, that on the sixth floor, "they use the good stuff, you will feel no pain." She and Pam went to the sixth floor to have the procedure done by Dr. #5, who when asked what medications would be given for pain and discomfort, said, "I do not use pain medications." The accompanying nurse said, "He's so good you won't even feel it." When Anna and Pam protested, knowing the agony she had already gone through in previous treatments at the BMT, Dr. #5 responded, "You may refuse treatment if you wish." Yeah, right!

The second bone marrow transplant was delayed because Anna developed a severe infection of blood sepsis from an "unknown" bacteria, probably a form of staph, received in the BMT unit. Her dangerous, weeklong recovery caused her to be weakened in [her] body and immune system, when the transplant process actually began, a week or so later. This time, Anna did not respond well as she had before. She had a severe headache for many days straight, which we were later told was caused by the immune suppressant drug that had worked the time before. This condition went on and on, leaving Anna in severe pain, until finally tests were done and determined that the "white matter in her brain had undergone changes." Anna was never herself after this experience.

The remainder of her time spent in the BMT unit was a constant descent into difficulties. Each physician in turn, as they changed rotations, took several days to get caught up on her condition, causing, in our mind, a temporary and unwelcome setback in her "care," until the physician could focus and get fully up to speed in decision making. When it was Dr. #2's turn to come onto the rotation, Anna's condition deteriorated to the degree that her kidneys began to decline and she gained forty-two pounds of fluid, swelling up like a whale, before adequate steps were taken to reduce the fluid substantially. [It] took several days to remove fluid buildup that we feel was not properly addressed in time to prevent further erosion in her condition. She was placed on dialysis and her liver began to fail as well, further complicating things. Her brain was not functioning correctly due to the white matter damage, her kidneys and liver were failing, and Anna descended into darkness, never to become conscious again.

She developed pneumonia and was placed on a ventilator. After many days, Anna's lungs improved to the point where they began to "work her off" the ventilator with a progression of hours of time for her to breathe "on her own." After several days of these attempts, one "pulmonary resident" physician gave the order for her to "breathe on her own" for a couple of hours, and then he would return to remove the ventilator. He never returned! The nurse paged him repeatedly, seven times throughout the day, to get instructions as to what was going to occur and find out if he wanted to keep her on the ventilator or if he planned to remove it. Anna had not eaten, and they do not want a patient to eat before removing the tube for fear of regurgitation. Anna was getting "tired" from the hours of breathing effort through the mechanism and tensions grew in the room as to why we, or the nurses, had not heard back from the "resident." After twelve hours, an angry resident returned to reprimand us that he was busy upstairs with "patients that were dying," and that he did not need to be hounded. He angrily scolded my wife and the nurse. This was witnessed by the BMT unit's floor nurse who took the physician to task for his lack of information regarding Anna, and that a simple page in return could have alleviated the entire situation. The "resident" physician was forced to begrudgingly apologize. The next day, the "attending" physician, Dr. #6, scolded my wife for her emotional hysteria! The nurse of the day before was so upset regarding the physicians' compounded lack of empathy and professionalism, she chose to take time off for her own emotional recovery.

In the days following the removal of the ventilator tube, Anna rallied slightly and then began a rapid descent. After the intravenous feeding had

*ceased, Anna never felt well enough to eat. Under Dr. #1's rotation, I asked her
if Anna didn't need to be placed back on some type of feeding intravenously,
since by this time, she had not had any nutritional nourishment for over three
weeks. She responded that, "No, I'm not worried about that; I don't think it will
matter." How can a patient rebuild white blood cells to fight rapidly growing
infections if she has no nutrients? Again, we felt that concern for basic emotional
and physical needs, was not delivered or addressed.*

*Anna descended quickly after this with continued breakdown of her liver,
kidney, lung, and brain functions. Also, the blood infection, sepsis, returned
with abandon. Finally we were told by Dr. #1 that she would not live for more
than forty-eight hours, and that we should gather the family and friends.
When we were told this, twenty-four hours had already passed, and we acted
quickly to prepare for her much unexpected demise. By seven o'clock in the
evening of May 9, Dr. #1 asked us to gather in the room because "it would be
anytime now." We all gathered by her bedside and held her hands and talked
to her as she declined. When three hours had passed and the day was ending,
Dr. #1 said to Pam, "I am embarrassed to say that I don't know your name,"
to a woman who had accompanied Anna on every visit as an outpatient
and lived continuously in her hospital room every day of her inpatient stays,
discussed every procedure, and received every patient report! When the clock
neared ten o'clock, motivated by what we assume was Dr. #1's desire to leave
for the day, she came in and said, "Anna, this is your night. Go to the light,
Anna. Go to the light!" When Anna didn't immediately expire at that time,
Dr. #1 suggested that if she turned off a blood pressure medication pump, the
fluid dynamics that were at work keeping her heart pumping, would allow
her to pass away more quickly. After Dr. #1 reached and turned the pump off,
Anna died within two minutes. Dr. #1 filled out the appropriate paperwork,
and we packed Anna's belongings and departed the hospital as quickly as we
could, never wanting to return ever again!*

*We returned to Tuscaloosa the following day and prepared for her funeral.
Several nurses attended the funeral and we received condolences from all the*

nurses in the subsequent days through cards signed and notes written on UAB stationery printed up just for such usage. To this day, we have never heard one word from any physician from UAB, either through phone call or written correspondence, after we spent two and a half years with them and the UAB bills have been paid in full!

Again, we say your physicians lack common courtesy and the decency to treat very ill patients with compassion or even respect. We feel as if, at every encounter with them, that it was an adversarial exchange. We would like to point out that after having consulted the "Patient Bill of Rights and Responsibilities" given to us when we entered the hospital for the first time many of its initial tenants were not adhered to, including:

All patients at UAB Hospital shall have the right to:

- *[R]eceive considerate, respectful, and compassionate care regardless of your age, gender, race, national origin, religion, sexual orientation, or disabilities. Given only a few of the examples listed within this letter, we declare that UAB Hospital and its physician staff failed this expected declaration.*
- *[R]eceive care in a safe environment free from all forms of abuse, neglect, or harassment.*
- *We declare that UAB Hospital and its physician staff failed this expected declaration.*
- *[B]e called by your proper name and to be told the names of the doctors, nurses and other health care team members involved with your care.*
- *Except as it applies to the nurses, we declare that UAB Hospital and its physician staff failed this expected declaration.*
- *To expect full consideration of your privacy and confidentiality in care discussions, examinations, and treatments. You may ask for a chaperone during any type of examination.*
- *We declare that UAB Hospital and its physician staff failed this expected declaration.*

- *To have your pain assessed, reassessed, and be involved in decisions about managing your pain.*
- *We declare that UAB Hospital and its physician staff failed this expected declaration.*

In conclusion, we would like to say that we did our part as patients and paid the bill in full. While medically, no one knows what the outcome will ever be, we fully expected to have a professional and compassionate experience with UAB and its physicians. Not only do we declare that we were disappointed, but we also feel it is our duty to our departed daughter to speak for her in her silence and testify that not only did we not receive this expectation, but we also received behavior more egregious than we could have ever anticipated. We [petition] you for satisfaction and for justice and we lay at your feet the responsibility for the actions of the physicians which you allow to create such an unsatisfactory environment, who go unchecked and seemingly unsupervised, answering to no one for their slights and lack of acceptable judgment in regard to human affairs and interactions.

Further, we request and expect a face-to-face discussion with you regarding your reactions to these declarations and your responses to them.

Sincerely,
Chris and Pam Gordon

* * *

I mailed the letter to Dr. Michael R. Waldrum on a Monday. He received it that Friday. I was sure when I mailed it that he might scan the letter, or even read it, but he definitely would throw it away or maybe file it with a thousand other complaint letters, never to be seen again.

My phone rang at 10:30 am that Monday. I was walking down the hallway at Bevill State Community College in Fayette, having just taught my first summer school class of the day. I answered it.

"Mr. Gordon? This is Dr. Michael Waldrum, CEO of UAB Hospital."

"Yes, sir," I said. "What may I do for you?"

"I've called because I received your letter and I want to talk to you about it, if I may."

"Yes, sir. That would be fine."

"I received it Friday and I've read it three times now. I must say that I have never received a letter like this before."

"Really, how so?"

"Well, I have daughters, too, and I have one who is a Spanish major at the University of Alabama. I think she knew Anna."

"Really…well, that's interesting."

"She tells me that Anna was quite the Spanish student. I can also tell you that as a father, myself, I understand the passion underlying your letter."

"Well, what did you think of it? I really thought that you would throw it away."

"Oh, no!"

"What is your reaction to our story, to what I told you?"

"I am shocked and embarrassed that a patient could be treated in this way at UAB. I assure you that I will look into this and see what I can do to make sure this does not happen again."

"What was the most disturbing thing that you read in the letter?"

"The behavior of Dr. #4. That humiliation of a young woman in front of all those male students is inexcusable. I can imagine how Pam felt when that incident took place."

"Thank you. I'm glad you understand."

"Yes, remember I have daughters, too. I'd like to schedule a time where you and Pam can come to my office and meet with me about some ideas I have. I want to have you advise me as I create these ideas I'm pondering. I promise, that if you give me some time, I will do my very best to make sure things like this, that happened to your family, don't happen again."

"Thank you," I replied, "we would be very happy to meet and work with you on this."

"I want to let you know that I am in charge of the hospital, its physical plant, and the nurses. But I do not hire the physicians or supervise them. That is another individual, who runs a foundation that hires and pays the doctors. I will have to set up a meeting with him to discuss this situation. I want him to be onboard with trying to reform the atmosphere in which these incidents occurred. I want to build a partnership with him. We must work together to build trust in the care we dispense at UAB. Give me a few weeks and when I have met with him, I'll have my office assistant get in touch with you and set up a time for our meeting together."

"Dr. Waldrum, I must confess that this phone call has been over and above anything that I ever imagined would happen. I really didn't think this could be possible. My wife will be glad to know that her feelings have been affirmed. Thank you for your time and your call. I look forward to hearing from your office assistant."

"Well, you're welcome. This will be my top priority until I get things to change. But I want to let you know that what I'm going to try to do will take a long time, and it will involve a lot of maneuvering, but I think I can make it happen. Just work with me, and be patient with me, please."

"Dr. Waldrum," I told him, "all we have is time."

* * *

Pam and I met with Dr. Waldrum many times over the next year. We discussed his plan. We spoke to the UAB's administrator of nurses, whom he called in to join our first meeting in his office. We thanked her for the work her nurses did with Anna. We suggested to her that she establish some mental health counseling services for her nurses who work in areas where high stress and emotional trauma are commonplace.

We told her of how tired her nurses are and how stressed. We told her of the nurse who had witnessed a very inhospitable interaction between Anna and a resident pulmonary physician—and we told her of the BMT charge nurse who took that doctor to task for allowing a bad situation to turn into an uproar when simply responding to a page would have rectified the problem. Anna's nurse had been quite stressed and emotionally overwhelmed; she took the next day off from work to recover her mental stability.

In other meetings, Dr. Waldrum gave us updates on the progress of his plan. He told us that he was going to have himself placed on the medical school's curriculum committee. What he wanted to do was to create a series of courses, one for each year of the curriculum, that taught doctors-in-training how to appropriately interact with cancer patients. He wanted to guide them to become more sympathetic and humane when interacting with patients and trying to understand the situation from their point of view. He informed us he would like to teach the fourth and final course in the series himself. He wanted to use Anna's journal as the course material, and he asked to borrow it so that he could make a copy. Additionally, his plan involved revamping the Kirklin Clinic so that all staff would be available per their established schedules; that all staff would respond to messages promptly; that all procedures would be performed when scheduled; that all personnel would be trained in sensitivity and support techniques regarding the specific types of patients they served; and that the clinic in general would adopt a more patient-sensitive philosophy.

Dr. Waldrum was planning massive change for the UAB medical service culture. I thought him ambitious in his plans and efforts, but I was not sufficiently encouraged to believe that those who were involved on the other end would readily accept the changes. In my opinion, Dr Waldrum's redesigns were going to take political savvy, timing, and luck in order to be implemented effectively. Pam quietly harbored the same reticence. We did, however, feel that Dr. Waldrum's rising passion was evident in his envisioning and developing of the multipronged plan. If nothing else, we felt encouraged that what Anna and we had collectively experienced as a family during our journey at UAB was not misguided or mistaken; nor had it been misinterpreted by Dr. Waldrum.

In the end, the Kirklin Clinic underwent the greatest and most sustained transformation possible regarding the care and sensitivity its staff provided its patients. The clinic's timeliness and efficiency, and the positive interpersonal interactions between the clinic's staff and the patients who received tests, consultations, and services, changed immediately—and these changes have been long-lasting. Additionally, Dr. Waldrum was appointed to a seat on the UAB School of Medicine's curriculum committee, and the four courses in patient sensitivity and interaction were presented and discussed, but they were never implemented.

Due in part to Dr. Waldrum's efforts to transform UAB's patient services, he was soon recruited as president and chief executive officer of the University of Arizona Health Network, where he supervised two different hospitals. He served in this capacity for only two years before other, larger, medical networks came recruiting. In 2015, he accepted the position of CEO of Vidant Health, a network of eight hospitals in eastern North Carolina. Also, he serves on the board of the Association of American Medical Colleges. In 2020, he was named chair-elect of the Council of Teaching Hospitals and Health Systems. In 2021, he was appointed as dean of the Brody School of Medicine at East Carolina University. He has been nationally involved in urging an increased sensitivity to—and awareness of—patients' perceptions of and emotional reactions to how medical care is dispensed within any given medical community, especially communities he directly supervises. His aim is to encourage and increase the capacity for sympathy, empathy, and humaneness within the hospital environment. To this day he continues his efforts to lead in this regard. Currently, he is engaged in writing a book using "Anna's words"—words and phrases from Anna's journal—as chapter headings. In each chapter, he advocates for specific administrative policies that reflect Anna's concerns regarding how a patient experiences individual interactions with physicians, nurses, and all members of the hospital community who deliver medical care and services.

*   *   *

Anna's Gordon's Journal Entries

4-6 through [4-]8-2010

My first few days in the Bone Marrow Transplant Unit were honestly so trau-matic, it has taken me three whole days to recover from them, to even begin to write them down. Mom and I moved our things into the BMT unit early on the morning of the 6th. Immediately, I was inundated with rules that I am required to follow during my stay. Although I am not usually upset easily, the complete loss of privacy and freedom, as well as the restrictions of small comforts from home, such as the use of my own sheets and lotion, simply tipped me over the edge into tears. Your every function is regulated here, and I often feel more like a specimen than I do as a person. After the initial culture shock of my new environment, I pulled myself together, determined to follow the rules as best I can and come out of this transplant like a true BMT champ.

It seems almost silly now in retrospect to write about how upset I was when I first arrived here. I know things like sheets and lotions are small things to sacrifice considering what struggles my doctors and I am going through to make me well again. But really, those things are symbols of the greater freedoms and quality of life that I have lost throughout my experience with cancer. Privacy, independence, health, modesty, control, security…when one views it that way, I'm not surprised at all that those emotions would spill out some time!

4-7-2010

This could quite easily be the worst day of my life! In the morning, while Mom and I were enjoying our coffee, Dr. #2, one of the BMT doctors, came in for rounds and very solemnly announced that she had a very high suspicion that my leukemia had returned and that, consequently, I would not be able to move forward with transplant. In other words, curing me would be a long shot. I felt as if I had been told to prepare to die. The odd thing was that I didn't even feel as frustrated or cry like I had done the day before over some stupid soap! I was completely stunned, exposed, nowhere to hide, no way to make myself feel better. I was like a deer caught in a hunter's path.

The doctor ordered an emergency bone marrow biopsy to check the presence of the leukemia, and miraculously, the test was normal. Although a more specific test called a flow cytometry test indicated about three percent immature white cells, that reading is considered to be normal. However, that news of the possibility of resurfacing leukemia still resonates with me...haunting me right down to the faulty marrow in my bones.

I'm doing my best now to stay upbeat, follow my instructions to keep myself healthy, like walking and doing my mouth care correctly, and push negative thoughts away. Afterall, I have absolutely no choice but to make it to the other side of this transplant. There is no hiding from it, putting it off, or waking up from this nightmare. I feel completely helpless, like falling and waiting to hit the ground. Living in the moment is my only defense against the fear I have about the future.

4-9 and 10-2010

On the 9th, Rob took over night duty and Mom retreated to the apartment. We entertained ourselves walking, watching movies, and playing games. Today, the 10th, was much of the same. Mom did bring new snacks for the room when she returned. I ate a whole bag of dill pickle potato chips! Diets and self-control are for healthy people. I did have P. F. Chang's for dinner...mmm. I'm trying to enjoy what is left of my appetite. These medical people keep threatening me with possibility of tube feeding and mouth sores worthy of needing a pain pump. Such cheery people they are.

4-14-2010

The inconsistency here drives me crazy, and it ultimately drives me not to trust my physicians and caregivers as much as I would like. Simply living day to day in the hospital is arguably just as challenging as any chemotherapy I have ever received.

4-12-2010

Let me confess that I really dread opening my mail these days. Not only that, but I feel guilty for feeling that way, too. I know people are trying to be nice, sending cards quoting scripture and giving their empty predictions for my future, but truthfully, these things irk me to the core. It's easy to tell others what to do when you've not walked in their shoes. If I ever get up the energy to write a book about this experience, here are a few words of advice about how not to care for your loved one with cancer.

1. It's about the patient: not about you!

Don't talk about yourself and your problems/complaints about your daily life. If you are visiting a cancer patient, remember the reason for your visit: that person. Save your own griping for someone who can better support you at this time, because frankly, you're cancer-stricken loved one couldn't care less about the pounds you put on over the holidays or how underappreciated you are at work. In all likelihood, your cancer loved one would do anything to keep food down, much less put on a few, or to have the opportunity to go to work each day, rather than waste away in a hospital room, feeling like someone's guinea pig in a big sterile cage. Get my drift?

2. Don't make predictions

Are you God? A doctor? A psychic? If you answered "no" to any of these questions, then why are you making predictions about the future? The truth is, no one knows the future of your cancer-stricken loved one, not even his or her doctors. So suppress the desire to say/repeat trite phrases such as, "This will be over soon," "Everything will turn out just fine, in the end." If everything were alright, your cancer patient wouldn't be in his or her situation, and he/she knows that. Try saying something more meaningful, such as: "I love you, and I'm here for you for as long as it takes to get you well again." Or "I know I can't take this burden away, but I'll do everything I can to make it easier for you to bear." These statements are so much more meaningful than those that cannot necessarily be counted upon.

3. Don't belittle your cancer loved one's pain/difficulty with fighting cancer.
Throughout my own cancer experience, I've noticed that people don't handle the permanence of cancer well. They belittle its impact verbally in hopes that such an action might lessen cancer's hurt on the person they love. Such verbal attempts often are similar to the following, "This cancer is just a bump in the road"—translation to a cancer patient—"Cheer up, this cancer is no big thing, besides, you've got plenty of life ahead, so quit your fretting." Such a statement to the cancer patient suggests to him or her that you disapprove of [the] fear, anger, or depression that he or she may feel throughout the treatment process. Instead, one should mirror and echo the feelings of the patient: not contradict them. What matters is the patient's reality—not yours.

4. I don't care what anybody says: Hair is important and plays a large role in the cancer patient's healing and recovery process.
Never trivialize that loss or make light of it in any way. Again, mirror the patient's attitude about the hair loss. If he/she adopts a light attitude about it, making mohawks with the remaining hair and sporting ridiculous hats as a new "do" to replace the old one—go with it. Offer to wear funny wigs, too, or help him/her order new hats to complement the new style. If he or she is anxious and insecure about hair loss, echo how sorry you are for his/her loss and that he/she has every right to feel put out about it. It is always appropriate to acknowledge that you couldn't possibly know how they are feeling during that time. Again, never trivialize or belittle the loss with phrases such as, "It's just hair," or "It will grow back, don't worry." If it's not your hair, you have no right to judge its value or impact on a person's identity or self-esteem.

5. Avoid talking about others you know who have gone through cancer treatment (both positive and negative stories).
In all likelihood, cancer patients are uninterested in the suffering stories of others: they have their own suffering to focus on. Besides, because each cancer patient is unique, two patients, as similar as can be, can have completely disparate experiences. There is no guarantee that because your childhood best friend's

mom recovered from her cancer, your cancer loved one will too. And vice versa, who the hell wants to listen to you tell stories you know of where cancer patients have died from their disease? Why in the world is that uplifting/encouraging to your loved one? Please, think before you speak. And if thinking is too difficult for you, quietly smile instead.

6. No, you can't possibly understand. I'm doing this alone.
Often friends and family members of cancer patients feel the need to communicate that they are on the same page as the patient. They try to express that, they, too, are hurting, and therefore, understand the patient's pain. This example of reasoning is false and erroneous. Although family and friends may be deeply involved in a patient's treatment and healing processes, the burden of the disease is the patient's, alone. It is the patient's body that experiences the treatment's physical effects. It is the patient's freedom, privacy, and independence that have been surrendered. It's the patient's mind that is burdened with fear of pain, anxiety over redefining one's personal identity, and above all, the realization of his/her own mortality and the tenuous nature of life here on earth. Please understand that your lame verbal commitments to "take cancer from the patient and put it upon yourself" are not only hypothetical in the most impossible sense, but they show the patient absolutely no true commitment on your part to ease his/her burden. Try promising more realistic commitments, such as performing caregiving duties or organizing fundraisers, and following through with them, rather than make lofty and dramatic promises that you could never fulfill anyway.

7. DO NOT try to reason about why cancer is now a part of your loved one's life.
Here are a few cardinal examples never to follow:

> *"This is God's will."*

> *"You are meant to be a vehicle of God's grace and an example to others to help strengthen their faith."*

> *"Others were meant to learn from your suffering, to better appreciate their blessings."*

"You did something in your past to deserve this burden."
"God is testing your faith, like Job."

* * *

On September 13, 2011, early in the fall semester at the University of Alabama, Dr. Robert E. Witt made good his promise to hold a memorial event for Anna Gordon on the quadrangle at Denny Chimes. At 4:00 p.m., the final hour of the workday, all those wishing to attend—university students, employees, and guests alike—assembled to remember Anna. Mr. Jason Beasley, our friend and organist at Christ Episcopal Church in Tuscaloosa volunteered to play the carillon housed within the campanile tower of Denny Chimes. Dr. John Ratledge, our friend, conducted the University Singers, and Dr. Witt gave a spoken remembrance.

The University of Alabama Remembers
Anna Elizabeth Gordon
June 5, 1987—May 9, 2011
September 13, 2011—4:00PM

The Chiming of the Hour	*Mr. Jason Beasley, Denny Chimes*
The University of Alabama Alma Mater	*Mr. Jason Beasley, Denny Chimes*
The Spoken Remembrance	*Dr. Robert E. Witt, President*
The University Singers	*Dr. John Ratledge, Conductor*
"I've Been in the Storm So Long" (Spiritual)	*Jeffrey Ames*
	Kasey Fuller, Soprano
The Playing of the Chimes	*Mr. Jason Beasley, Denny Chimes*
"For the Beauty of the Earth"	
"Praise to the Lord, the Almighty"	
"Minuet"—J. S. Bach	
"Joyful, Joyful, We Adore Thee"	
The Chiming of Remembrance: Twenty-Three Years	*Mr. Jason Beasley, Denny Chimes*

* * *

On August 8, 2012, the University of Alabama honored the memory of Anna Gordon when the director of undergraduate admissions, Rick Funk, officially opened the Anna E. Gordon Living Room inside the office complex where Anna worked as an admissions counselor for Alumni and Volunteer Recruitment in 2011. In addition to staff offices, the complex has five living rooms where staff, like Anna, meet visiting students and their families when they arrive on campus. In this welcoming space, the counselor and the prospective students and their families are refreshed and made comfortable before the beginning of campus tours, testing, interviewing, and any other orientation activity.

Anna Gordon loved the University of Alabama and it loved her in return. Through The Anna Gordon Memorial Endowed Scholarship in Psychology and the Anna E. Gordon Living Room housed in the Office of Admissions, she will continue to have an impact on future generations of higher education students. She would be pleased—"Well Done!"

Chapter 15

GRIEF IS A REAL THING. IT IS DIFFERENT THAN regret, or fear, or anxiety, or stress, or depression. These emotions reflect feelings of a potential future doom. Grief comes after the unspeakable happens. There is no changing the outcome, avoiding calamity, or softening the blow. Grief follows a death, the ripping away of known reality, plunging a person, a relationship, a friendship, a confidence, a hope into the unknown. The transition itself, the death, is peaceful, serene, a stoppage of all physical torment and adversity for the one who is transitioning. It is the dying that is hard, the physical decline that is so violent, so unfair, so destructive, and so full of struggle against that outcome—the struggle to stay here in this experience! Death itself, when it comes, is peaceful, respectful, poignant, almost a physical representation of our hope of continuing, of going on, of still existing, of being whole, transitioning to a different but definite experience. For me, when I witnessed Anna travel through that passage, I got the same feeling of awe I experienced when she was born: once again, she was transitioning from one place or experience to another. I felt both moments were a brief, fleeting, glimpse of a greater reality.

Grief comes just after. Grief is an overwhelming pain. It shortens breath, buckles knees, and loses rationality and repose, replacing itself with pure despair, as the perceived permanence of a relationship is ripped from you, against your will, never to be replaced. This void is what one feels as reality. What you knew as reality is turned into memory and all the evidence that you have that the relationship existed, was real, is your memories. Memory is both sweet and sour, pain and comfort, hope and despair, and it vacillates between the two extreme opposites, apportioning them differently at any given time. What I do know is that the harder you love, the more valuable the relationship, the more meaningful and important the bond, the deeper and the more intense will be the pain from the loss.

Grief is a noun that describes the pain of loss. Mourning is a verb that refers to the processing of that loss, the struggle to explain, to find reasons, to ask why, to wrestle with the new rules of a different reality in one's day-to-day existence. The process of mourning varies from person to person. There is no timeframe, no designated length of days or degree of recovery that marks its closing. It is what it is, and it will be what it needs to be within each individual who experiences it. Again, the greater the loss, the greater the mourning process. In my experience, the loss of a child is the most painful and deep grief of any grief a person can bear, because as a good parent, the birth changes you. It changes you from an entity of self-interest into an entity of selfless sacrifice. When you love a child, you love and value that child and its welfare above your own self. You love that child more than you love yourself. Therefore, when there is death and separation, a parent's despair is a permanent part of their reality. It never goes away because the love you have for that other person and the self-sacrificing instincts you possess to prosper that child never go away. While the mourning process may lead to ways of keeping the pain and loss from becoming debilitating when performing daily tasks, the loss is still ever-present, a companion throughout your daily experience.

In my experience, the loss of a certainty that informs your actions, provides meaning, and directs your purpose from the moment of loss onward, accompanies the loss of the relationship with your child. The inner feeling of certainty you rely on to guide your process of discernment is like a toolbox you acquire over a lifetime by embracing ideas that seem certain. These tools seem to be a gift of truth and direction and they give you the ability to choose how to act in this world, how to feel. These certainties are now missing, and the tools you formerly used have no practical use now. Tools like belief in the goodness of God, like prayer, like a master plan that you melt into and become a part of, a divine guidance for those who seek, accept, and obey; these anchors of action and truth are, in one moment, spilled on the floor, jumbled and broken, lost and left in a useless disarray. Your light, your hope, your certainty is violated. I was left with anger, confusion, and distrust, in a manner similar to what one feels when experiencing a robbery or home invasion. The sense of safety has been removed, and we have been disappointed. The worst part of the ordeal is that you are left feeling disappointed with the best thing: that idea that held you fast and strong and sure—the idea of a loving, giving, ever-present, knowing, sure defense—a God! A God who will fight our battles, smite our enemies, miraculously change our circumstance, and make things better when we cannot, if we only trust and ask. This concept of God was not what I experienced, not what I expected, or wanted to admit was my truth.

You read, you study, you evaluate, and you accept the idea of God as you progress through a life experience. You read, you study, you memorize, and you glean a truth or certainty from the rational acceptance of paradigms contained within sacred Scriptures that tell you it is so. A host of family, of friends, of ancestors, of neighbors, of strangers even, tells you it is so, as they act as witnesses to how these truths have played out in their experience. These tools for initiating action are held sacred and holy because of the truth they contain, and this host advises that a wise man is the man who accepts these premises and acts accordingly, building the history of his life through the informed action of these writings and sacred tenets. In our experience, at least in the midst of the process of mourning, the process of enduring, of analyzing, and of sifting through the pain to find a path—they are not true!

It is precisely at this time, the time of most immediate need, that you require those tools to work. Your most precious possession, the living breathing manifestation of goodness and light in your life and of meaning for your world, has been taken from you. In our case, Anna's death took a struggle of over two years. We could see the immediacy of the moment. We knew how important the fight. The battle with a disease unearned, unfair, and unwelcome, created the most intense and desperate struggle of not only her life, but of all of our family's lives. This was the time to pull out the tools we had collected, use them, believe in them, and wield them against every negative aspect of the disease in order to win the battle and to conquer—to conquer the threat of death.

Two of the tools we and all those who came to our support and aid used were belief and prayer. We prayed from March 2nd of 2009 until 11:00 at night on May 9, 2011. I prayed, Pam prayed, Tori prayed, Anna prayed. Practically every person we knew, and many more we did not know, prayed individually and in groups for healing. Hundreds and hundreds of people of varying faiths, values, and life circumstances joined us and added their sincere soulful efforts toward the beseeching of the divine to intervene, to heal and to restore Anna's life as well as her body and to provide for her a future, one that surely would bear the best fruit she could share with all, just as she had every day of her life leading to that moment. In the end, although Anna valiantly fought, struggled, and suffered more than any human should have to suffer; although she conquered obstacle after obstacle the disease threw in her path—even those artificially created by others around her—she died. She lost the battle, or as Dr. Robert Witt said at her memorial service held on the University of Alabama's quadrangle, "Anna didn't lose, she just ran out of time."

"My God, My God, why hast Thou forsaken me?"..."Ask and it shall be given unto thee, seek and you shall find, knock and it shall be opened unto you..."..."Whatever you ask in my name it shall be given unto you." Tools to use, certainties to assure—were not true. In our experience, it was not true. We wanted it to be true. Who wants to say that their beliefs and those actions entered into in the sincere and genuine attempt to claim those promised results did not work, did not restore, and did not comfort as the Scriptures promised? No one wants to willingly abandon the tools given to them to use in times of challenge and crisis. But, at a time when you need God most, you find there is no reprieve, no help, no mercy, no restoration, and no change.

This is a disturbing place to be after the dust has settled. Your mental and emotional state is at odds with all of the surroundings you are interacting with. You ask yourself, "What good is it?" This is where you find yourself, and these are the questions to which you must respond and the rules you must rewrite, the toolbox you must rebuild for use the next time.

Our natural reaction to the hurt and disappointment of our apparent abandonment by the "Almighty" was real. Our spiritual disappointment combined with the actual pain of losing Anna was truly devastating. When we said so, especially in public forums like Facebook, we received true caring, empathy, and understanding by many who had gone through a similar experience. They knew, they understood. But from a multitude who had not directly experienced what we experienced, we received comments attacking us and accusing us of not being faithful enough, of not believing enough, of not accepting the situation enough, and of not endorsing a "Plan" that we "cannot know now, but one day we will understand." While these people may have had the best of intentions, saying what they said out of their hopes to ease our suffering, in truth they infuriated us with what we felt was a callousness and an over-simplification regarding what our intended actions should be, even though the people who wrote these hurtful comments had no direct experience that could be compared to our experience: they had no direct way to comprehend what we were feeling and saying. They merely felt insulted themselves that someone would actually say something that went against their core beliefs, even if their experience—the experience that apparently caused such fierce belief—was insulated from real pain. I guess they attack with such fierceness because they want their beliefs to be correct. Perhaps they feel that if they are not correct, then they, too, would be destroyed by similar circumstances?

The offensive responses fell into several categories. The first category consisted of comments such as "Miracles should occur with those who pray for them *if* they believe hard enough" or if you are "a good enough

'Christian,' " or "if you have earned God's favor," with the implied tag line—
"like me!" This category of response was received by us as a judgment of our
spiritual character; therefore, they were infuriating! The second category of
response was "God has a plan, and this was His plan. We will know it one
day." Or, "It is God's will. 'Not my will but Thine be done, O Lord.' " The third
(and worst) category comprised comments espousing the notion that "Anna
must have deserved this; it must be punishment for something she did or
said or felt." Or, "The world is all cause and effect, you know." Our ultimate
reaction to these ideas was: for however long we last on this earth, there will
be no comfort for our loss. We can only hope for time to cover the emotional
wounds we bear. Our view of the future was one of joyless noncreativity and
nonproductivity, stretching on day after day until there were no more days.

We also heard suggestions regarding how to get over our pain from certain Facebook followers who were less offensive in their comments. But those
comments declared, in essence, that we must forget about Anna in order to
avoid more pain, so that we would not continually pick at our emotional scab
by dwelling on her memory and reliving events. We should let it go, release
it into the hand of God or fate or the "Plan" and move on. But move on to
what? I guess these mildly sympathetic souls believed there was a limit in
regard to how long they should have to hear of your grief. They wanted you
to get better, return to who you were before the illness and become, again,
the person that they knew and liked prior to the tragedy. I suppose that in
their experiences with death and grieving they had felt bad for only a few
days, an appropriate amount of time set aside to reflect, and then they went
on acting as they had before—forgetting and removing from the forefront
of their mind the probably distant friend or relative they had lost to death.
These people, too unaccustomed to real tragedy, were too disturbed by our
pain to hang around anymore. Again, in my book, the harder you love, the
deeper and more valuable the relationship, and the harder, longer, and deeper
you grieve. They must not know of that kind of pain.

In reality, you cannot release pain and accept loss without deliberately thinking less often of the one you lose! The parental instinct is to remember, to hold on to, to talk about, and to include in life experiences; in our case, it is to preserve our family experience as a unit of four, not three. But when you act as if you are four, you face the reality of the absence of the missing one—and the reoccurrence of the pain associated with that absence—on a daily, even hourly basis. This we cannot avoid. It seems to be our future, even if it is because we choose it to be this way. The choice to remember, even when it is accompanied with its sorrow, is somehow more comforting than the less painful choice of forgetting.

In the middle of swimming in the ocean of uncertainty that is a consequence of the grieving and mourning process, I have experienced the desire to reassemble my life's toolbox. Doing so is necessary to my survival. But you can't just repack the toolbox with the same instruments that led to the disappointment you find so uncomfortable now. When one grieves, the emotional struggle and the physical suffering are such intensely motivating experiences that you become desperate to reconfigure your understanding so it may prove useful in the times that surely lie ahead. This feeling of desperation forces one to reevaluate every notion, every principle and supposition one makes in order to assess its continued place in your toolbox. I was forced to fully engage my mind and openly reassess the tenets of my faith, ultimately reorganizing some, discarding some, and placing new emphasis on others. Finally, I theorized some new tenets, replacing those that now seemed to be unsound with those that reflected the facts of our experiences, both emotionally and physically.

I felt that it was important that I codify my own theology, based on my truth and the truths that spoke to me, informed me, and inspired me. Right or wrong, I felt that this step was necessary because the toolbox I had previously been given and that I had previously accepted had so painfully disappointed me when it was needed most. To me, the theology I had inherited, although well-meaning and potentially filled with truth, was full of holes and inconsistencies, and that it was difficult to reconcile with reality. My child needed truth in order to feel comfort and to have peace while she endured her situation and her continued suffering. She had looked for it, looked to me for it, and what I was able to offer her in the heat of her battle was not adequate to the experience. Now that she was gone, I could forget and put aside the memory of her struggle and its philosophical inadequacies and continue on in my daily life of apathy and ignorance, or I could put in the effort to investigate, prioritize, evaluate, and create my personal theological mythology and square it with the self-evident truths I still held that were contained in the inherited theology.

I chose, like Martin Luther of old, to use my reasoning and apply it to my very salvation and take responsibility for what my mind's eye saw. Just as Martin Luther believed, I do not mean for others to follow until they do what Luther commanded his followers to do—reason for themselves! And so Martin Luther published his theological theses for all to read and reason through the soundness of his thinking for themselves before they acted. This self-reasoning represents the heart of humanism, of Protestantism, of the Renaissance, and ultimately of the Enlightenment's philosophies. Man must use his senses and experience to reason his way forward through informed action.

I realized that I must do what others have done for centuries; I must take responsibility for what my mind tells me and to trust it boldly. I remembered that just like Martin Luther, like Galileo, and even like the more recent Dr. Martin Luther King, I must do what they did. These men used their God-given power of reason to discern, to the best of their abilities, what was correct and just and accurate. In each of these cases, they offended the established religious and theological powers of their day, striking out on an individual course, even risking their own "salvation," at least as it was viewed by their conservative peers. Yet because they took the risk to think and to trust their conclusions, others' lives were enhanced and set free from the constrictions common in their day. I must be willing to risk the security I found in my previous concept of salvation, in order to find a more useful, consistent, and meaningful peace that would allow me to move forward. So it was in this spirit of independent purpose that I began what I had to do if I were to continue to be a believer at all.

I started with the principle of prayer and the commands given us to pray. I understood the Scripture's instructions regarding "Ask what you will…" and all of the conventional Christian wisdom that supported that commandment. Until now, its validity in my mind was self-evident. But that assurance was housed in a life experience that preceded the vital necessity of using that principle as instructed. When the need came to use the tool and the instruction, it did not work. The reality was that the more I looked at others' situations—situations where prayer was involved, requested, or offered up by one person for someone else's benefit—more times than not, it did not work. Statistically speaking, this is not good news. It does not reassure the user of this particular tool. In fact, to my mind, when requested through prayer the manifestation of beneficial results in regard to another person's difficulty seemed no surer than the occurrence of those same results by random chance.

Anna thought the universe was lawful. Once, when in the hospital discussing the power of prayer, she rightfully stated that "the universe is a lawful place. Gravity works all of the time, not just some of the time. The universe is full of laws that can be depended on to keep order. My problem with prayer is that if it were truly a physical and spiritual principle that could be used by people for the benefit of people, it would work all of the time, not some of the time." When I first heard her say that I literally stopped talking. There was nothing I could say that was more self-evident than what she had just uttered, and it stunned me. I was not prepared to think that prayer might not work for Anna, or for anyone. The promise of prayer in the Scriptures was too great, too comforting, and too familiar to cast it into the harsh light of statistical reality. Inside, I wanted to point out each occasion with which I was familiar where prayer had worked; at the same time I could also think of as many or more occasions where it had not. Internally accounting for the sincerity and qualifying factors of the people doing the praying in each unsuccessful instance, I was left with the underlying truth of what she had matter-of-factly stated.

The more I thought about this revelation the more destruction my toolbox endured. Why does prayer not work predictably? The answers that came to me from out of my past reminded me of many different statements I had heard throughout the period of my religious upbringing and training. My memories ran the gamut of theological ideas held by Christians regarding prayer. *"You have to believe. If you don't have enough faith, then it won't come to pass." "You have not lived a righteous enough life for God to hear your entreaties." "You're answer is NO from God. He knows best, NOT YOU." "Be happy with the answer you have been given and don't expect God to be a genie going around granting wishes." "Everything happens for a reason, honey. One day you will understand."* While the people from my past (and present) who spoke these words may have come to their opinions based on various Scriptures they cited as justification for the recipe they believed should be used to ensure one's prayer requests were successful, I realized that God's perceived response to each of my prayers using the yardstick of their explanations was—NO, regarding my stated request! To me, their perceived reality flew in the face of direct, unarguable commands to "Ask what you will…and pray without ceasing."

I concluded that prayer as a discipline is good for the one who prays. It creates opportunities for internal growth in the areas of empathy, sympathy, and selflessness, and it increases concern for others. It seems to me that when these internal traits are encouraged to grow and mature, good works can have the opportunity to come from the one who prays, increasing the chances of real, helpful action. I am not convinced that just because one prays for a change in another person's physical condition or another person's circumstances, God steps in as a result of the prayer itself to make the requested changes, simply because the request has been made. In regard to the many scriptural passages referring to prayer, I think there is too much conflicting information and too meager specific instructions available to achieve consistent, predictable, measurable results.

Moreover, I believe that life on this earth is often random. Why do some people have car accidents that have horrible results, and some do not? Why do some people contract a debilitating disease while many do not? Why do bad things happen to good people while many bad people seem to enjoy all that life has to offer? I do not know! But I can't help but feel that life is full of randomness. Chance occurrences and inexplicable, random events occur in peoples' lives, both positive and negative. I do not think that God punishes certain people or gives them tests or even challenges their faith through trials while letting others off unhindered, living in apparent uninterrupted prosperity and ease.

I believe that God is an unknowable concept, an idea, an initiator, a creator, the first and the last, the totality of what is and to whom we must return when our life experience is over. I believe that the term *God* is used by people when they do not know what else to call something. I believe that the term *God* reflects, for me at least, everything that is good and just and right and kind and fair and loving, even if I seem alone in my journey through life's circumstances and trauma. My job is to discipline my free will in order to minimize my sense of selfishness and learn to maximize my selflessness. In doing so, I have the opportunity to become a conduit for love through my deliberate action, and God as goodness, as kindness, as rightness, and as fairness, becomes manifest in the world for the benefit of others through my choosing to act. I have become useful love. I have chosen to become the hands and feet of God for another person in this world, in this place, and at this time.

This notion came to me when I contemplated how "God" has interacted with me in my life experience. It dawned on me that "God" never came to me in a lightning strike or booming voice. No unearthly miracle such as a "burning bush" or "pillar of fire" ever got my attention and changed my circumstance. Rather, whenever I remember help coming to me to actually change my circumstance, it came to me in the form of another person, a person actually doing something for my benefit that was not required for their betterment. Someone listened to me talk, someone dried my tears, someone gave me money, someone spoke words of encouragement, someone mowed my lawn or brought me food or water, cut fallen trees from out of my driveway and my yard with chainsaws after a tornado, lifting and carrying away wood. Neighbors and friends came to my house and packed my belongings after an EF4 tornado ripped through my neighborhood circle and left trees in my living room so that they could place tarps on the holes in my roof to keep the rain out before the darkness of night came and more rain arrived. I did not ask these people for help. I could not ask these people for help. I could not help myself. But they came. Immediately they came from next door, across town, and from campus. From other cities, many miles away, loaded with tools and gas and food they came. "God" was helping me, providing for me, saving me through these people! These people, who saw a need, who selflessly put aside their comfort and chose to act, were becoming "God's" blessing to me and my family at a time when we could not help ourselves. This realization changed my life!

I saw it all during 2009, 2010, and 2011. During the years that followed Anna's leukemia diagnosis, people individually and in groups thought, planned, organized, and provided for me and my family over and over again. As a family, we were barely able to focus on anything other than getting done what was necessary for Anna's treatment and for the improvement of her situation. Without significant consultation with us, friends, neighbors, colleagues, and even strangers acted to ease every burden they could. Multiple fundraisers were organized, raising enough money to pay for all of Anna's medical bills not covered by insurance. Throughout the two-and-a-half-year ordeal, prayer events were hosted and maintained in multiple towns involving multiple churches of various denominations. The most powerful example of selfless sacrifice was embodied in the efforts of the twelve-year-old girl from Gordo, AL, who had been a piano student of Pam's prior to Anna's illness. That young girl began to knit purses that she would sell to adult women. With each order she received, she began another purse, knitting at night and on the weekends. She collected the money she made from creating and selling the purses, and she donated it to Anna's fund. In the end, she donated more than one thousand dollars, selling purses at a price of twenty dollars each! The purity of heart combined with the physical effort necessary to knit that many items over that long a period of time was—and is—stunning to me. I could not have been more humbled, embarrassed, and ashamed that I could point to nothing I had done in my fifty years of life as generous or magnanimous as what this child had done for our family. The lesson was powerful, self-evident, and life changing for me.

There was good in the world! There was kindness, love, empathy, compassion, caring, and strength, and it came through people—people who chose to act, to love, to feel another's hurt, to care, to sacrifice, to help, and to support. Not merely once, but continuously over the long haul and even after, during the recovery. This is what we are supposed to do. This is the perfect plan, a masterful system for the transformation for both parties, the helper and the one in need. I finally got it, understood its simplicity and purity. Because of others, I realized what I consider to be the true nature of life's purpose.

To my mind, free will is given to me to choose my outlook through my attitude. My task is to master my choices to the degree that allows nature to no longer constrict my free will with its demand for self-survival and self-prosperity. Selfish choices, while gratifying to me and allowing me to prosper, actually blind me to the needs of others, and they give me the illusion of separateness, of the need to compete, and of self-aggrandizement through the intoxication I get as the result of my successes and the self-interested boosting of my self-image and perceived self-worth. When I discipline my free will to act unselfishly, it allows me the opportunity to exercise my selfless efforts, thereby becoming a conduit of kindness, caring, and assistance to someone else. They are helped and assisted in a real sense, and I am helped and assisted for having chosen to help. My task is to learn to be selfless rather than selfish;

in doing so, over time, until it becomes my first instinct rather than my last instinct, my creator's investment in me will bear fruit. I will become the salt of the earth, and the "talents" that I have been given, as in the parable, will increase. I can return to my creator the talents given to me with interest. I am made useful, for I can take on more responsibility because I can be trusted to be a surrogate for Christ in the world, becoming "I in you and you in me." As Scripture also states, "I am the vine, and you are the branches."

The spiritual reality flooding my mind had nothing to do with church attendance, denomination selection, dogma, or politics. It had nothing to do with cultural popularity or family traditions. It had to do with the essence of me as an individual spirit and the quality and usefulness of my existence. It was dawning on me that I could choose to be love in the world. That was my ideal. Of course I would fail, I would fall victim to selfishness and self-interest, but now I had a goal, one that I fully understood and one that made sense, one that could become an undeniable beacon of hope for not only the perfecting of myself but also for the bringing of help and hope and peace to others.

I also recognized that I was late to come to this realization. Many around me and multitudes before me understood this. It is because of them that anything good had occurred at all in the world. The simplicity of this notion was beautiful to me, elegant, and very comparable to what my experiences as a husband and parent had been. Because I knew beyond all doubt the correctness of this concept as witnessed in my life of family, for the first time, what the Scriptures had promised was resonating in my heart and mind—a sense of deep and abiding peace. Peace not born of religion or culture, or family, or righteousness, as understood from my Southern Protestant cultural teachings, but a soft and sure confidence that felt right: this peace was now what I leaned on in the uncertainty of my life experience after my child's death, a death that seemed unjust, full of extreme suffering and disturbing disillusionment with fate.

I had been taught a lesson, one most valuable and rare, by hundreds of people in west Alabama whether they knew they were teaching it or not.

As my mind began to formulate the meaning of all that had happened to us over twenty-six months, the central purpose of my life that had been ripped away and destroyed with Anna's death was now being replaced with a purpose I could accept, a purpose I could use as the reason to continue to live and act and love throughout the remainder of whatever days I was given. I am grateful!

Chapter 16

My Spiritual Theses,
or Wisdom, or Toolbox—Today

1. My life is my experience alone. I was born to learn and grow, to be made more useful in my surroundings and circumstance. I am given my senses, my intuition, and my reasoning ability as tools to learn, use, and trust while experiencing each day.

2. I am given free will to act and to feel.

3. Regarding feelings, emotions, and inner thoughts, I can choose my attitude each day and even each moment, and this attitude will govern the feelings, emotions, and thoughts I experience in my head. The act of choosing my attitude, and the resulting conversation in my mind and body, will drive my experience.

4. I also get to choose my ideal, my goal, my constant, my "North Star." This choice is what is referred to in common language as "what I believe," meaning "to Be," and "to Live" (referring to and informing my action), creating the word *believe*, which is a verb, reflecting the actions associated with my ideal, as well as the word *belief*, which is a noun, referring to the meaning of my choice of ideal.

5. I travel my life and its experience alone, acting with "hope," which informs my choices, my thinking, and my feelings (or emotions.) I

am allowed to change my mind and select another "ideal" as a touch-stone when my reasoning dictates the need for a change.

6.   I do not "know" the ultimate truth. I only experience "my truth," which describes what "feels true" within myself. No one knows the ultimate truth while on life's journey. So, I will not give more credence to another's knowledge of "truth" above my own percep-tion of it. I will respect their journey as their own and I will do my own internal thinking and reasoning and perceiving. Occasionally, I will come across other people who understand and reflect my perception of "truth," and I will find encouragement and example in their journeys.

7.   I am no better, but no worse, than any other individual I encounter, regardless of their chosen "beliefs" or resulting actions. I should offer them respect, honor their journey, and offer help, encouragement, and support in whatever way I am able. I believe that they have "God" in them as I am a part of "God" myself. Whatever I do to or for them, I do to my perception of "God," and to myself.

8.   I believe my actions, and my choices that inform and motivate those actions, have consequences. These consequences aid or hinder my progress in experiencing and growing my understanding of my ideal. Hinderance leads to repeating the lesson, or opportunity to choose and act again. When I choose and act in accordance with my "ideal," I grow toward my own "salvation," which means that I accept the good that comes to me when I act toward myself and others in a manner that reflects my "ideal." I discipline my choosing, which brings rewards in my physical circumstance and in my sense of well-being.

9.   I am not left to my own mind alone when choosing. I also have "inner knowing," also called *intuition*. This, I believe, is what is scripturally referred to as the "still small voice." When I identify the difference

between my own thoughts and the impressions of the intuitive voice within me, I realize that the intuitive voice within me is one that can be trusted, one that never leads me to action that will hinder or harm me and is a voice that will always guide me toward continued progress in my intended journey. In my experience, the more I listen to my intuition, the easier its voice is to identify within the cacophony of my thoughts, and the more I will hear its speaking to me. This always brings peace, softening the inner doubt and fear of making a wrong choice. I learn to trust the guidance of that "still small voice."

10. I believe fear is an internal lack of confidence and a hinderance to progress within my journey, and a disrupter of my peace.

11. I believe that when I act in accordance with my ideals, consistently, that this is my faith and defines my faith.

12. I respect others' journeys and choices as reflections of their individual paths. I will not try to convince them of the correctness of my life journey, life choices, and purpose. I believe that their journey and purpose is as valuable and meaningful as my own and that it is arrogant of me to think I know best for anyone other than myself. All I am called to do is to travel my own path, discover its own meaning, and be of help and comfort to others as I encounter them. My ideal is to leave them in better shape after my encounter with them than I found them. This is my example.

13. I will not experience everything in my single life's journey. Therefore, I cannot "know" everything. I will remain open to the wisdom of others' examples and "truths" when I encounter them.

14. The best attitude I can select every day when I rise is that of gratitude. I will be thankful for what I have now, for who I am now, and for what I am becoming. I will rejoice (or re-joy) in the possibilities of this day's lessons, gifts, and encounters.

15. I will be open to acceptance. In other words, I will learn to accept the gifts that come my way each day, no matter their form.

16. I will choose the perception of abundance each day. This is the knowledge that I have (or have access to) everything that is necessary to sustain my journey and allow it to prosper. I will never lack because I can always ask for help in regard to any negative aspect of my life.

17. I will foster communication with my intuition and inner guiding voice. I will express and demonstrate thanks through gratitude. I will find peace in the knowledge that I may ask for help or resources or guidance. Once I have made a request, I will act as if the thing is already created and on its way into my perception for my use, and I will accept this reality and wait upon its arrival to me in faith. I will feel certain that I may request my betterment. I will also request help and betterment for others, but I will not always know if my request will appear for their betterment. I accept that I do not have a complete understanding of how this exchange of request (or prayer) and answer works. I believe only that I am responsible for my journey and my prayers.

18. I believe there is more that exists than I can experience and "know" in this body.

19. I believe that I existed before I was born into my present-day experience and that I will continue in some manner when my body releases me. I do not "know" how or all the "whys" of this, I only "know" that this feels correct, and the idea rings true to my perception of "truth." My experience with this concept is reflected in my perceptions at the moment of each of my children's births and in the deaths of those I have witnessed. The two "opposite" experiences, that of an entity entering this realm and that of the same entity exiting this realm, bear witness to the continuation of an entity's journey,

arriving somewhere and then departing for somewhere else; they are not the beginning or the ending of that spirit, soul, or entity, in my perception. I accept that it is not my prerogative to "know" the "truth" of these things.

20. I believe that everyone's journey will be best served if they make their own list of decided truths that they use when selecting their goals, ideals, and interactions with others they encounter. Having done so, one's actions can be more purposeful. I also believe that everyone, including myself, should be open to change in regard to the "truths" within that list when experience and the "inner voice" leads one to more convincing "truth." Be open, be flexible, always learn and grow.

How to Love

1. I believe that one has to choose to love.

2. I believe that love is a verb, an action.

3. I believe that people confuse the experience of love as a feeling, usually a romantic or platonic one. This feeling is the precursor to love, in that the feeling causes me to act in a loving manner toward the person or thing being loved. But I believe the feeling is a call to action, and if an action does not occur, then love is not transferred onto the person or thing being loved. I must complete the circle, or complete the call to action, by actually taking action.

4. I believe that my "ideal" is to love everyone I encounter because in doing so, I act lovingly toward God because God is in all things—"I am the vine and ye are the branches." Therefore, all that I encounter—human, animal, plant, or earth—is God.

5. I know this concept to be true because I experience God in my journey through what others have done to or for me.

6. I believe that love begets love. In other words, the more you experience love from others, the more you want to love in return as gratitude for the love expressed, and transferred, toward you.

7. I believe there is a formula built into the system of life. The formula is:

8. I have a calling to act in a loving manner toward another.

9. My response to that calling is to act toward another.

10. The one I act towards receives my action.

11. And because of my love, that person is left with that same calling, the same one from which I initiated my action.

12. I believe that the more love I give out in my journey, the more I will receive in my life. I am in control of this process through my choosing.

13. I believe the feeling I ultimately receive after an action from another, directed toward me, is a higher sense of gratitude. The more love I receive, the more gratitude I feel—and the more I am called to perform actions of love, not only to the one who loved me, but to anyone, and everyone.

14. I believe that this is the design of not only this life experience, but of all creation.

"WHEREVER YOU GO, NO MATTER THE WEATHER, ALWAYS BRING YOUR OWN *sunshine*"

Epilogue

I CANNOT END THIS TALE WITHOUT TRYING TO incorporate an ending that represents a neat and tidy conclusion, something profound and of vital worth that will make the suffering, anxiety, ugliness, and unfairness of what took place more palatable for the reader. The moral of this story does not concern Anna Gordon. In the end, the telling of her life is meant to illustrate my spiritual growth. My understanding was the byproduct of what happened to her. This is the wisdom I wish to leave the reader—the secret to life well-lived. The story of the helpers, the encouragers, that is the moral, their story is the wisdom, the secret.

It is wisdom to understand that one must use one's life to make a difference, to do good, to help those in need without hesitation or judgment, to give other people the best you have—all people, not merely some people. Become, take responsibility for your soul, your joy, your happiness by relieving pain, suffering, injustice, need, lack, and ignorance in the world. Share others' burdens. While here on earth, there is no permanence to positive things, nor to negative ones. It is a constant cycle between positive and negative.

Life is the journey, and that journey is accomplished through changes in circumstance. But the journey forces us to choose how to respond to circumstances. Sometimes you may be the helper; sometimes you may need the help. You do not get to control circumstances. But you navigate circumstances with hope as a constant. Live on purpose, with purpose, growing your awareness of opportunities to "love one another." Then muster the courage and develop the will to habitually do it! In the end, there is only hope or despair. Choose hope. Hope is all there is. I know this…and Anna Gordon knew it before me.

* * *

Dear Donor,

Never in my life had I ever imagined myself in the position to be writing this letter of thanks to you. It is so strange and disconcerting how cancer can creep into a healthy life so unexpectedly. Only a year ago I was living like any healthy young person would—with the worries and stresses that are normal for people of that age. However, now, as a leukemia patient, I find myself with different worries and stresses than those trivial trials of my previous daily life, such as a loss of independence, privacy, and the wavering promise of a long and prosperous life ahead.

But because of you, I now have reason to hope that I can soon renew my citizenship card to the "real world," and once again enjoy those things which are not available to those like me who have been forced to live their lives sustaining their lives, rather than enjoying them. Because of you, I have regained much of my strength, energy, and autonomy that were once lost. Because of you, I am making my way back to life—I am applying for jobs rather than leaving them. I am enjoying the outdoors, rather than remaining quarantined in a hospital room. I am hugging and kissing the ones that I love rather than distancing myself from them out of fear of infection. Because of you, I am becoming whole again, rather than continuing to fall apart.

But most importantly, because of you, I now have hope; hope that I can again go back to school, fall in love, celebrate birthdays, travel the world, and begin a new life of my own. Because of you, I have hope that I can remain someone's sister, daughter, niece, granddaughter, and friend. But more importantly, because of you, I have hope that I can someday become someone's wife, mother, aunt, grandmother, and new friend as well.

I have never known the kind of love that it took to do what you have done for me—a love for a faceless stranger—but I am thankful now to know that kind of love exists. I know it exists because I have witnessed it. In fact, it lives in me, and it will for the rest of my life. Thank you for showing me—your faceless, nameless, stranger—that kind of love by sharing your life with me, so that I might live to love others. Although we are strangers for now, we are connected both in body and spirit, and I look forward to the day that we might meet one another.

From the very marrow of my bones (literally), thank you for giving me life, thank you for giving me love, thank you for giving me hope.

—Your Recipient

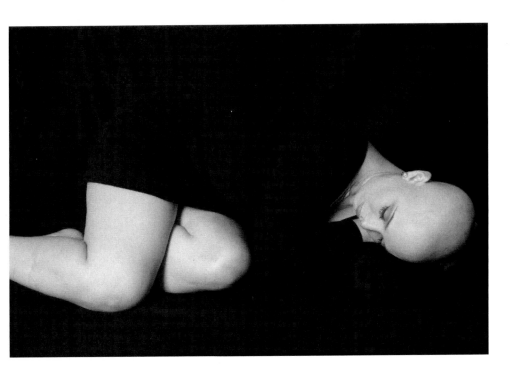